PROGRESSIVE

Complete
Learn To Play
GUITAR CHORDS
Manual

by
Peter Gelling and Gary Turner

PROGRESSIVE COMPLETE LEARN TO PLAY GUITAR CHORD MANUAL
I.S.B.N. 978 1 86469 317 7
Order Code: CP-69317
Acknowledgments
Cover Photograph: Phil Martin
Photographs: Phil Martin

For more information on this series contact;
L.T.P. Publishing PTY LTD
email: info@learntoplaymusic.com
or visit our website;
www.learntoplaymusic.com

Published by ™
KOALA MUSIC ™
PUBLICATIONS

CONTENTS

CHORDS

SECTION 1: Triads

OTHER TRIAD TYPES

SECTION 2: Four Note Chords

SECTION 3: Extended Chords, Altered Chords

CONTENTS CONTINUED

INTRODUCTION

Progressive COMPLETE LEARN TO PLAY GUITAR CHORD MANUAL is the ultimate Guitar Chord manual. It assumes you have no prior knowledge of music or playing the Guitar, and will teach you everything you need to know about chords and how to use them. By the end of the book you will be able to play and understand in any style, and will be ready for any musical situation.

The book is divided into five sections. The first section deals with basic chord types such as **major** and **minor**, along with other three note chords (triads). The second section covers four note chords such as sevenths. The third section extended and altered chords, and the fourth and fifth sections show you how to understand and use all the various chord types in a musical context The accompanying CDs contain all the examples in the book so you can play along with them. At the end of the book there are also several jam-along tracks for you to practice your chords with.

Through the book you will have learned many different chord types in many musical styles, so you may wish to learn more about some of them.

* To learn more about Rhythm guitar and its related styles, see
    Complete Learn to Play Rhythm Guitar Manual.
* To learn more about Blues guitar and its related styles, see
    Complete Learn to Play Blues Guitar Manual.
* To learn more about Jazz guitar, see
    Complete Learn to Play Jazz Guitar Manual.
* To learn more about Rock guitar and its related styles, see
    Complete Learn to Play Rock Guitar Manual.
* To learn more about lead guitar and improvising, see
    Complete Learn to Play Lead Guitar Manual.
* To learn more about fingerpicking with the right hand, see
    Complete Learn to Play Fingerpicking Guitar Manual.
* To learn more about Classical guitar, see
    Complete Learn to Play Classical Guitar Manual.

All guitarists should know all of the information contained in this book.
The best and fastest way to learn is to use this book in conjunction with:
1. Buying sheet music and song books of your favourite recording artists and learning to play their songs. There is no substitute for playing real music.
2. Practicing and playing with other musicians. You will be surprised how good a basic drums/bass/guitar combination can sound even when playing easy music.
3. Learning by listening to your favourite CDs.

Also in the early stages it is helpful to have the guidance of an experienced teacher. This will also help you keep to a schedule and obtain weekly goals.

For More books and recordings by Peter Gelling, visit: **www.bentnotes.com**

USING THE COMPACT DISCS

This book comes with **two compact discs which contain all the recorded** examples in the book. The book shows you where to put your fingers and what technique to use and the recording lets you hear how each example should sound. Practice the examples slowly at first, gradually increasing tempo. Once you are confident you can play the example evenly without stopping the beat, try playing along with the recording. You will hear a drum beat at the beginning of each example, to lead you into the example and to help you keep time. To play along with the CD your guitar must be in tune with it. If you have tuned using an electronic tuner (see below) your guitar will already be in tune with the CD. A small diagram of a compact disc with a number as shown below indicates a recorded example.

 **23.0** ← CD Track Number

ELECTRONIC TUNER

The easiest and most accurate way to tune your guitar is by using an **electronic tuner**. An electronic tuner allows you to tune each string individually to the tuner, by indicating whether the notes are sharp (too high) or flat (too low). If you have an electric guitar you can plug it directly in to the tuner. If you have an acoustic guitar, the tuner will have an inbuilt microphone. There are several types of electronic guitar tuners but most are relatively inexpensive and simple to operate. Tuning using other methods is difficult for beginning guitarists and it takes many months to master, so we recommend you purchase an electronic tuner, particularly if you do not have a guitar teacher or a friend who can tune it for you. Also if your guitar is way out of tune you can always take it to your local music store so they can tune it for you. Once a guitar has been tuned correctly it should only need minor adjustments before each practice session. To learn how to tune your guitar to itself or another instrument, see page 208

Electronic Tuner

TUNING YOUR GUITAR

Before you commence each lesson or practice session you will need to tune your guitar. If your guitar is out of tune everything you play will sound incorrect even though you are holding the correct notes. On the CD the **six notes on track 1** correspond to the **six strings of the guitar**. If you don't have a tuner, you can tune your guitar to these notes.

 **1. 6th String**
E Note (Thickest string)

 5th String
A Note

 4th String
D Note

 3rd String
G Note

 2nd String
B Note

 1st String
E Note (Thinnest string)

WHAT IS A CHORD?

A **chord** is a group of three or more notes that are played together. Chords are used to accompany a singer, or an instrumentalist who is playing the melody of song.

CHORD TYPES

The most common types of chords are:

CHORD SYMBOL	CHORD SYMBOL	CHORD SYMBOL
1. MAJOR	**2. MINOR** m	**3. SEVENTH** 7

From these chords other chords called **extended chords** are formed. These chord types are also quite common.

CHORD SYMBOL	CHORD SYMBOL	CHORD SYMBOL
4. SIXTH 6	**5. MINOR SEVENTH** m7	**6. MAJOR SEVENTH** maj7

Here are four other chord types used in **Pop/Rock** music. Although less common you will come across them.

CHORD SYMBOL	CHORD SYMBOL
7. AUGMENTED +	**8. DIMINISHED** o
9. SUSPENDED sus	**10. NINTH** 9

For **Jazz** and **classical** music more complex chord types can be used. The chord shapes for these chord types are generally more difficult to play. The most important of these chord have been included in this book.

For playing **Rock**, **Pop** and **Country** styles of music you should be familiar with the 10 chord types listed above.

CHORD SHAPES

There are three main group of chord shapes a guitarist will encounter.

1. OPEN CHORDS

These chord shapes are found within the first **four** frets and contain at least one open (i.e. not fretted) string. These chord shapes are the first shapes you should learn to play. They are commonly used to play **Pop, Rock, Country** and **Blues** music. Open chords sound particularly good played on acoustic guitars either strummed (Rhythm Guitar) or Fingerpicked. In this book the easiest open chord shapes have a box around them. There are about 25 basic ones and you should know how to play all of them as they are very useful. These open chords are also the basis for **Bar chords and other moveable shapes**. With these open chord shapes and knowledge of substitution (page 11), transposing (page 18) and use of a capo (page 19) you will be able to play almost every song ever written.

CHORD DIAGRAMS

Chords are written on a **chord diagram**. This chord diagram shows you exactly where to place your left hand fingers in order to play a particular chord. A chord diagram is a grid of horizontal and vertical lines representing the strings and frets of the guitar. The chord diagram and the photograph below illustrate an **open E major** chord.

LEFT HAND FINGERING

1 Index Finger
2 Middle Finger
3 Ring Finger
4 Little Finger

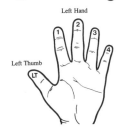

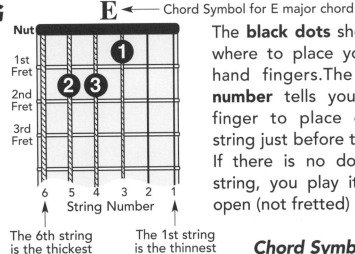

E ← Chord Symbol for E major chord

The **black dots** show you where to place your left hand fingers. The **white number** tells you which finger to place on the string just before the fret. If there is no dot on a string, you play it as an open (not fretted) string.

The 6th string is the thickest

The 1st string is the thinnest

Chord Symbol

E

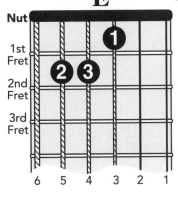

E Major Open Chord Shape

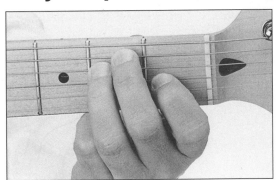

To play the **E** chord place your:
1 **First finger** just behind the **first** fret of the **3rd** string.
2 **Second finger** just behind the **second** fret of the **5th** string.
3 **Third finger** just behind the **second** fret of the **4th** string.

The other chord diagram symbols used in this book are summarized with the following two open chord shapes.

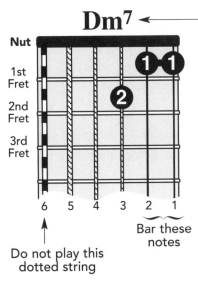

Dm⁷ ← Chord symbol for D minor seventh chord.

Bar these notes

Do not play this dotted string

A **dotted** string indicates that string is not to be strummed. A small **bar** connecting two black dots indicates they are held down by the same finger. This is called **barring**.

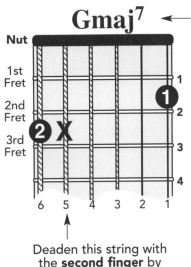

Gmaj⁷ ← Chord symbol for G major seventh chord.

Deaden this string with the **second finger** by lightly touching it.

An **X** on the string indicates that string is to **deaden** by another finger lightly touching it. The string is still strummed as a part of the chord but it is not heard.

8

2. BAR CHORDS

A **bar chord** has no open strings and can be played anywhere on the fretboard. The first finger of the left hand is used to Bar across all six strings of one fret and the other fingers are used to form the chord shape as shown in the Bar chord diagram and photograph of the **G** major Bar chord below.

Bar chord are based on open chords, e.g. This **root 6 G** chord is an **open E major** chord played after a Bar across the 3rd fret.

G

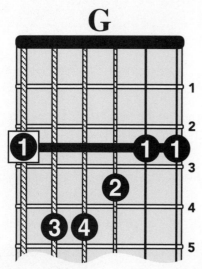

G Major
Root 6 Bar Chord Shape

⬛ **Root Note**   The note after which the chord is named is called the **root note**, e.g. G is the root note of the G major chord. The G major Bar chord shape above is a **root 6** shape because the root note is on the 6th string. If the root note is on the 5th string as in the C maj seventh (Cmaj7) Bar chord below the chord shape is called a **root 5** shape.

Cmaj⁷

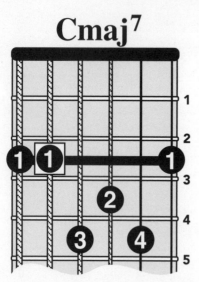

C Major Seventh
Root 5 Bar Chord Shape

Bar chords are commonly used in **pop** and rock music and when played on an electric guitar with loud volume and amplifier distortion, Bar chords (and parts of Bar chords called power chords) are the basis of heavier rock styles, e.g. **heavy metal**. Bar chords are easier to play on an electric guitar but are also played on acoustic guitars. Bar chords shapes are called **moveable** shapes because they can be played with the first finger Bar on any fret, e.g. if the above **G** major Bar chord shape was moved two frets higher it would be an **A** major chord. If the above **Cmaj7** Bar chord shape was moved two frets higher it would be a **Dmaj7** chord. Bar chords and all other moveable chord shapes in this book have the root note indicated with a box ⬛ .

3. MOVEABLE CHORDS

There are many moveable chords which do not involve the first finger barring all the strings. In the book these chords are simply called **moveable chords**. Many seventh chords and higher extensions commonly occur as moveable shapes and are often called **Jazz chords**. They are sometimes harder to play but songs and chord progressions containing these chord shapes have a unique sound that cannot be achieved by with open or Bar chords. The moveable chords given in this book are shown with the root note (indicated with a box ⬛). The G major seventh (Gmaj7) chord shape below is a root 6 chord. The C minor seventh (Cm7) is a root 5 chord.

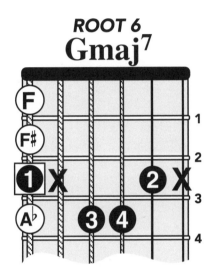

ROOT 6
Gmaj⁷

G Major Seventh
Root 6 Jazz Chord Shape

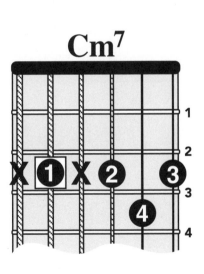

Cm⁷

C Minor Seventh
Root 5 Jazz Chord Shape

Many moveable chord shapes contain '**deadened**' strings as indicated by the **X** on the string. All strings are strummed but the 'deadened' strings are not heard. The strings are deadened by lightly touching them with another finger in the chord shape, e.g. in the G major seventh chord shape above the 5th and 1st strings are deadened by the first finger lightly touching them.

CHORD SYMBOLS AND ALTERNATIVES

In sheet music notation, there is a lack of uniformity in writing chord symbols. For example, the C major seventh chord can be written as either "Cmaj7" (used in this book), "CØ7" or "CM7". The table below outlines the symbols used in this book, together with correct pronunciation and alternative symbols used for each chord type if applicable.

Symbol Used In This Book	Chord Name	Alternative Symbols
(None)	Major	Maj, M
–5	Major Flat Five	♭5
m	Minor	min, mi
sus	Suspended	sus4
+	Augmented	♯5, +5, aug
6	Major Sixth	Maj6, △6, M6
6/9	Major Sixth Add Nine	6(add9), 6/9 , Maj6(add9), M6(add9)
m6	Minor Sixth	mi6, min6
7	Dominant Seventh	Dom 7
7sus	Seven Suspended	sus7, 7sus4
7♯5	Seven Sharp Five	+7, 7+5
7♭9	Seven Flat Ninth	7–9
7♯9	Seven Sharp Ninth	7+9
m7	Minor Seventh	mi7, min7
m7♭5	Minor Seven Flat Five	ø7, mi7♭5, min7♭5, m7–5
o	Diminished Seven	o7, dim7, –7, dim
maj7	Major Seventh	△7, M7
m(maj)7	Minor Major Seven	m(Maj7), m(△7), mi(+7), min(+7)
m9	Minor Ninth	mi9, min9, –9
maj9	Major Ninth	△9, M9
m11	Minor Eleventh	mi11, min11, –11
13	Thirteenth	M13, M7(add6)

HOW TO READ SHEET MUSIC

Most of the sheet music you will buy in a music store will be arranged for piano. Piano music is written using two or three staves, with the chord symbols written above the top staff. It may also contain unfamiliar symbols and terms. At this stage you need only look at the top staff, which contains the melody line (tune), the lyrics and the chords. In some sheet music chord diagrams may also be included. As most sheet music is arranged by keyboard players quite often the guitar chord shapes given are incorrect, unnecessary or impractical, and many piano arrangements of guitar based songs do not sound anything like the recorded version. Guitar tablature versions of sheet music are gradually becoming more popular and in many cases are very accurate arrangements of the song. If you want to learn more about reading music and tablature see **Progressive Complete Learn to Play Guitar Manual.**

Also many piano arrangements are in difficult keys for a beginning guitarist and quite often use unnecessary chords. Piano sheet music also gives no indication of how to strum the chords. So piano sheet music is only a guide for a guitarist but is useful for lyrics and a general chord guide.

If the song contains chords that you are not familiar with you can:

1. **Learn how to play this new chord as shown in this book.**
2. **Change the key of the song** (see transposing page 18).
3. **Substitute an easier chord.**

   Use the easy chord table below which lists the type of chord you may see in the sheet music (on the left of the table) and the simpler chord you can substitute (on the right of the table). If you know how to transpose (see page 18) and substitute chords you can play almost every song ever written using only a few basic chord shapes. As your knowledge of chords increases, you can gradually add in all the other chord types.

EASY CHORD TABLE

Chord Written on Sheet Music		Use This Chord Instead (First Choice)	Use This Chord Instead (Second Choice)
–5	Major Flat Five	Major	Major
add9	Major Add Ninth	Major	Major
sus	SUSPENDED	Major	Major
+	AUGMENTED	Major	Major
6	MAJOR SIXTH	Major	Major
6/9	Major Sixth Add Nine	Sixth	Major
m6	Minor Sixth	Minor	Minor
7	SEVENTH	Major	Major
7sus	Seven Suspended	Suspended	Major
7♯5	Seven Sharp Five	Seventh	Major
7♭9	Seven Flat Ninth	Seventh	Major
7♯9	Seven Sharp Ninth	Seventh	Major
m7	MINOR SEVENTH	Minor	Minor
m7♭5	Minor Seven Flat Five	Minor Seventh	Minor
o	DIMINISHED SEVENTH	Major Flat Five	Major
maj7	MAJOR SEVENTH	Major	Major
m(maj)7	Minor Major Seven	Minor	Minor
9	NINTH	Seventh	Major
m9	Minor Ninth	Minor Seventh	Minor
maj9	Major Ninth	Major Seventh	Major
11	ELEVENTH	Ninth	Seventh
m11	Minor Eleventh	Minor Ninth	Minor Seventh
13	THIRTEENTH	Eleventh	Ninth

Here is an example of simplifying a chord progression, by using the chord substitutions outlined above. Chord Substitution is covered in detail on pages 187 to 196.

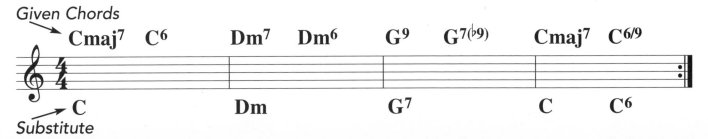

HOW TO READ MUSIC

There are two methods used to write guitar music. First is the **traditional music notation** method (using music notes, ♩) and second is **tablature.** Both are used in this book but you need only use one of these methods. Most guitarists find Tablature easier to read, however, it is very worthwhile to learn to read traditional music notation as well. Nearly all sheet music you buy in a store is written in traditional notation.

TABLATURE

Tablature is a method of indicating the position of notes on the fretboard. There are six "tab" lines each representing one of the six strings of the guitar. Study the following diagram.

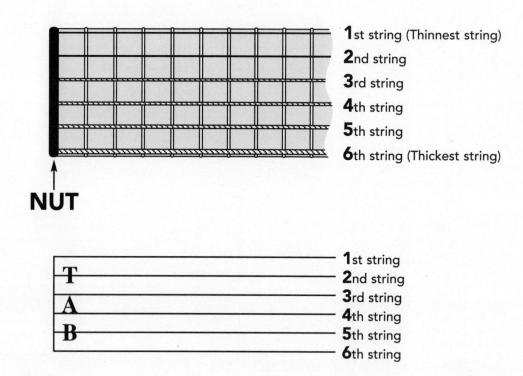

When a number is placed on one of the lines, it indicates the fret location of a note e.g.

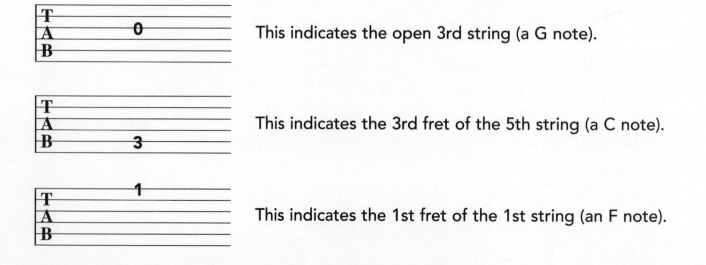

This indicates the open 3rd string (a G note).

This indicates the 3rd fret of the 5th string (a C note).

This indicates the 1st fret of the 1st string (an F note).

MUSIC NOTATION

These five lines are called the **staff** or the **stave**.

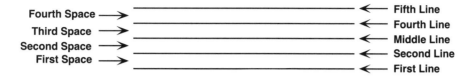

Fourth Space → / Fifth Line
Third Space → / Fourth Line
Second Space → / Middle Line
First Space → / Second Line
/ First Line

THE TREBLE CLEF

 This symbol is called a **treble clef**. There is a treble clef at the beginning of every line of guitar music.

THE TREBLE STAFF

A staff with a treble clef written on it is called a **treble staff**.

MUSIC NOTES

There are only seven letters used for notes in music. They are:

A B C D E F G

These notes are known as the **musical alphabet**.

Guitar music notes are written in the spaces and on the lines of the treble staff.

The Quarter Note

← stem

← note head

This is a **quarter note**. A quarter note lasts for **one beat**.

NOTES AND REST VALUES

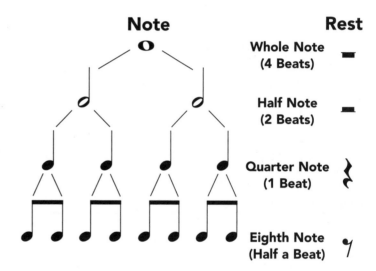

Note	Rest

Whole Note (4 Beats)
Half Note (2 Beats)
Quarter Note (1 Beat)
Eighth Note (Half a Beat)

To remember the notes on the lines of the staff, say:
Every **G**ood **B**oy **D**eserves **F**ruit.

The notes in the spaces spell:
F A C E

BAR LINES are drawn across the staff, which divides the music into sections called **BARS** or **MEASURES**. A **DOUBLE BAR LINE** signifies either the end of the music, or the end of an important section of it.

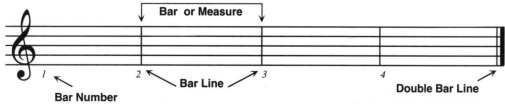

Bar or Measure

Bar Number · Bar Line · Double Bar Line

RHYTHM SYMBOLS

Count **1** 2

This is a **half note strum**. It lasts for **two** beats. There are **two** half note strums in one bar of ⁴⁄₄ time.

V

Count **1**

This is a **quarter note strum**. It lasts for **one** beat. There are **four** quarter note strums in one bar of ⁴⁄₄ time.

V∧

Count **1** +

These are a pair of **eighth note strums**. Each strum lasts for **half a beat**. There are **eight** eighth note strums in one bar of ⁴⁄₄ time. Play the larger downward strum louder.

V∧V∧

Count **1** e + a

These Strums are a group of **sixteenth note strums**. Each strum lasts for **one quarter** of a beat. There are **sixteen** sixteenth note strums in one bar of ⁴⁄₄ time. Play the larger downward strum louder.

RHYTHM NOTATION

As well as traditional music notation and tablature, guitar music sometimes uses **rhythm notation**. This is similar to traditional notation, except that the notes have a diagonal line instead of a notehead. This tells you that instead of playing individual notes, you will be strumming chords. An example of rhythm notation is shown below.

Count: 1   +   2   +   3   +   4   +   1   +   2   +   3   +   4   +

TIME SIGNATURES

At the beginning of each piece of music, after the treble clef, is the **time signature**.

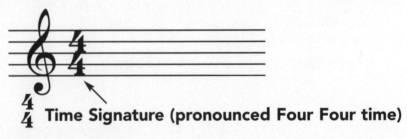

⁴⁄₄ **Time Signature (pronounced Four Four time)**

The time signature indicates the number of beats per bar (the top number) and the type of note receiving one beat (the bottom number). For example:

4 – this indicates 4 beats per bar.

4 – this indicates that each beat is worth a quarter note (crotchet).

Thus in $\frac{4}{4}$ time there must be the equivalent of 4 quarter note beats per bar, e.g.

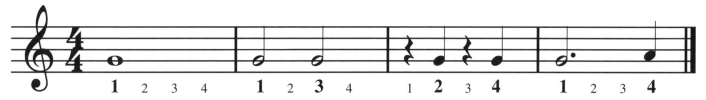

$\frac{4}{4}$ is the most common time signature and is sometimes represented by this symbol called **COMMON TIME**.

Most Rock/Pop songs are in $\frac{4}{4}$ time.

Some other common time signatures are $\frac{3}{4}$, $\frac{2}{4}$ and $\frac{6}{8}$. These are demonstrated below.

COMMON TIME

$\frac{3}{4}$ indicates 3 quarter note beats per bar, e.g.

$\frac{2}{4}$ indicates 2 quarter note beats per bar, e.g.

$\frac{6}{8}$ time indicates 2 dotted quarter note beats per bar, which can be divided into two groups of eighth notes as such:

CHORD CONSTRUCTION

All chord types are based upon a unique formula which can be related back to the major scale that has the same letter name as the chord, e.g. C chords are based upon a formula that can be measured against the C major scale. Here is the C major scale written in standard music notation and **tab** (tablature). If you play these notes you would get the familiar **Do Re Mi Fa So La Ti Do** sound.

The letter name of each note is written below the note on the staff ($\quarternote$). The number written below the letter name is the degree number of the note in the scale. These thirteen note degrees are all that is needed to create all chord types. Each chord type will have its own unique formula.

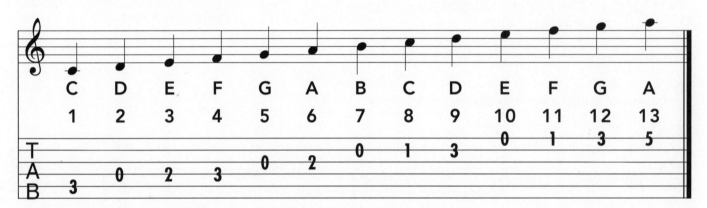

The formula for the **major** chord is **CHORD FORMULA** $\boxed{1 \quad 3 \quad 5}$ which means that the major chord consists of the **first**, **third** and **fifth** notes of the major scale, e.g. the C major chord consists of the 1st, 3rd and 5th notes of the C major scale, i.e. the **C E G** notes. These notes can be in any order and can be duplicated but there must be at least one of each of those notes, e.g. in the adjacent C major chord shape there are two C notes, three E notes and one G note.

The G major chord consists of the 1st, 3rd and 5th notes of the **G** major scale, i.e. the **G B D** notes.

The formula for a **minor** chord is **CHORD FORMULA** $\boxed{1 \quad \flat3 \quad 5}$ which means that the minor chord consists of the first, flattened third and fifth notes of the major scale.

e.g. the **C minor (Cm)** chord consists of the 1st, 3rd and 5th notes of the **C** major scale, i.e. **C E♭ G**. So even though it is a minor chord the chord formula still relates back to the major scale.

The chord formula chart on the right lists all the chord types in this book along with its formula (relative to the major scale) and an example based upon **C**.

A full understanding of chord construction is very useful as your playing ability advances as it is particularly useful when improvising, substituting or writing an accompaniment for a song or piece of music.

You will need to know about major scales, keys, key signatures, sharps(♯) and flats(♭). All this information and everything you need to know about useful theory for guitar can be found in *Progressive Guitar Method : Theory*

CHORD FORMULA CHART

The following table lists all the types of chords in this book and the note degrees from the major scale required for each chord. As an example each chord type is also shown in the key of **C**. Study the diagram below and its relationship to the **C major** scale on the opposite page.

Chord Name	Chord Formula	Example (C)
Major	1 3 5	C E G
Major Flat Five	1 3 ♭5	C E G♭
Major Add Ninth	1 3 5 9	C E G D
Minor	1 ♭3 5	C E♭ G
Suspended	1 4 5	C F G
Augmented	1 3 ♯5	C E G♯
Major Sixth	1 3 5 6	C E G A
Major Sixth Add Nine	1 3 5 6 9	C E G A D
Minor Sixth	1 ♭3 5 6	C E♭ G A
Seventh	1 3 5 ♭7	C E G B♭
Seven Suspended	1 4 5 ♭7	C F G B♭
Seven Sharp Five	1 3 ♯5 ♭7	C E G♯ B♭
Seven Flat Ninth	1 3 5 ♭7 ♭9	C E G B♭ D♭
Seven Sharp Ninth	1 3 5 ♭7 ♯9	C E G B♭ D♯
Minor Seventh	1 ♭3 5 ♭7	C E♭ G B♭
Minor Seven Flat Five	1 ♭3 ♭5 ♭7	C E♭ G♭ B♭
Diminished Seven	1 ♭3 5 ♭♭7	C E♭ G B♭♭
Major Seventh	1 3 5 7	C E G B
Minor Major Seven	1 ♭3 5 7	C E♭ G B
Ninth	1 3 5 ♭7 9	C E G B♭ D
Minor Ninth	1 ♭3 5 ♭7 9	C E♭ G B♭ D
Major Ninth	1 3 5 7 9	C E G B D
Eleventh	1 3 5 ♭7 9 11	C E G B♭ D F
Minor Eleventh	1 ♭3 5 ♭7 9 11	C E♭ G B♭ D F
Thirteenth	1 3 5 ♭7 9 13	C E G B♭ D A

♯=Sharp (raise note one fret), ♭=Flat (lower note one fret), ♭♭=Double flat (lower note two frets)

TRANSPOSING

Transposing (or **Transposition**) is the process of changing a song or piece of music from one key to another.

There are two reasons for transposing into another key:
A.   If the song is too high or too low to sing, the song can be changed into a lower or higher key. Changing the key of a song does not change the sound, pattern or timing of the melody but simply changes how high or how low it is sung.

B.   If the song is hard to play or contains difficult chords you can transpose it to a key with easier chords. e.g. If a song is written in the key of **B flat** (**B♭**) **major** (which many songs are) it would contain chords like **B♭**, **E♭** and **Cm** which may be difficult for a beginning guitarist. If the song is transposed into the key of G major the chords would then be **G**, **C** and **Am**, which are easier for a guitarist to play.

HOW TO TRANSPOSE

If the sheet music is in the key of **E flat** (**E♭**) **major** and contains difficult chord shapes, you can transpose it to another major key with easier chord shapes. Keys that contain easy shapes for beginners are **C major** and **G major**, or if the song is in a minor key, **A minor** (**Am**) or **E minor** (**Em**).
Write down the chromatic scale (see page **53**) of the key the sheet music is in (usually the first chord is the key chord). Then underneath it write down the chromatic scale of the key you wish to change to. E.g. to change a song from the key of **E♭** to the key of **G**, write down the chromatic scale starting with the note **E♭** and then underneath it write down the chromatic scale starting on the note **G**.

E♭ chromatic scale:	E♭	E	F	G♭	G	A♭	A	B♭	B	C	D♭	D	E♭
	↓	↓	↓	↓	↓	↓	↓	↓	↓	↓	↓	↓	↓
G chromatic scale:	G	G#	A	A#	B	C	C#	D	D#	E	F	F#	G

The letter name of the chord is written on the top line and the letter name of the new chord in the new key (in this case **G**) will be directly underneath it.

Note that the chord type never changes. If the chord is a minor chord in the key of **E♭ major** it will also be a minor chord in the major key it is transposed to.

e.g. an **E♭** chord in the key of **E♭ major** becomes a **G** chord in the key of **G major**.
e.g. an **A♭** chord in the key of **E♭ major** becomes a **C** chord in the key of **G major**.
e.g. a **Cm** chord in the key of **E♭ major** becomes an **Em** chord in the key of **G major**.
e.g. a **B♭m** chord in the key of **E♭ major** becomes a **Dm** chord in the key of **G major**.

The easiest keys for guitar are:
G major, C major, D major, A major, E major, A minor and **E minor**. These keys contain chords that have open strings in them and are generally easier shapes to hold.

If a guitarist wants to transpose a song into a different key to enable the use of easier chord shapes but the singer prefers to sing the song in the original key e.g. E♭, a capo may be used.

THE CAPO

The **capo** is a device which is placed across the neck of the guitar (acting as a moveable nut). It has 2 uses:
1. To enable the use of easier chord shapes, without changing the key of a song.
2. To change the key of a song, without changing the chord shapes.

Capos come in various shapes and sizes.

E.g.**1.** If a song is in a key which is within your singing range, but involves playing difficult chord shapes, e.g. in the key of **E flat (E♭)**, a capo may be used. The capo allows you to play the song in the same key, yet at the same time use easier chord shapes. Consider a Turnaround in **E flat (E♭)**:

E♭	Cm	A♭	B♭

If you place the capo on the third fret, the following easier chord shapes can be played without changing the song's key.

C	Am	F	G

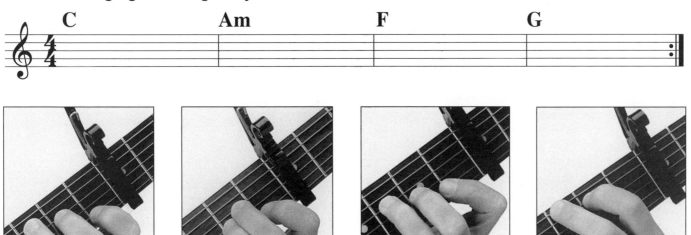

(C chord shape with capo)	**(Am chord shape with capo)**	**(F chord shape with capo)**	**(G chord shape with capo)**

If you have studied bar chords, you will notice that the capo is acting as a bar. To work out which fret the capo must be placed on, simply count the number of semitones between the "capo key" you have selected to change to (eg: **C**, as used in the above example) and the original key (i.e. **E♭** as above). Hence **C** to **E♭** = 3 semitones, and therefore the capo must be placed on the third fret.

Eg: **2.** If the song is in a key that already has easy chord shapes but is out of range to sing, you can change the key by placing the capo on a particular fret and still use the easy chord shapes. Eg: if you start with the above Turnaround in the **key of C** but wish to change it to the **key of E♭**, place the capo at the third fret and play the same **C Am F G** chord shapes. When you play these chord shapes with the capo at the third fret they become **E♭ Cm A♭ B♭**.

Section 1
Triads

As you learnt on page 6, a **chord** is a group of three or more notes played simultaneously. Different types of chords can be formed by using different combinations of notes. The most basic type of chord contains three different notes and is called a **triad**. The most common triads are **major chords**. All major chords contain three notes taken from the major scale bearing the same letter name as the chord. These three notes are the **1** (first), **3** (third) and **5** (fifth) degrees (notes) of the major scale, so the **chord formula** for the major chord is: **1 3 5**. This is demonstrated below with a **C major triad** (usually just called a **C** chord).

Chord Symbol

C

The C Major Chord

Notes in Chord

C	E	G
1	3	5

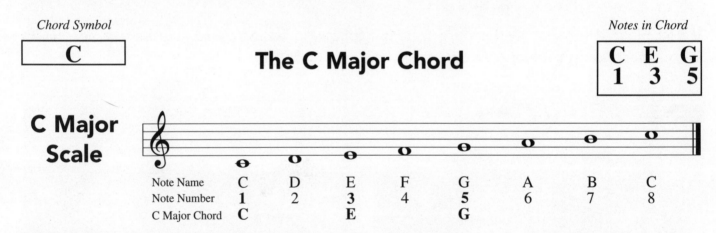

C Major Scale

Note Name	C	D	E	F	G	A	B	C
Note Number	**1**	2	**3**	4	**5**	6	7	8
C Major Chord	**C**		**E**		**G**			

Once you have the correct notes for a C chord (or any chord) they can be arranged in any order. As long as the notes are still C, E and G, you still have a C chord. E.g. a C chord could be played C E G, or E G C, or G C E, or even G E C. These various arrangements of the notes within a chord are called **inversions**. It is also possible to **double** notes within a chord. E.g. the diagram below shows a common way of playing a C major chord on the guitar. It contains two C notes and two E notes. It is still a C major chord because it only contains notes called C, E and G. **Doubling** notes is common when playing chords on the guitar.

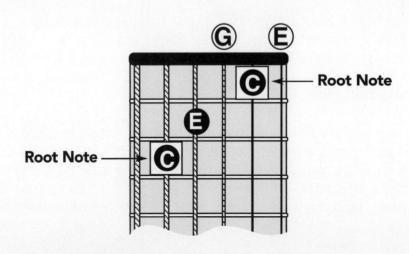

CHORD SYMBOL	MAJOR	CHORD FORMULA
maj		**1 3 5**

OPEN CHORDS

As mentioned on page 6, the term "open chords" refers to chord shapes which contain at least one open string. There are occasional exceptions in this book, but all chord shapes shown under an open chords heading will occur in the first four frets. Where there is more than one option for a particular chord, the easiest version is boxed.

Throughout the book, chord shapes are given from all twelve possible root notes used in music. It is recommended that you learn each shape and then transpose it to all the other keys. This will result in you being able to play any chord anywhere on the fretboard.

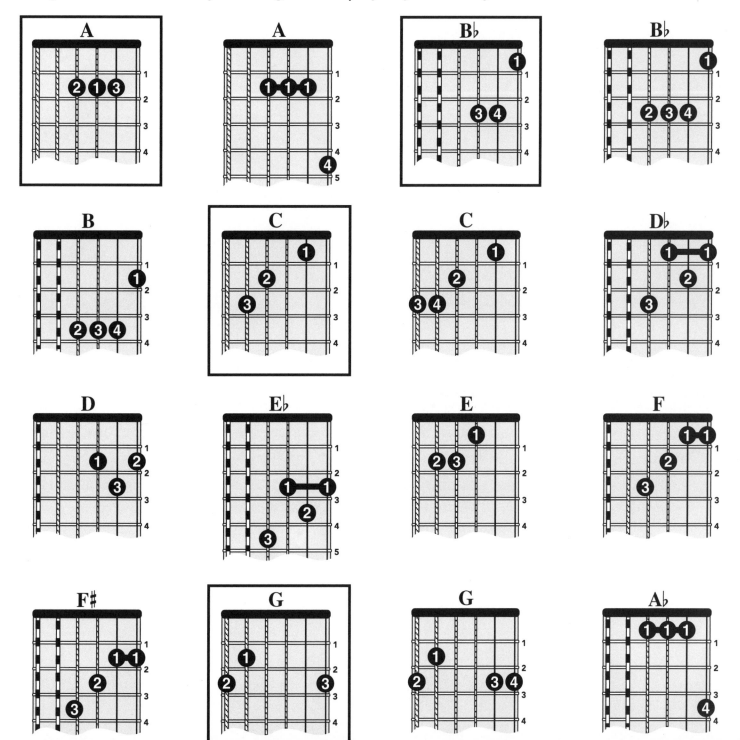

CHORD PROGRESSIONS

The following example is called a **chord progression**, meaning **a series of chord changes.** Chord progressions are common in all styles of music, and the more you know, the more songs you will be able to play.

RHYTHM PATTERNS

Instead of writing the strumming above each bar of music, it is easier to write it as a **rhythm pattern**. This indicates which strumming pattern to use in each bar throughout the song. The rhythm pattern above the following example shows two quarter note strums followed by a half note strum.

2.0

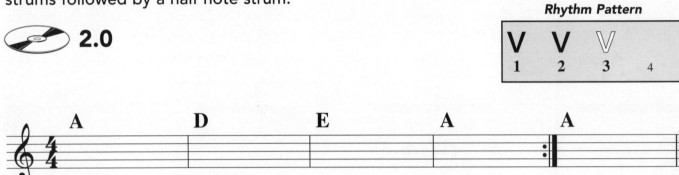

2.1

This chord progression contains four different chords and is played with a rhythm pattern using both quarter and eighth note strums. If you have trouble with the strumming pattern or are unfamiliar with reading rhythms, see *Progressive Complete Learn to Play Rhythm Guitar Manual*.

RHYTHM NOTATION

As well as traditional music notation and tablature, guitar music sometimes uses **rhythm notation**. This is similar to traditional notation, except that the notes have a diagonal line instead of a notehead. This tells you that instead of playing individual notes, you will be strumming chords. Rhythm notation is commonly used in Jazz charts.

2.2

Rhythm Notation

ARPEGGIOS

An **arpeggio** is a chord played one note at a time. Arpeggios enable you to play parts which fit chord progressions perfectly, since every note of an arpeggio is a note of the accompanying chord. Written below is a **C major arpeggio** which consists of the notes **C, E** and **G**. These are the **root, third** and **fifth** of a **C major chord**. To play this arpeggio, simply hold down a C chord shape and pick the notes individually.

3.0

Here is an example which makes use of arpeggios. Hold down the chord shapes indicated by the chord symbols as much as possible, except when playing notes which are not in the chords (e.g. the B note at the end of bar 2). Take care with your picking and make sure all your notes are clear and even.

3.1

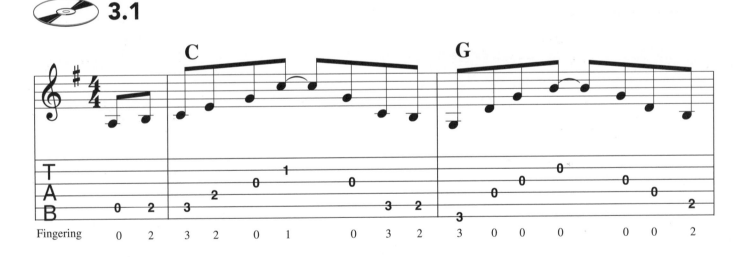

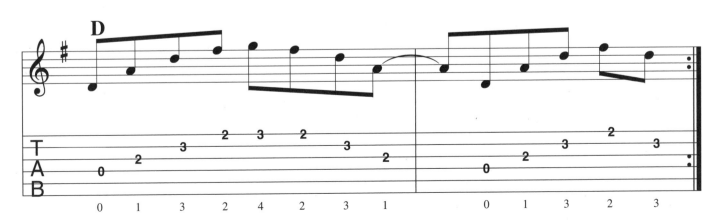

BAR CHORDS

The term "bar chord" means that the first finger acts as a **bar** (sometimes called a **barre**) across all, or some of the strings. The fact that there are no open strings in a bar chord means it is possible to move the one shape to any position on the fretboard and to play in every key. The term "position" refers to the fret your first finger is at. E.g if your first finger is at the **3rd fret**, you are in the **third position**. If your first finger is at the **8th fret**, you are in the **eighth position**. The diagram and photo below demonstrate an **F major** bar chord (played in the **first position**). Notice that this chord is simply an E chord shape played with the 2nd, 3rd and 4th fingers, with a first finger bar behind it.

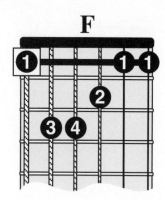

LEFT HAND TECHNIQUE

Bar chords can be difficult to play at first and will require a great deal of practice before they are comfortable to use. Try to keep the first finger of the left hand straight and parallel to the fret. It is also important to keep the other fingers arched and use only the tips of the fingers. The left hand thumb must be kept behind the neck.

Keep first finger straight.

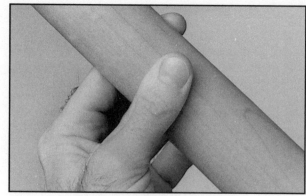

Keep thumb behind neck.

ROOT 6 BAR CHORDS

As with open chords, there are several different types of bar chords, including major, minor and 7th chords. The bar chord shape shown above is referred to as a **root 6** major bar chord because the **root note** (name note) of the chord is on the **6th string**. The root 6 major bar chord can be played at any fret with the name of the chord depending on which note the first finger is fretting on the sixth string. E.g. at the **3rd fret**, this shape would be a **G chord**. At the **5th fret**, it would be an **A chord**, etc. as demonstrated on the following page.

CHORD SYMBOL

maj

MAJOR

CHORD FORMULA

1   3   5

ROOT 6 BAR CHORDS

To find any chord when using **root 6** bar chords, simply move the shape up or down the fretboard. The chord will be named from the **root note** under your **first finger** on the **6th string** as demonstrated below. The root note can also be found on the 1st and 4th strings.

BASIC OPEN CHORD SHAPE

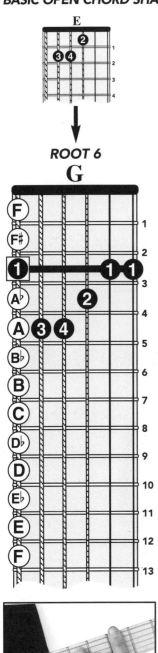

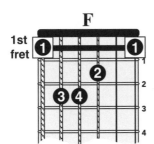

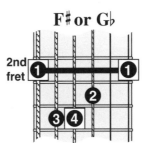

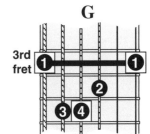

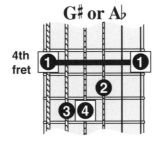

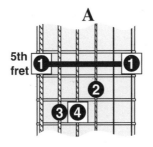

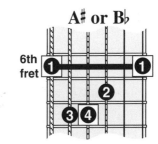

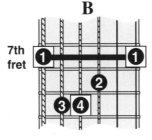

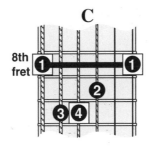

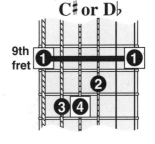

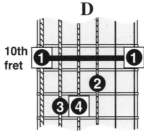

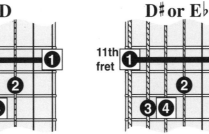

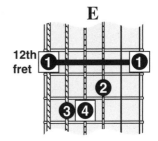

NOTES ON THE SIXTH STRING

In order to determine exactly where to place your first finger for any particular bar chord, it is essential to know the notes on the sixth string from memory. The diagram below shows the notes on the sixth string up to the 13th fret where the F note repeats an octave higher than the first fret. It is rare to play bar chords any higher than the 12th fret.

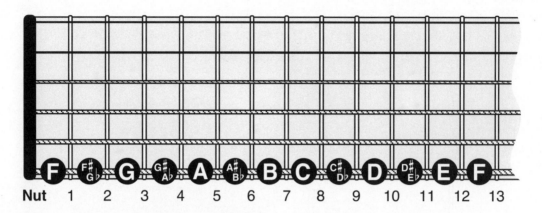

4.0 Root 6 Bar Chords

Practice playing bar chords at different frets at random until you can instantly name the chord at any fret. Once you can do this, try the following example, which moves the same shape up and down the neck to form all the chords in the progression.

PERCUSSIVE STRUMMING

An important rhythm technique used in many styles of music is the **Percussive Strum**. This is achieved by forming a chord shape with the left hand and placing it on the strings, but **without** pressing down on the frets. A percussive strum is indicated by using an **X** in place of a notehead.

This technique can be applied to any type of chord. The following example features **percussive strumming** with root 6 bar chords. Wherever percussive strums occur, release the pressure with your left hand, so that the fingers lift up off the fretboard but still remain in contact with the strings. **Keep the bar chord shape** so you are ready to press down again to play the next chord as soon as it occurs.

4.1

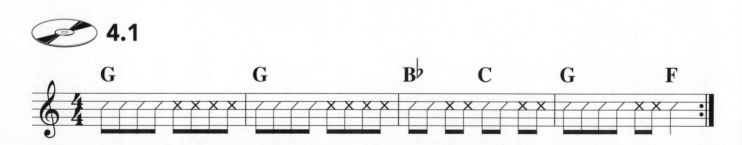

ROOT 5 BAR CHORDS

As the term **root 5** suggests, the root note of these chords can be found on the fifth string, fretted with the first finger bar. Like all bar chords, the same shape can be moved up or down to any position on the fretboard. Below is the basic shape for the root 5 Major bar chord shown in two positions. You will need to have patience with this chord shape, as the combination of the first finger bar and the partial bar with the third finger is particularly difficult at first. Make sure the third finger sounds the 4th, 3rd and 2nd strings, but **not** the 1st string.

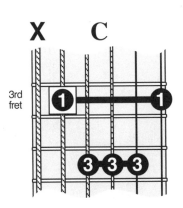
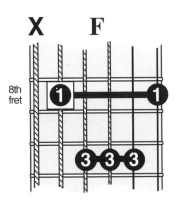

NOTES ON THE FIFTH STRING

To find root 5 bar chords easily, it is essential to know the notes on the 5th string from memory. The diagram below illustrates all notes on the fifth string up to the 13th fret. Try naming a chord and moving to the correct fret. Practice this until you can do it without hesitating or having to think ahead.

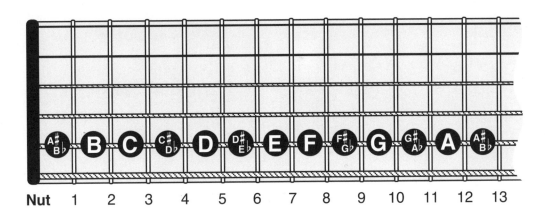

4.2 Root 5 Bar Chords

Here is an example which makes use of root 5 bar chords. Notice once again the use of percussive strumming.

CHORD SYMBOL

> maj

MAJOR

CHORD FORMULA

> 1 3 5

ROOT 5 BAR CHORDS

To find any chord when using **root 5** bar chords, simply move the shape up or down the fretboard. The chord will be named from the **root note** under your **first finger** on the **5th string** as demonstrated below. The root note can also be found on the 3rd string.

BASIC OPEN CHORD SHAPE

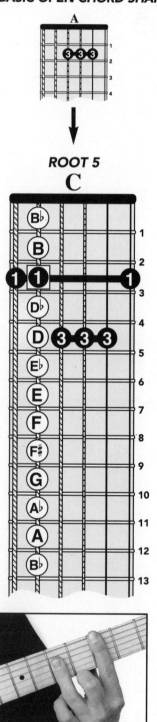

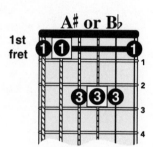

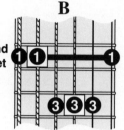

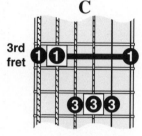

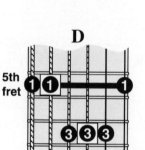

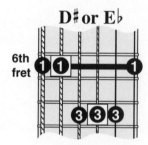

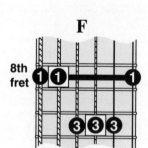

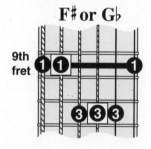

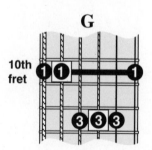

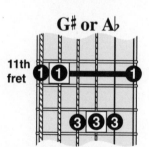

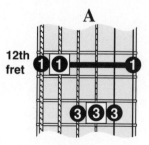

CHANGING BETWEEN SHAPES

Once you know how to play both root 6 and root 5 bar chords, the next step is learning how to combine them. The exercise below will help you gain control of changing between the two major bar chords. The **G** chord is **root 6** while the **C and D** chords are **root 5**. These are chords Ī, ĪV and V̄ in the **key of G** (Using roman numerals to describe chords is explained on page 153) These are the most common chords in any key. You could also move the chords to other positions on the fretboard and play a song using these chords in any key. This becomes even easier when you learn the following pattern, which applies to all keys.

If **chord Ī is root 6,** then **chord ĪV will be root 5 at the same fret,** and **chord V̄ will be root 5 two frets higher up the neck.**

 **5.0**

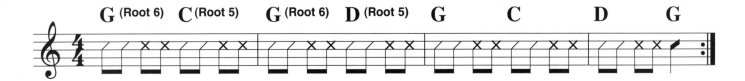

It is also possible to play this progression beginning with a root 5 chord. If **chord Ī is root 5,** then **chord ĪV will be root 6 two frets lower,** and **chord V̄ will be root 6 at the same fret as chord Ī.** This pattern also applies to **all keys.** Listen to the CD to hear the difference between this example and the previous one.

 **5.1**

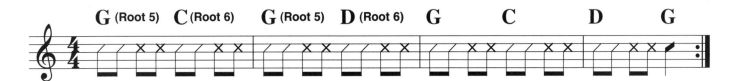

 **5.2**

Here is another example which will give you more practice at changing between root 5 and root 6 bar chords. Notice the use of **staccato** here. Staccato with bar chords is achieved by quickly lifting the fingers off the fretboard but not off the strings immediately after strumming the chord. If you are not familiar with staccato playing, see *Progressive Complete Learn to Play Rhythm Guitar Manual.*

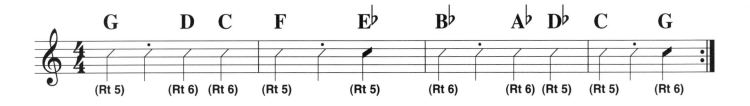

LEARNING THE WHOLE FRETBOARD

When using moveable chord shapes, it is important to be able to quickly find the correct fret at which to play each chord, and also to be able to play equally well in all keys. The best way to achieve this is to memorize the names of all the notes on the fretboard. This may seem a daunting task, but it can be done and will be well worth it. More advanced guitar playing requires the use of many different chords, which may take their name from **any** of the six strings, so you need to learn them all equally well.

Notes on the

Here is a fretboard diagram of all the notes on the guitar. Play the notes on each string the open note e.g. the open 6th string is an **E** note and the note on the 12th fret of the

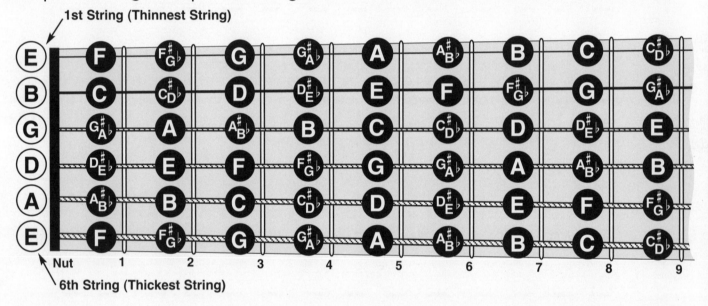

A good way to learn all the notes is to take one string at a time. Call the "in between" notes sharps as you progress up the fretboard and flats as you go back down. The diagram below shows notes on the 4th string only. To practice naming the notes, slide your first finger up one fret at a time and say the name of each note out loud as you go. When you reach the 12th fret where the notes begin to repeat, move back down one fret at a time. You can use any finger to do this exercise, it is the note names that are important, not the fingering.

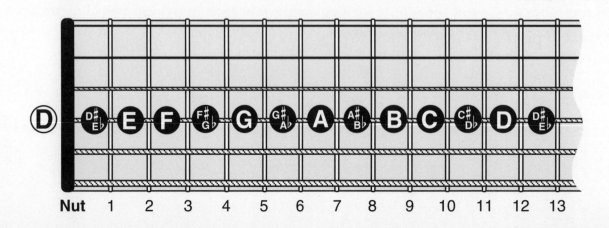

The dots on your guitar are good points of reference. You can use them to help the memorizing process.

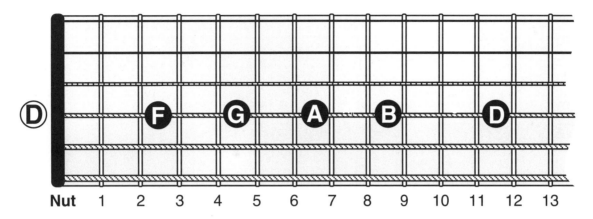

Nut   1   2   3   4   5   6   7   8   9   10   11   12   13

Guitar Fretboard

from the open notes to the 12th fret. The note on the 12th fret is one octave higher than 6th string is also an **E** note, but is one octave higher.

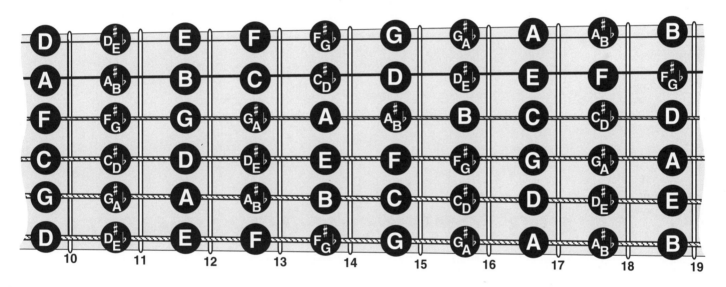

Once you are confident you know the names of the notes along a particular string, pick the name of any note at random and find it on that string as quickly as possible. When this becomes easy, move on to the next string.

Another useful exercise is to find the same note on every string, remembering that a note usually appears twice on each string unless it is at the 11th fret.

Finally, name and play the notes across each fret. Once again use sharps as you go higher in pitch and flats as you go back down.

NOTES IN MORE THAN ONE PLACE

Once you start playing notes all over the fretboard, you quickly realize that you can find the same notes in more than one place. E.g. the **E note** which is the **open first string** can also be found at the **5th fret** on the **second string**, the **9th fret** on the **third string** and the **14th fret** on the **fourth string** (on electric guitars it can also be found at the **19th fret** on the **fifth string**). Once you are comfortable with all the locations of a note, it is easy to play the same melody in many different places on the fretboard. This is valuable when you are improvising or reading music. Practice naming any note and then finding it in as many places on the fretboard as possible. Keep doing this for a few minutes each day, until you are confident you can quickly find all the locations for any note.

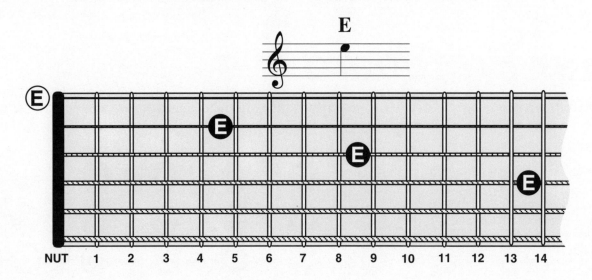

HIGHER AND LOWER OCTAVES OF NOTES

Another valuable exercise for improving your knowledge of the fretboard is to find all possible octaves of any given note. Remember that an **octave** is the distance between any note and its next repeat at a higher or lower pitch.

An example of this would be the note **C#**, which can be found at the **9th and 21st frets** on the **sixth string**, the **4th and 16th frets** on the **fifth string**, the **11th fret** on the **fourth string**, the **6th and 18th frets** on the **third string**, the **2nd and 14th frets** on the **second string**, and the **9th and 21st frets** on the **first string**. These positions are shown in the diagram below. Practice choosing notes at random and finding each one in all possible positions, until you are confident you can instantly find any note in any position.

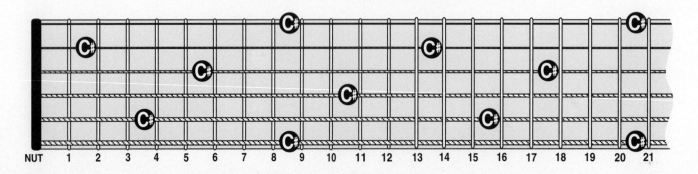

MOVEABLE CHORD SHAPES IN FIVE FORMS

To become a good guitar player, it is important to have a system for identifying moveable chord shapes all over the fretboard in any key. Most moveable chord formations are closely related to the **five basic major chord shapes** shown below.

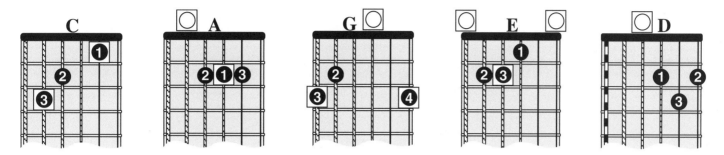

You already know the E form bar chord (root 6) and the A form bar chord (root 5). The C, G and D chords can also be used as the basis for bar chords. There are also many other moveable chord shapes based on these 5 shapes which are useful for Blues playing. The **five basic bar chord forms** are shown below. Notice the order of these forms - **C**, **A**, **G**, **E** and **D**. This order is easy to memorize if you think of the word **caged**.

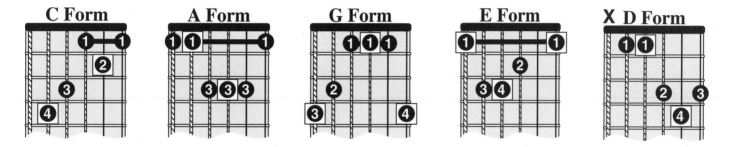

When these five forms (shapes) are placed end to end in the one key, they cover the whole fretboard. E.g. if you start with an **open C chord**, the **A form** bar chord at the **3rd fret** is also a C chord. The **root note** on the **5th string** is shared by both chord forms. The A form chord then connects to a **G form** C chord beginning on the **5th fret**. The **root note** on the **3rd string** is shared by both chord forms. The G form then connects to an **E form** C chord at the **8th fret**. This time there are **two root notes** shared by both forms – one on the **6th string** and one on the **1st string**. The E form then connects to the **D form** at the **10th fret**, this time the shared **root note** is on the **4th string**. To complete the pattern, the D form connects back to the **C form** at the **12th fret**. The shared **root note** between these two forms is on the **2nd string**. This C form is **one octave higher** than the open C form. After this, the whole pattern repeats. The example below demonstrates **all five forms being played as C chords.**

 **5.3**

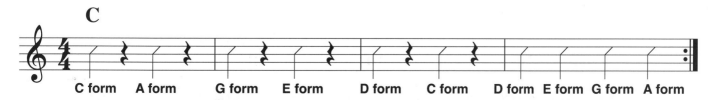

THREE NOTE CHORD VOICINGS

Some of the chord forms shown on the previous page are difficult to play, particularly the G form. The most important thing is to be able to **visualize** these shapes, especially the positions of the root notes. Remember that major chords are made up of three different notes. Any more notes in a chord shape are just doublings of those notes. This means it is possible to play just **three notes** from any of these chord forms instead of using the whole shape. Some common examples of **three note voicings** on the 1st, 2nd and 3rd strings are shown below, along with an example which makes use of them. Once you have learnt them, try transposing them to other keys by moving them up and down the fretboard.

THE HALF BAR

The term **half bar** means the first finger is barring some strings, but not all six. The first G chord shape shown below is played with the first finger barring the 1st and 2nd strings. The second G chord shape is played with the first finger barring the 1st, 2nd and 3rd strings. Practice playing them separately until you can sound all the notes clearly. Then play the example below which uses these shapes to play the chords **G**, **C** and **D**.

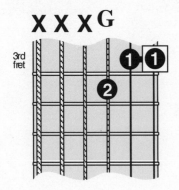 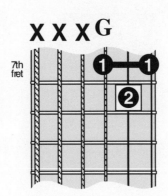 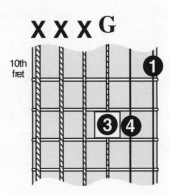

 6.0

This example uses the three shapes shown above. The particular shape used for each chord is indicated above the TAB.

INVERSIONS

All triads contain three different notes. These notes can be duplicated and/or played in a different shape. When the lowest note in each of these three chords is the root note, the chord is said to be in **root position**. When the third (3) is the lowest note of the chord shape, the chord is said to be in **first inversion**. When the fifth (5) is the lowest note of the chord shape, the chord is said to be in **second inversion**. The following example demonstrates the three inversions of a D Major chord, which contains the notes **D**, **F♯** and **A.** The fingerings here are mostly derived from a the C form of a **D major** chord shown in the diagram below.

 6.1 **Inversions of a D Major Chord**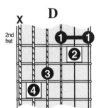

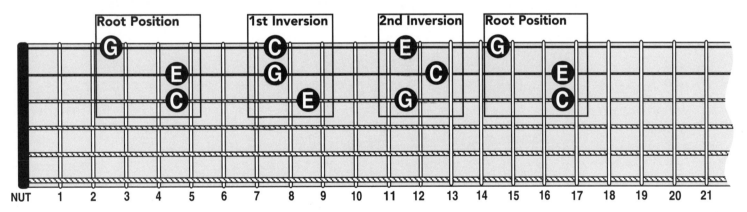

INVERSIONS ALONG SETS OF STRINGS

Because there are three notes in a major chord, it is possible to find all three inversions of any major chord along any set of three adjacent strings. The diagram below demonstrates this with a **C** chord on the **1st**, **2nd** and **3rd** strings.

Here are the above inversions shown as individual chord shapes. Each of them can be used to play **any** major chord.

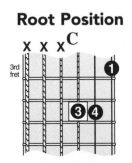
Root Position

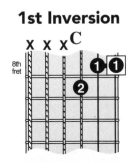
1st Inversion

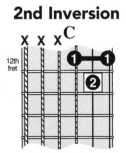
2nd Inversion

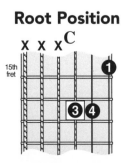
Root Position

Here are the shapes for the three inversions of a **C** chord on the **2nd**, **3rd** and **4th strings**.

Root Position	1st Inversion	2nd Inversion

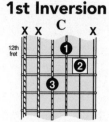
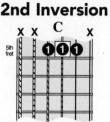

Here are the shapes for the three inversions of a **C** chord on the **3rd**, **4th** and **5th strings**.

Root Position	1st Inversion	2nd Inversion

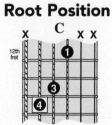
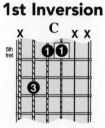
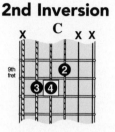

Here are the shapes for the three inversions of a **C** chord on the **4th**, **5th** and **6th strings**.

Root Position	1st Inversion	2nd Inversion

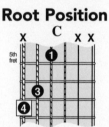
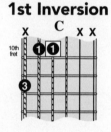
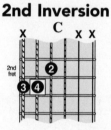

USING INVERSIONS

One of the reasons inversions are useful is that they enable you to find chord shapes which are close together on the fretboard, as demonstrated in the following example which uses various inversions of the chords **D**, **G** and **A** on the 2nd, 3rd and 4th strings. By using inversions which are close together on the fretboard you can create a smoother transition between chords. The way the individual notes connect in chord changes is called **voice leading**. This is dealt with on page 161.

 **6.2**

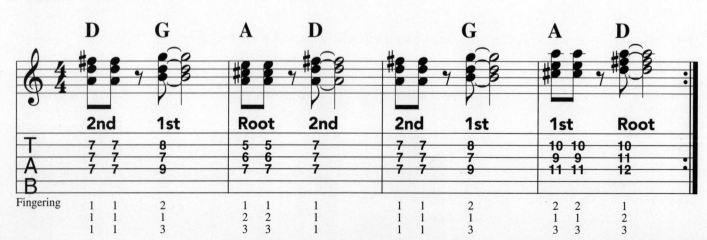

CHORD SYMBOL	MAJOR	CHORD FORMULA
maj		1 3 5

MOVEABLE INVERSIONS

If you add up all three inversions on each set of three strings (4 sets) you come up with 12 different shapes. These are shown below, each with a different root note. Since there are 12 different notes in music, there are 12 possible root notes for any chord type. Learn each shape from memory and then transpose it to the other 11 keys by moving the shape up or down the strings.

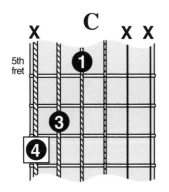
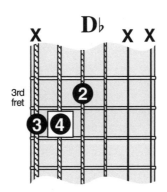
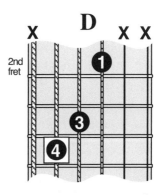
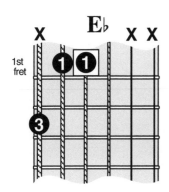
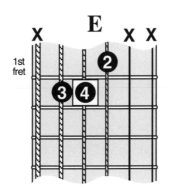
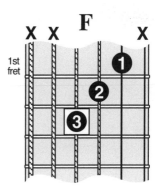
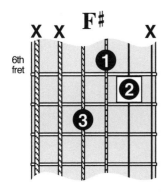
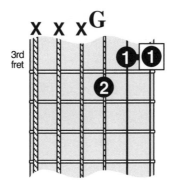
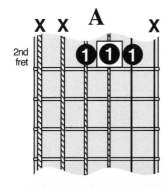
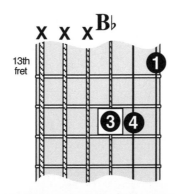
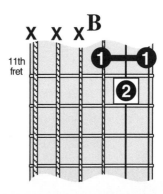

OPEN VOICINGS

By moving the middle note of any triad up an octave, you get what is called an **open voicing**. This has the effect of giving the chord a more open sound. The process is demonstrated below using a first inversion **C** chord. The diagrams below the music show some common open voicings. Learn each one as a **C** chord and then transpose it to all the other keys. You should make a habit of doing this with every new chord voicing you learn.

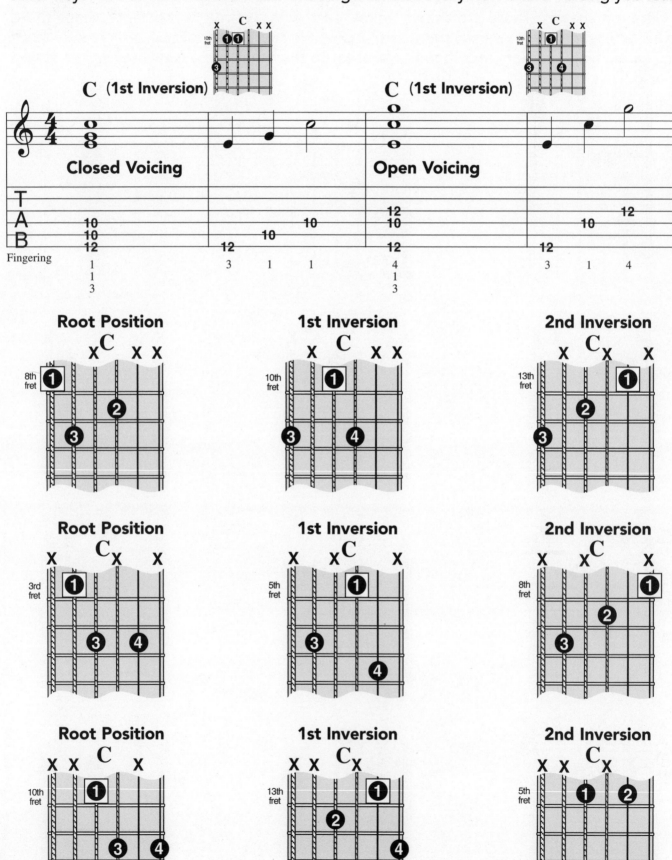

FOUR NOTE VOICINGS

To create a bigger sound, it is common to double one of the notes of a triad, thus creating a **four note voicing**. Two common four note voicings are shown below along with an example demonstrating a guitar part created from them. To change between these chords, all you need to do is play the **D** chord and then place the second and third fingers ahead of the first finger bar to form the **G** chord, as shown in the third diagram here.

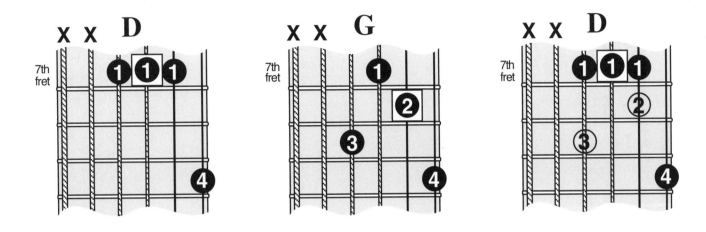

🔘 **6.3**

The first two bars of this example alternates between the two chords shown above and then moves down two frets where the chord shapes become **C** and **F**. Try making up your own parts using these chords. Don't forget to transpose them to all the other keys.

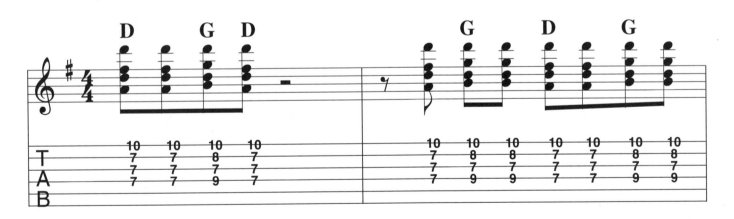

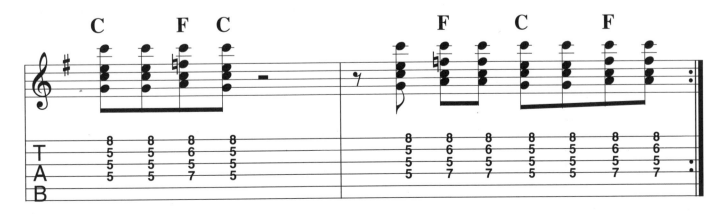

MOVEABLE CHORDS (FOUR NOTE VOICINGS)

Shown below are 16 four note voicings of major chords. They are all derived from the five basic chord forms shown on page 33 (**C A G E** and **D**). Be careful not to confuse the name of the chord with the name of the basic form which the chord shape is derived from.

The term "form" refers to the positions of the root notes and how they relate to an open chord shape. The name of the actual chord depends on the name of the root note. E.g. if the root of a major chord shape at a given fret is a **D note**, then it is a **D major chord** regardless of the pattern formed by the root notes in the shape (which is what determines the name of the form).

Each shape is shown here as a **D** chord, but as always, it is essential to transpose them to all the other keys by sliding them up or down the fretboard to find the root note of the desired chord. The more you do this, the easier it gets, and the more comfortable you will feel playing anywhere on the fretboard.

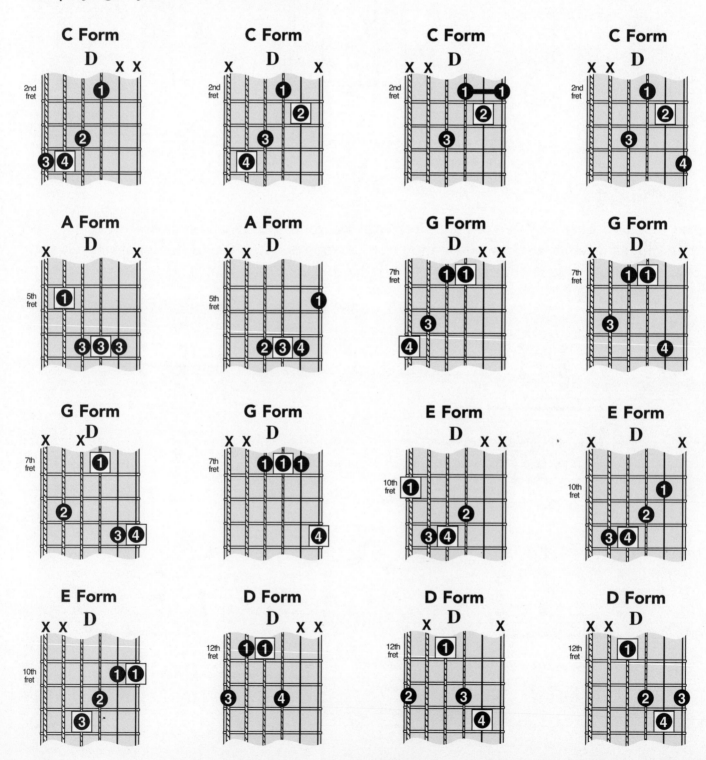

CHORD SYMBOL	MINOR	CHORD FORMULA
m		**1 ♭3 5**

A **minor** chord can be created by flattening the 3rd degree of any major chord. E.g. a **C major** chord contains the notes **C**, **E** and **G**, (**1**, **3** and **5**) while a **C minor** chord contains **C**, **E♭** and **G**, (**1**, **♭3** and **5**). Shown below are some common open minor chord shapes.

OPEN CHORDS

Where there is more than one option for a particular chord, the easiest version is boxed.

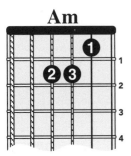 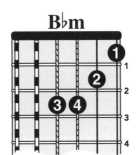 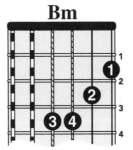 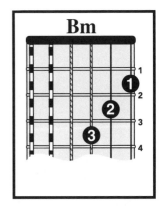

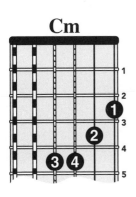 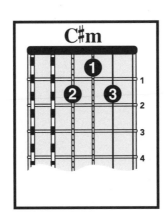 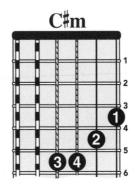 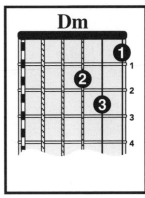

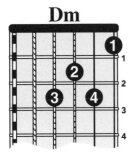 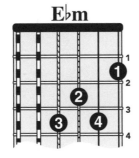 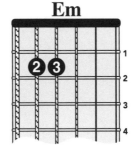 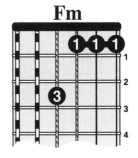

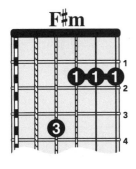 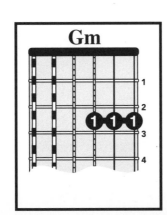 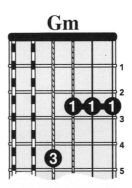 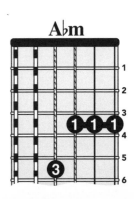

PROGRESSIONS USING OPEN MINOR CHORDS

Here are some progressions which use minor chords and major chords based on the five fundamental forms (**C A G E** and **D** forms). The first one contains both an **A major** and an **A minor** chord. Notice that the root note (**A**) is in the same position for both chords.

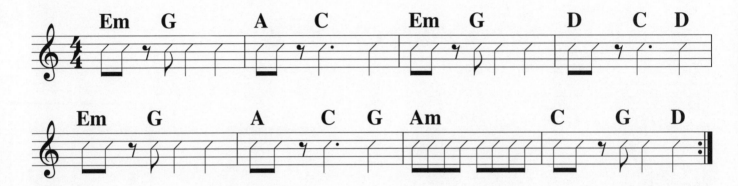

TIES

A **tie** is a curved line that connects two notes with the **same** position on the staff. A tie indicates that you play the **first** note only, and hold it for the length of both notes. For a more in-depth study of ties, see *Progressive Complete Learn to Play Rhythm Guitar Manual*.

MINOR ARPEGGIOS

For every type of chord there is a corresponding arpeggio. Shown below is a **C minor arpeggio** which consists of the notes **C**, **E♭** and **G** which are the **root**, **flattened third** and **fifth** of a **C minor chord**.

8.0 C Minor Arpeggio

 **8.1** **G Minor Arpeggio**

This is a **G minor arpeggio** which consists of the notes **G**, **B♭** and **D**. These are the root, third and fifth of a **G minor chord**.

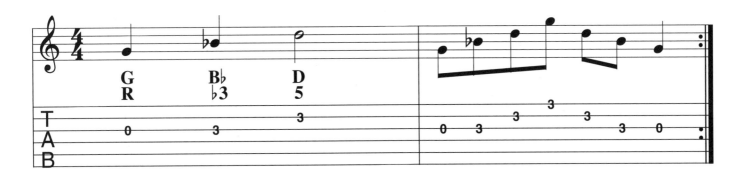

 **9.**

Here is an example which makes use of both major and minor arpeggios. Remember to hold the whole chord shape down as you play each bar. Listen carefully and make sure all the notes sound clearly and evenly.

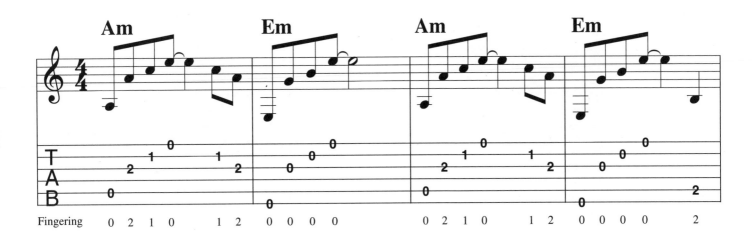

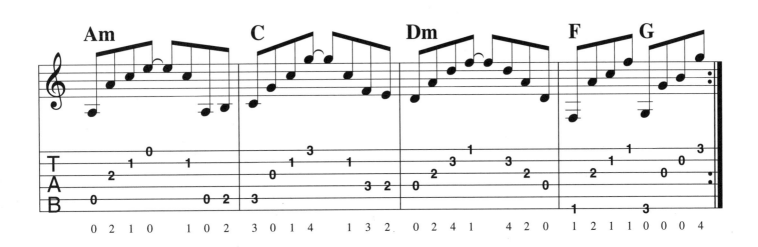

CHORD SYMBOL	MINOR	CHORD FORMULA
m		**1** **♭3** **5**

BAR CHORDS

Bar chords work the same way regardless of whether the chord is major or minor. Shown below are **root 6 minor** and **root 5 minor** bar chords As with major bar chords, simply move the shape up or down the fretboard to find the root note of any minor chord. If you are holding a **root 6** minor bar chord shape, the root note will be on the **6th string**. If you are holding a **root 5** minor bar chord shape, the root note will be on the **5th string**.

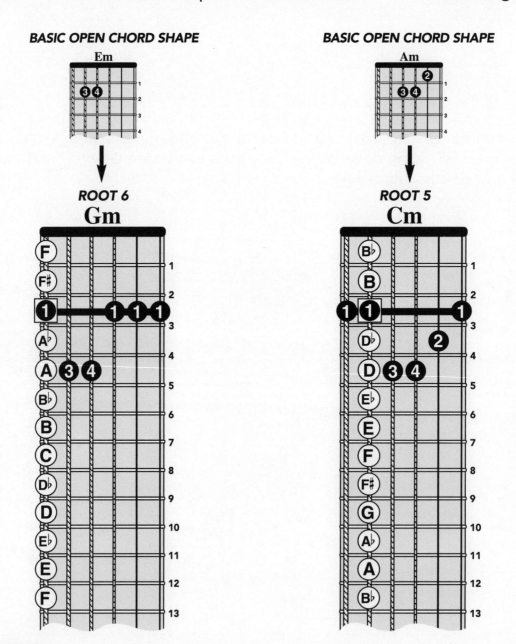

 **10.0**

This example is played using the root 6 and root 5 minor shapes shown above, along with a root 5 major bar chord.

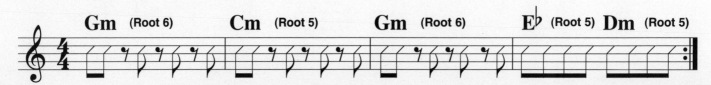

 **10.1**

Here is the same progression played as arpeggios and using different chord shapes. It is important to experiment with different ways of playing every new progression you learn.

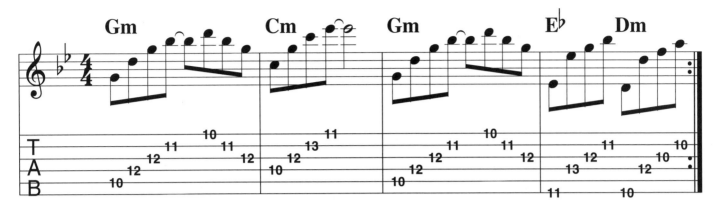

MOVEABLE MINOR CHORDS

Once you know the basic system of moveable major chord shapes (the **C**, **A**, **G**, **E** and **D** forms) it is possible to alter some of the notes to create other chord types, e.g. minor chords. **The positions of the root notes remain the same regardless of the chord type.** Shown below are the five basic forms as open position minor chords.

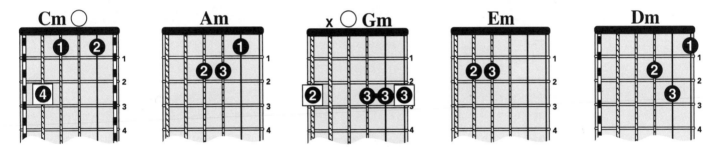

Like major chords, these minor forms can be joined end to end in the same order (CAGED) to cover the whole fretboard. Shown below are the five basic forms of moveable minor chords.

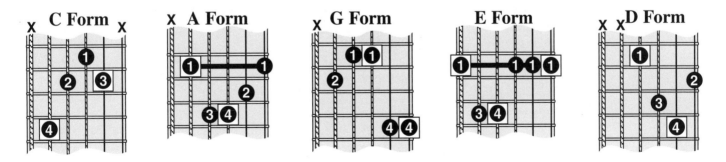

The example below demonstrates **all five forms** played as **C minor chords.** Practice them slowly and memorize the shapes and positions of the root notes. When you can do this easily, transpose them to other keys.

 **10.2**

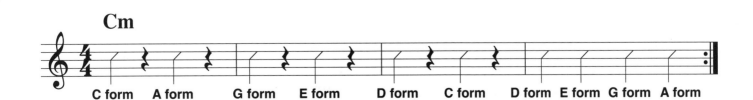

CHORD SYMBOL	MINOR	CHORD FORMULA
m		**1 ♭3 5**

MOVEABLE INVERSIONS

As mentioned previously, any chord type can be arranged into inversions. Like major chords, minor chords have three possible inversions named according to the lowest note. The diagrams below show a C minor triad (notes **C**, **E** and **G**) in root position, first inversion and second inversion on four sets of strings. As always, each one can be used to play twelve different minor chords, built from each note of the chromatic scale (see page 137).

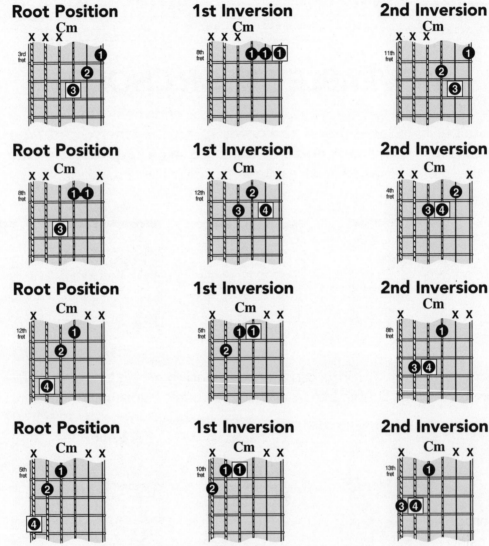

MINOR OPEN VOICINGS

Like major chords, it is possible to create open voicings from minor chord inversions by moving the middle note up an octave. Shown below are three open voicings of a **Cm** chord at the 5th position (fret). These are all within the basic G form of a C minor chord.

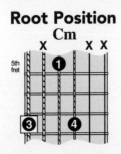
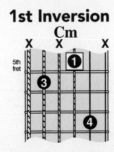
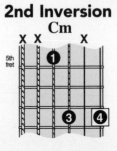

MOVEABLE MINOR CHORDS (4 NOTE VOICINGS)

Each shape is shown here as an **A minor** chord (**Am**), but as always, it is essential to transpose them to all the other keys once you have memorized the shapes.

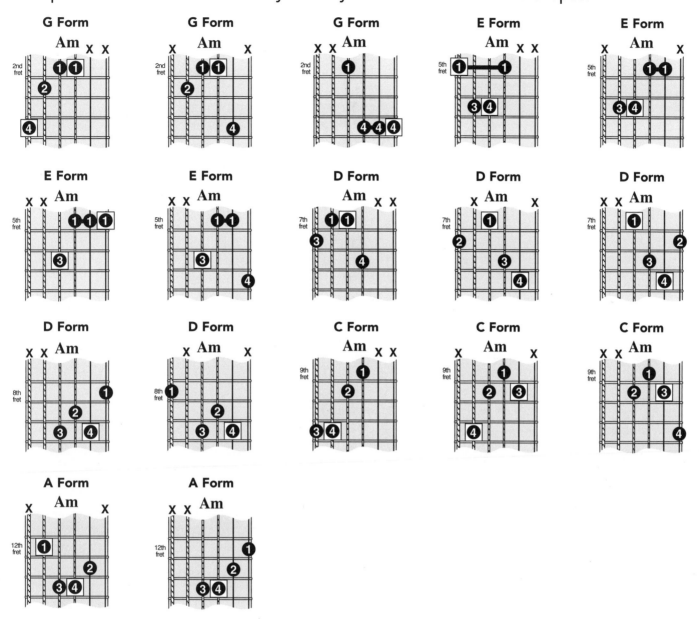

The following progression uses moveable four note voicings on the first four strings. It is played with a rhythm using **sixteenth notes** (four notes per quarter note beat). If you are not familiar with sixteenth note rhythms, see *Progressive Complete Learn to Play Rhythm Guitar Manual*.

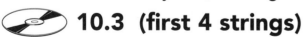

10.3 (first 4 strings)

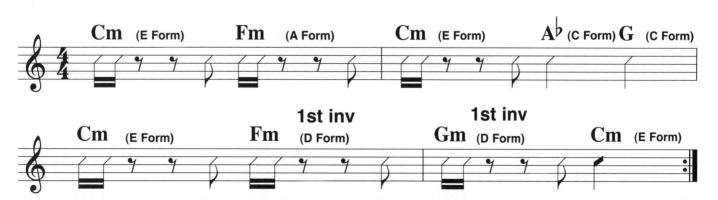

CHORD SYMBOL
sus

SUSPENDED

CHORD FORMULA
1 4 5

A **suspended** chord can be created by substituting the 4th degree of a chord for the third. E.g. a **C major** chord contains the notes **C, E** and **G, (1, 3** and **5)** while a **C suspended** chord contains **C, F** and **G, (1, 4** and **5)**. Shown below are some common open suspended chord shapes.

OPEN CHORDS

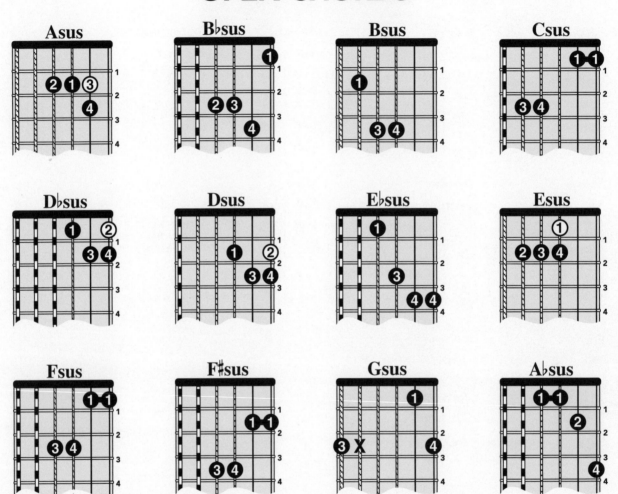

When using suspended chords, it is common to alternate them with the major chord of the same name. This is demonstrated in the following progression which uses shapes shown above, along with open major chords.

11.0

CHORD SYMBOL
sus

SUSPENDED

CHORD FORMULA
1   4   5

BAR CHORDS

Like major and minor chords, suspended chords can also be played as bar chords. The diagrams below demonstrate how root 6 and root 5 bar chords can be formed from open **Esus** and **Asus** chords. Like all bar chords, you simply move the shape along the fretboard to find different chords.

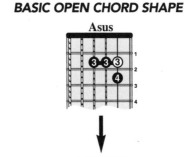

BASIC OPEN CHORD SHAPE   **BASIC OPEN CHORD SHAPE**

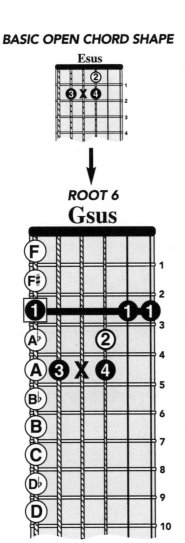
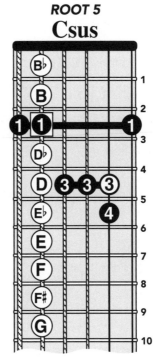

ROOT 6 — Gsus   ROOT 5 — Csus

 **11.1**

This progression is the same as the one on the previous page, but this time it is played using bar chords. The **A** and **Asus** are **root 6** bar chords. All the **D** and **E** chords are **root 5**. The **G** and **Gsus** can be played as either root 6 or root 5.

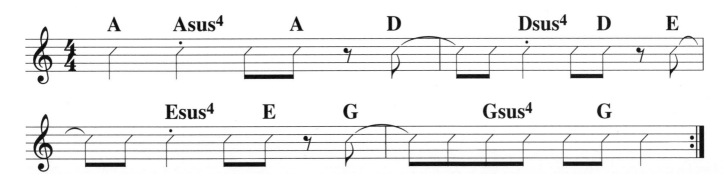

CHORD SYMBOL	SUSPENDED	CHORD FORMULA
sus		1 4 5

MOVEABLE CHORDS

Here are some of the most commonly used three note open voicings, and four note voicings of suspended chords. Each voicing is shown as an **Fsus** chord, and as always they can all be transposed to 11 other keys by locating the appropriate root note.

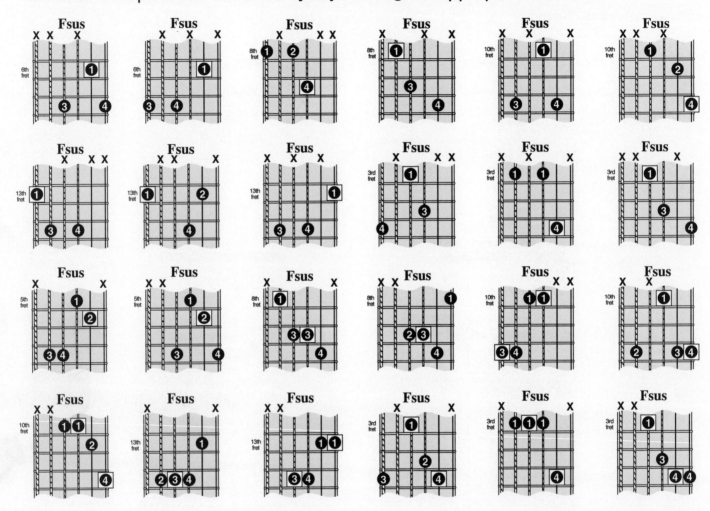

The following progression uses a second inversion suspended chord shape on the first three strings which is derived from the open D form. The shape is simply moved up the fretboard to change between the chords.

 11.2

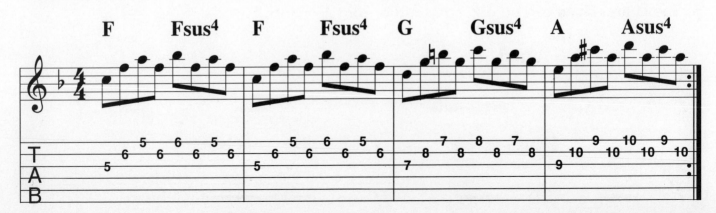

CHORD SYMBOL	MAJOR	CHORD FORMULA
- 5 or (♭5)		1 3 ♭5

As its name suggests, a **Major flat five** chord can be created by **flattening** the **5th** degree of any major chord. E.g. a **C major** chord contains the notes **C, E** and **G**, (**1, 3** and **5**) while a **C-5** chord contains **C, E** and **G♭**, (**1, 3** and **♭5**). Shown below are some common open major flat five chord shapes.

OPEN CHORDS

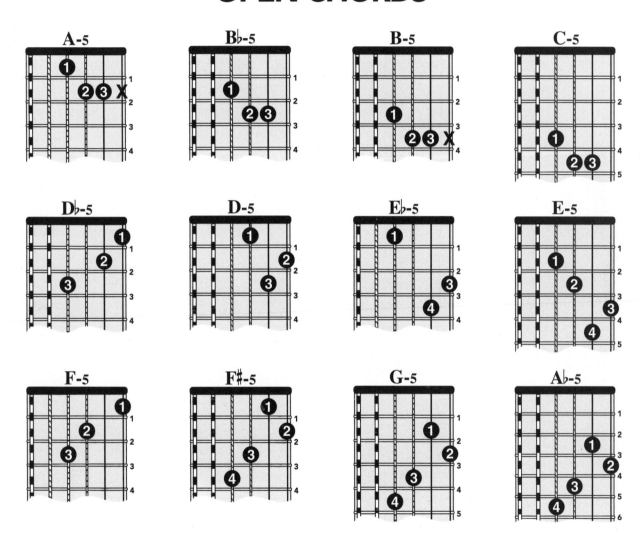

🔘 **12.0**

This progression uses the **D-5** chord shown above.

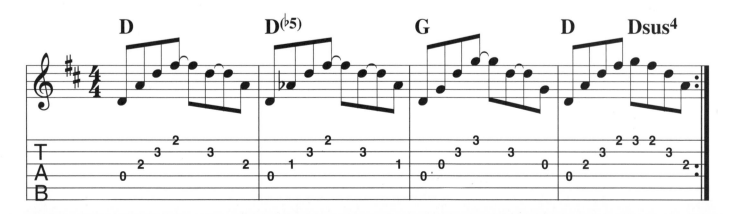

CHORD SYMBOL	MAJOR	CHORD FORMULA
- 5 or (♭5)		1 3 ♭5

MOVEABLE CHORDS

Here are some moveable three note open voicings, and four note voicings of major flat fiver chords. Each voicing is shown as a **G(♭5)** chord, and as always they can all be transposed to 11 other keys by locating the appropriate root note.

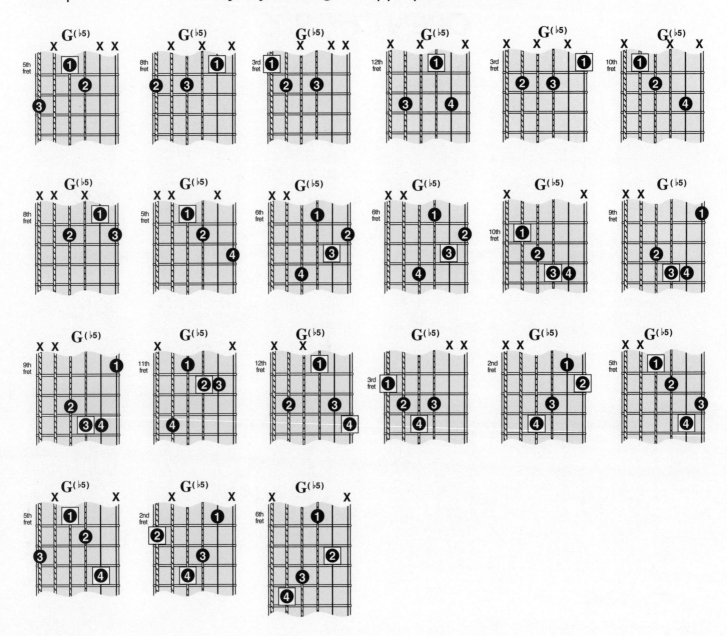

 **12.1**

This example can be played with one shape moved up and down the strings. On the recording it is played with an A form chord, but experiment with all the shapes shown above.

CHORD SYMBOL
+

AUGMENTED

CHORD FORMULA
1   3   ♯5

An **Augmented** chord can be created by **sharpening** the **5th** degree of any major chord. E.g. a **C major** chord contains the notes **C**, **E** and **G**, (**1**, **3** and **5**) while a **C+** chord contains **C**, **E** and **G♯**, (**1**, **3** and **♯5**). Shown below are some common open Augmented chord shapes.

OPEN CHORDS

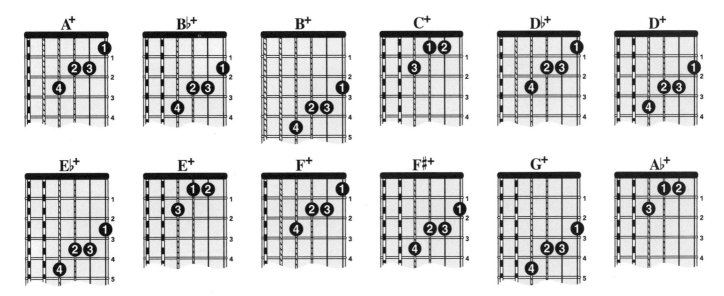

THREE CHORDS IN ONE

If you look at the diagrams above, you will notice that only one shape is required to play all twelve possible augmented chords. This is because the augmented chord is a **symmetrical chord** which means that any of the notes in the chord can be the root note. Therefore, each augmented chord has three possible names (or sometimes more counting enharmonic notes - e.g. **B♭ = A♯**). There are really only **four** augmented chords, each one having at least three names. They can all be played by forming an augmented chord and then moving the shape up the neck one fret at a time. After the fourth chord you get back to a repeat of the first one as demonstrated below.

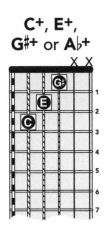

C+, E+, G♯+ or A♭+

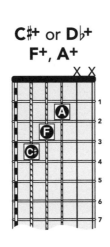

C♯+ or D♭+ F+, A+

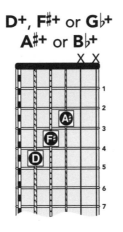

D+, F♯+ or G♭+ A♯+ or B♭+

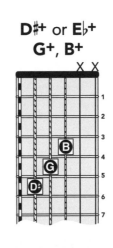

D♯+ or E♭+ G+, B+

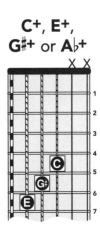

C+, E+, G♯+ or A♭+

CHORD SYMBOL	AUGMENTED	CHORD FORMULA
+		1 3 ♯5

MOVEABLE CHORDS

Here are some useful three note open voicings, and four note voicings of Augmented chords. No names or root notes are shown because **any** of the notes in each shape can be the **root note** and therefore the name of the chord. Each time a shape is moved, it will have at least three possible new names. Learn to name each shape from all of its notes. The examples below the chord shapes demonstrate some typical uses of augmented chords.

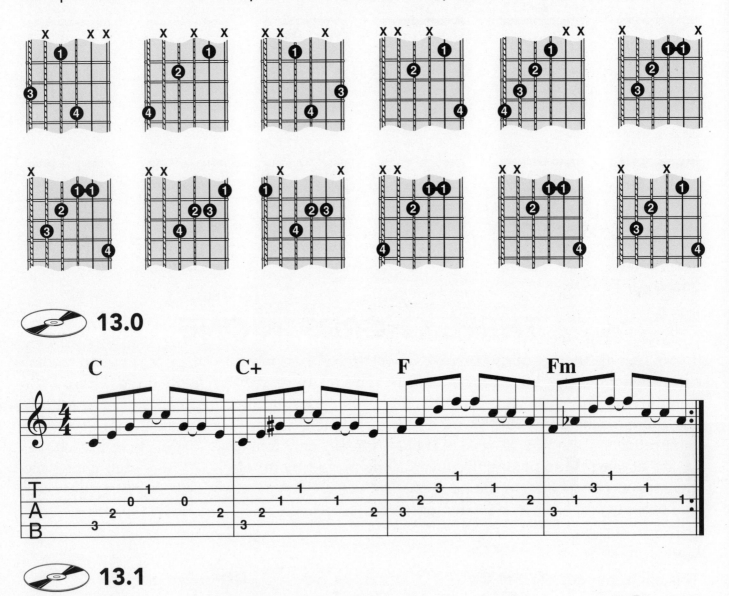

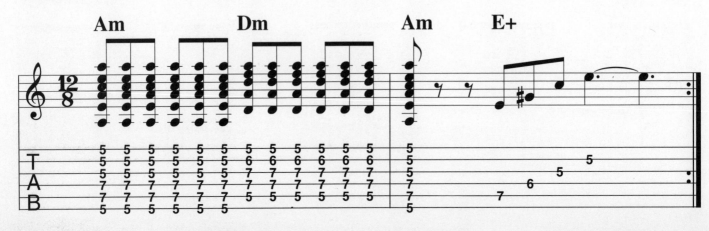

CHORD SYMBOL
O or Dim

DIMINISHED

CHORD FORMULA
1   3   ♭5

There are two types of diminished chords which are often interchangeable. The ones shown here contain three notes (triads). The other type is the diminished 7th chord. It contains four notes and is demonstrated in the next section. The shapes below show diminished triads in various inversions built on twelve different root notes. The bottom line of chords demonstrate some open voicings built on the notes **D**, **A**, and **E**. These can be transposed to all the other keys.

DIMINISHED TRIAD SHAPES

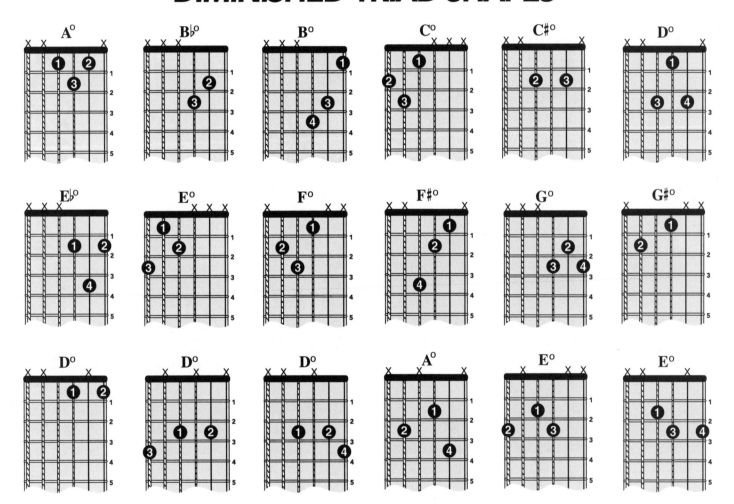

14.

This example uses the **Bdim** chord in root position as shown in the diagram above.

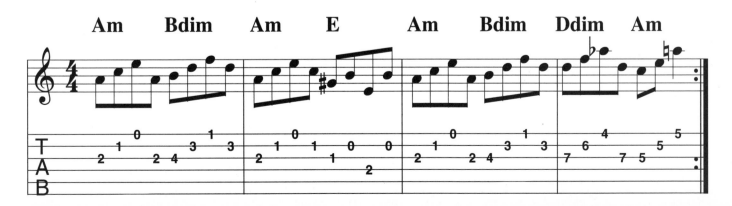

Section 2
Four Note Chords

This section covers many new chord types which contain **four different notes**. They are all created by adding one extra note to the various types of triads you learnt in section 1. From here on, there will be only **two** categories of chord diagrams - **open chords** and **moveable chords**. Bar chords will be included in the moveable chords section as they are a particular type of moveable chord.

The most common four note chords are the various types of **7th chords**: e.g. Major, minor and dominant 7ths. Seventh chords are created by adding a **7th degree** on top of a triad. The type of seventh chord depends on the type of triad, and whether the seventh is natural (e.g. a **B** note in C major) or flattened (e.g. a **B** note in C major). There are also other four note chords such as **6ths** and **add9** chords. Each of these types is introduced in section 2 with its particular formula and many useful fingerings, along with examples demonstrating the use of each chord type.

INVERSIONS OF FOUR NOTE CHORDS

Like triads, four note chords can be played in various inversion. Because there are four notes, there are also four possible inversions - **Root Position** (root in bass), **First inversion** (3rd in bass), second inversion (5th in bass) and **Third inversion** (7th in bass). This is demonstrated below with a **C7 chord** which contains the notes **C**, **E**, **G** and **B♭.**

C7	B♭ G E C	C B♭ G E	E C B♭ G	G E C B♭
	Root Position	**1st Inversion**	**2nd Inversion**	**3rd Inversion**

MORE ABOUT OPEN VOICINGS

Closed voicings of four note chord inversions are not very practical on the guitar because they require large finger stretches. Because of this, open voicings are commonly used. The following diagrams demonstrate this with a **first inversion C7 chord** in closed position followed by an open voicing.

C7 First Inversion Closed Voicing

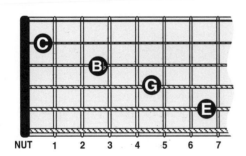

Open Voicing

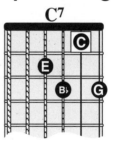

4 NOTE INVERSIONS ALONG GROUPS OF STRINGS

By using open voicings, it is possible to find comfortable fingerings for all inversions of four note chords along groups of strings. The following diagrams demonstrate some practical voicings for inversions of a **C7** chord on the first four strings.

1st Inversion

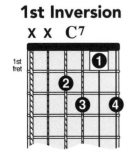

2nd Inversion

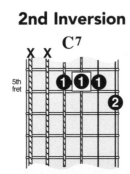

3rd Inversion

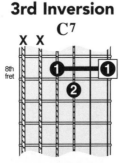

Root Position

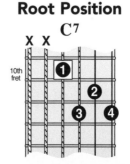

1st Inversion

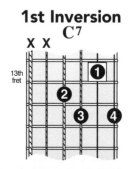

CHORD SYMBOL

add 9

MAJOR

CHORD FORMULA

| 1 | 3 | 5 | 9 |

A **major add9** chord is created by adding a **9th** degree to any major chord. E.g. a **Cadd9** chord contains the notes **C**, **E**, **G** and **D** (**1**, **3**, **5** and **9**). Shown below are some common open major add9 chord shapes.

OPEN CHORDS

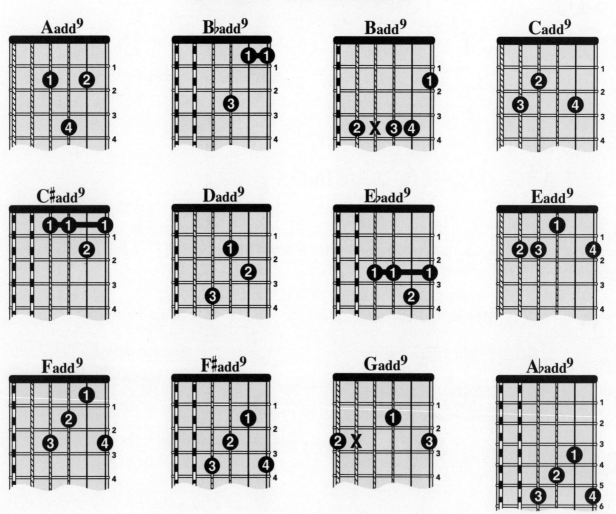

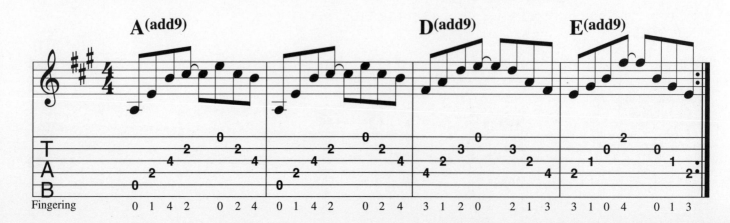

15.0

This example uses three of the major add9 chord shapes shown above.

CHORD SYMBOL	MAJOR	CHORD FORMULA
add 9		**1 3 5 9**

MOVEABLE CHORDS

Here are some moveable fingerings for **major add9** chords, shown here as **Aadd9**. The fingerings on this page are all on groups of four adjacent strings. With all four note chords, it is possible to find three such groups - **top four**, **middle four** and **bottom four.**

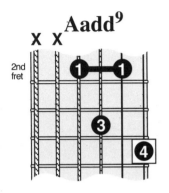
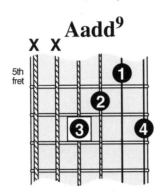
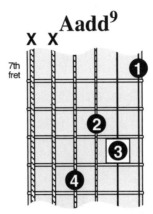
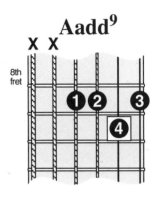

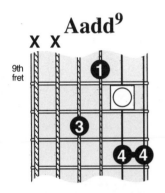
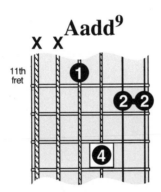
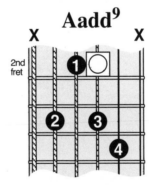
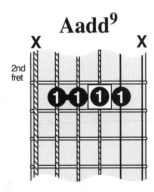

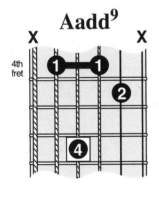
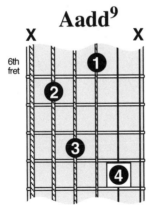
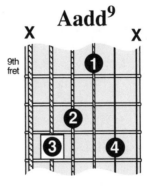
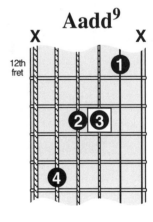

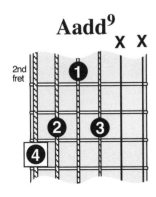
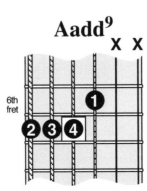
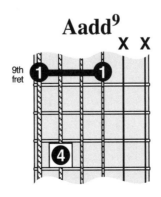
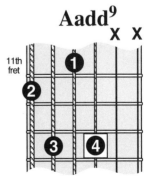

CHORD SYMBOL	MAJOR	CHORD FORMULA
add 9		**1 3 5 9**

MOVEABLE CHORDS

Here are some more moveable fingerings for **major add9** chords. These ones are not on groups of four adjacent strings, but all are commonly used shapes. Some contain doubled notes - usually the root or 5th of the chord. Although quite a few fingerings are shown here, there are always more possibilities. Memorize the chord formula and then experiment with all possible combinations of the notes to come up with your own fingerings.

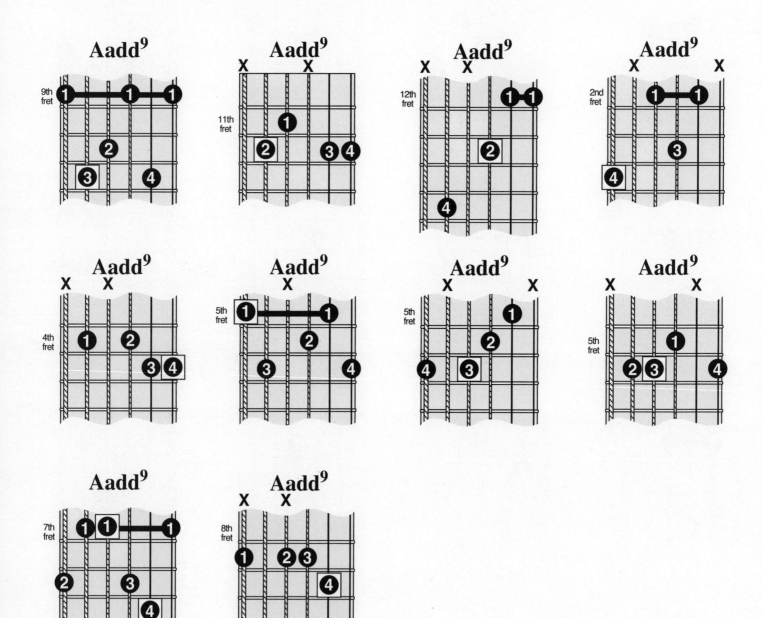

CHORD SYMBOL

m add 9

MINOR

CHORD FORMULA

1 ♭3 5 9

A **minor add9** chord is created by adding a **9th** degree to any minor chord. E.g. a **Cmadd9** chord contains the notes **C, E♭, G** and **D** (**1, ♭3, 5** and **9**). Shown below are some common open minor add9 chord shapes.

OPEN CHORDS

Amadd⁹

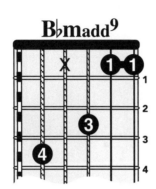
B♭madd⁹

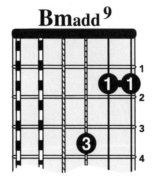
Bmadd⁹

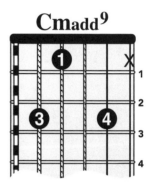
Cmadd⁹

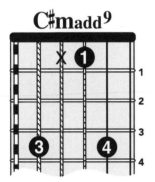
C♯madd⁹

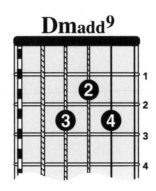
Dmadd⁹

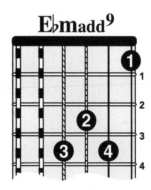
E♭madd⁹

Emadd⁹

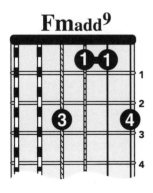
Fmadd⁹

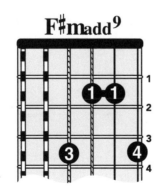
F♯madd⁹

Gmadd⁹

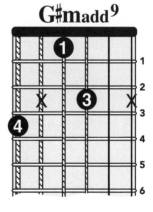
G♯madd⁹

CHORD SYMBOL

m add 9

MINOR

CHORD FORMULA

1 ♭3 5 9

MOVEABLE CHORDS

Here are some useful moveable fingerings for **minor add9** chords, shown here as **Am add9**. Each of these shapes can be related back to the five basic forms (C A G E D) As with all chord types, learn the shapes shown here, then memorize the chord formula and then experiment with all possible combinations of the notes to come up with your own fingerings.

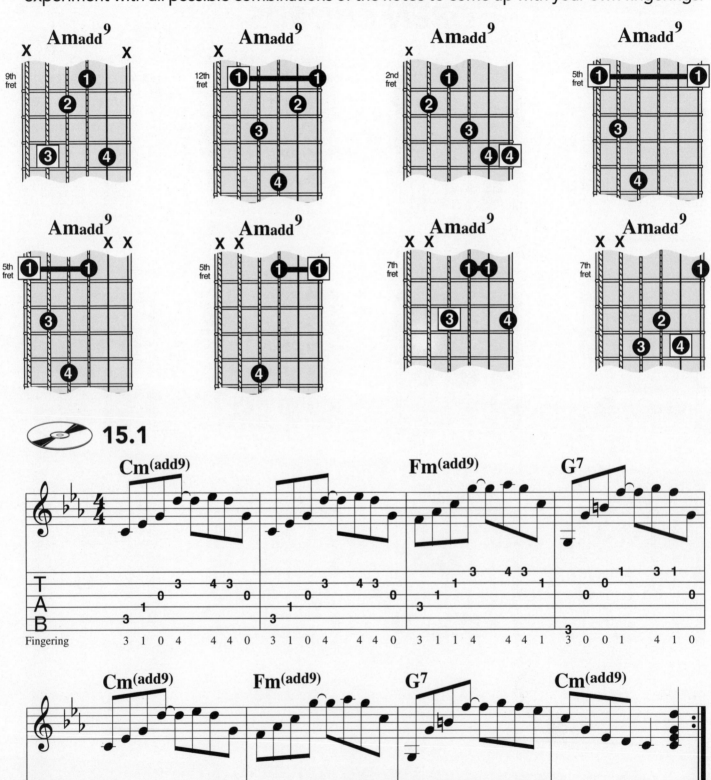

CHORD SYMBOL
6

SIXTH

CHORD FORMULA
1   3   5   6

A **major 6th** chord is created by adding a **6th** degree to any major chord. E.g. a **C6** chord contains the notes **C**, **E**, **G** and **A** (**1**, **3**, **5** and **6**). Shown below are some common open major 6th chord shapes. Where there is more than one option for a particular chord, the easiest version is boxed.

OPEN CHORDS

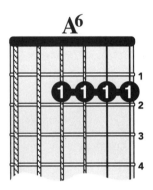
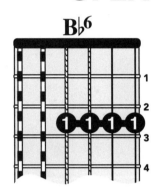
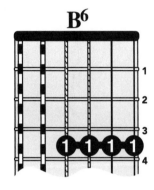
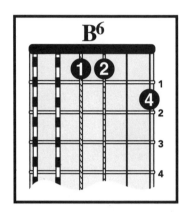

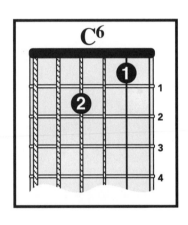
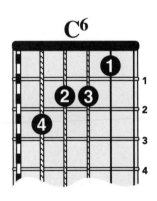
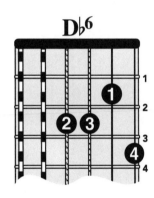
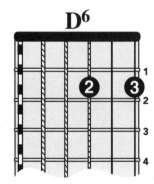

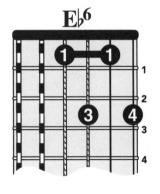
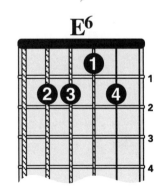
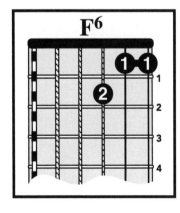
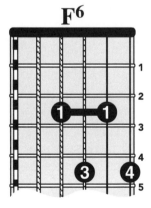

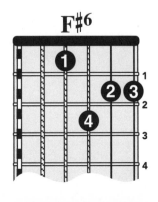
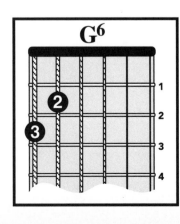
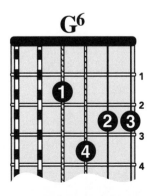
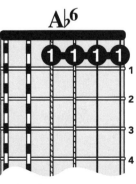

6

SIXTH

CHORD FORMULA

1 3 5 6

MOVEABLE CHORDS

Here are some moveable fingerings for **major 6th** chords, shown here as **B♭6**. The fingerings on this page are all on groups of four adjacent strings - **top four, middle four** and **bottom four. The shapes on the following page** are not on groups of four adjacent strings, but all are commonly used shapes. Each one relates to one of the five basic forms. As with all chord types, these are determined by the positions of the root notes.

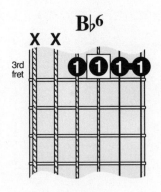

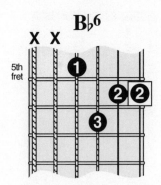

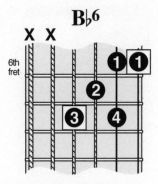

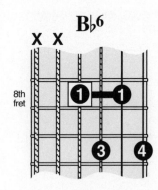

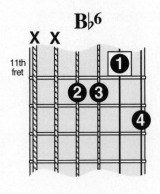

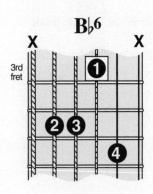

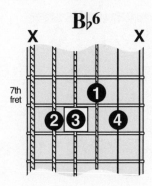

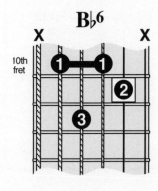

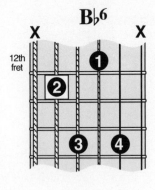

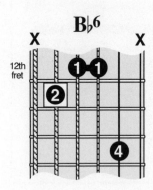

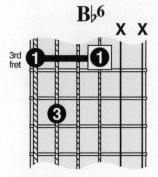

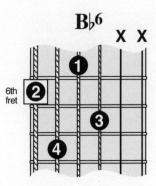

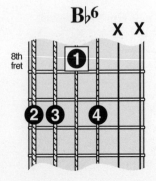

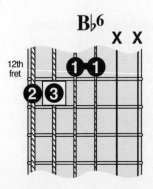

CHORD SYMBOL
6

SIXTH

CHORD FORMULA
1 3 5 6

MOVEABLE CHORDS

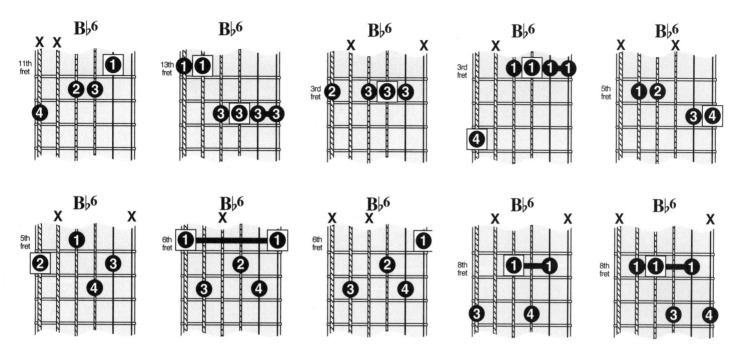

 16.0

Here is a guitar part using **major 6th** chords. The eighth notes in this example are swung, as indicated by the above symbol. If you are not familiar with swing rhythms, see *Progressive Complete Learn to Play Rhythm Guitar Manual*.

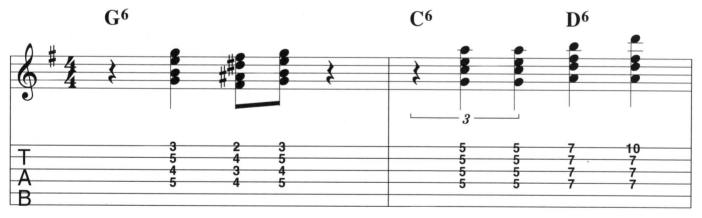

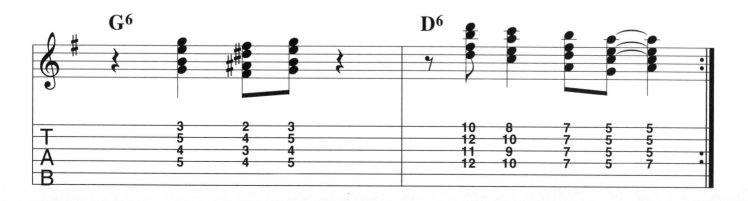

CHORD SYMBOL

m^6

MINOR SIXTH

CHORD FORMULA

1 $\flat$3 5 6

A **minor 6th** chord is created by adding a **6th** degree to any minor chord. E.g. a **Cm6** chord contains the notes **C**, **E**$\flat$, **G** and **A** (**1**, $\flat$**3**, **5** and **6**). Shown below are some common open minor 6th chord shapes.

OPEN CHORDS

Am^6
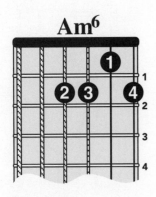

B$\flat$m^6
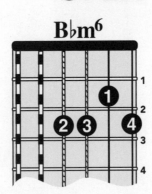

Bm^6
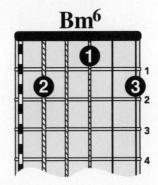

Cm^6
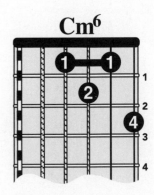

C$\sharp$m^6
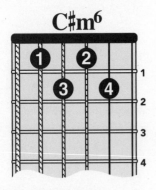

Dm^6
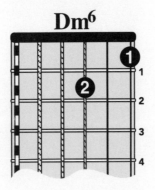

E$\flat$m^6
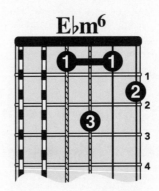

Em^6
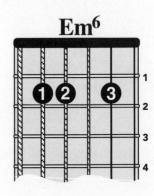

Fm^6
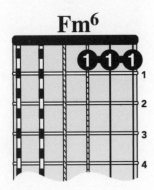

F$\sharp$m^6
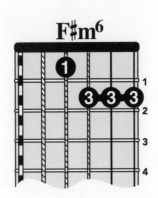

Gm^6

A$\flat$m^6
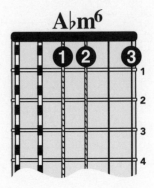

CHORD SYMBOL
m⁶

MINOR SIXTH

CHORD FORMULA
1 ♭3 5 6

MOVEABLE CHORDS

Here are some moveable fingerings for **minor 6th** chords, shown here as **B♭m6**. The fingerings on this page are all on groups of four adjacent strings - **top four**, **middle four** and **bottom four. The shapes on the following page** are not on groups of four adjacent strings, but all are commonly used shapes which relate to the five basic forms.

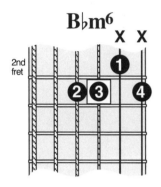
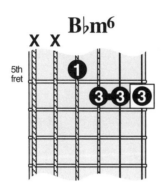
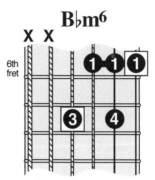
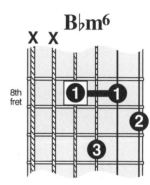

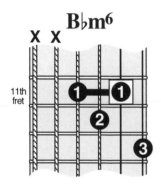
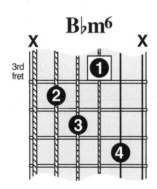
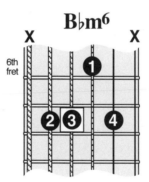
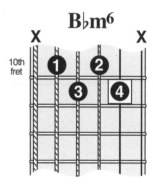

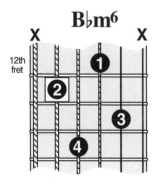
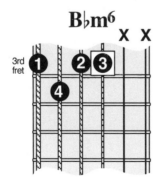
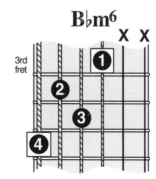
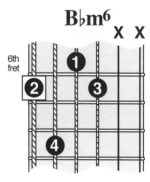

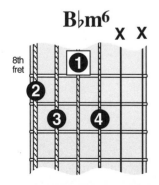
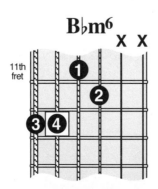

68

CHORD SYMBOL
m^6

MINOR SIXTH

CHORD FORMULA
1 ♭3 5 6

MOVEABLE CHORDS

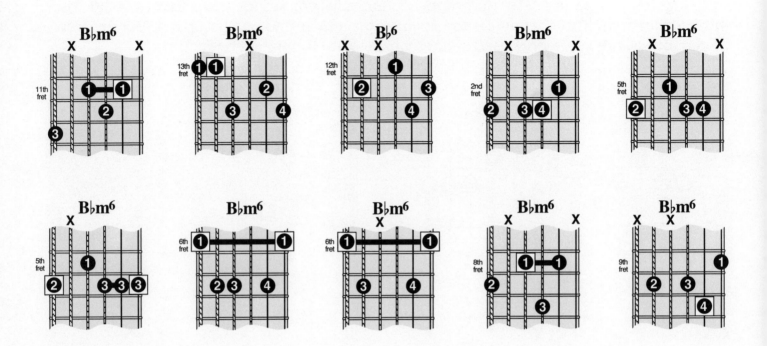

Here are some examples demonstrating the use of **minor 6th** chords. Learn them and then experiment with the ideas presented to come up with your own parts and progressions.

 **16.1**

 **16.2**

SEVENTH CHORD TYPES

By adding extra notes on top of the basic triads, it is possible to create various types of **seventh** chords. The **7th degree is** either a major or minor third interval above the basic triad. Intervals are explained in detail on pages 145 to 152. The formulas for the **five basic types** of seventh chords are shown below.

Major Seventh
Chord Formula

Chord Symbol

| CMaj7 |
| or |
| CØ7 |

1   3   5   7

Notes in Chord

C	E	G	B
1	3	5	7

Dominant Seventh
Chord Formula

Chord Symbol

| C7 |

1   3   5   ♭7

Notes in Chord

C	E	G	B♭
1	3	5	♭7

Minor Seventh
Chord Formula

Chord Symbol

| Cm7 |

1   ♭3   5   ♭7

Notes in Chord

C	E♭	G	B♭
1	♭3	5	♭7

Minor Seven Flat Five
Chord Formula

Chord Symbol

| Cm7♭5 |
| or |
| CØ7 |

1   ♭3   ♭5   ♭7

Notes in Chord

C	E♭	G♭	B♭
1	♭3	♭5	♭7

The final type of seventh chord is the diminished seventh. This chord is unusual in that it contains a **double flattened 7th** degree (♭♭7). This note is actually the same as the 6th degree (A) but it is technically called B♭♭7 because the interval has to be some kind of seventh rather than a sixth because the chord is a type of **seventh** chord.

Diminished Seventh
Chord Formula

Chord Symbol

| C°7♭ |

1   ♭3   ♭5   ♭♭7

Notes in Chord

C	E♭	G♭	B♭♭
1	♭3	♭5	♭♭7

CHORD SYMBOL

maj⁷ or Ø

MAJOR

CHORD FORMULA

| 1 | 3 | 5 | 7 |

A **major 6th** chord is created by adding a **7th** degree to any major chord. E.g. a **Cmaj7** chord contains the notes **C**, **E**, **G** and **B** (**1**, **3**, **5** and **7**). Shown below are some common open major 7th chord shapes.

OPEN CHORDS

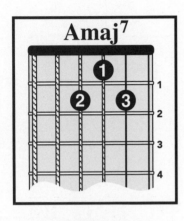

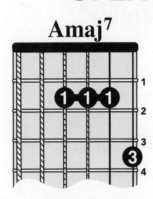

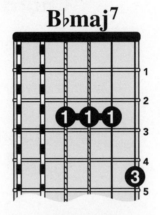

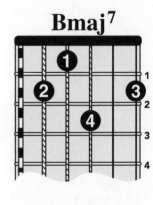

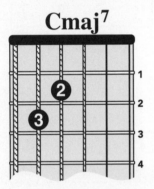

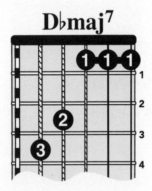

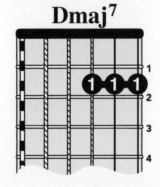

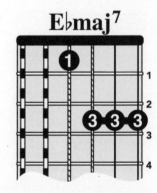

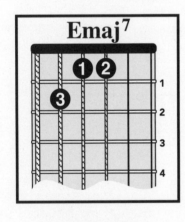

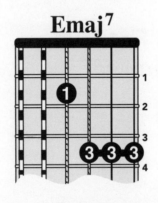

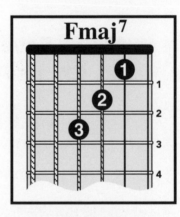

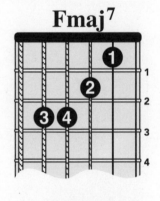

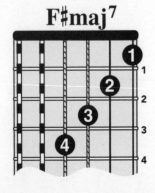

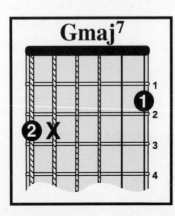

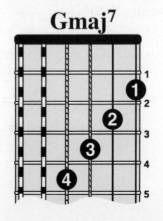

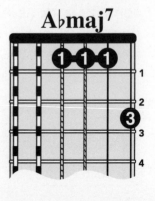

CHORD SYMBOL
maj⁷ or ∅

MAJOR

CHORD FORMULA
| 1 | 3 | 5 | 7 |

MOVEABLE CHORDS

Here are some moveable fingerings for **major 7th** chords, shown here as **Bmaj7**. As before, voicings on four adjacent strings are shown first, followed by other useful shapes which relate back to the five basic forms. Don't forget to transpose them to all keys.

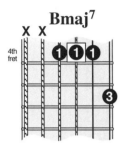 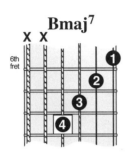 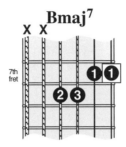 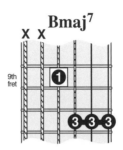 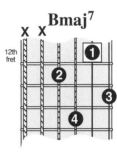

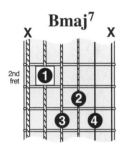 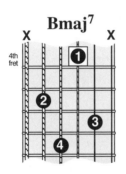 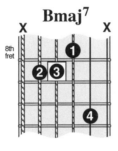 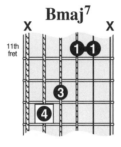 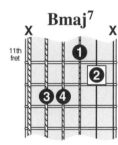

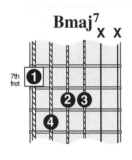 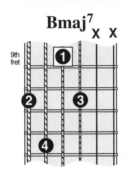 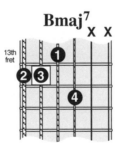 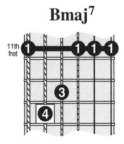 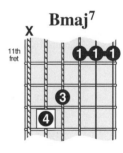

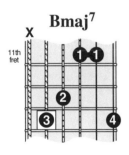 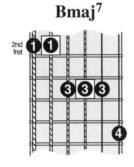 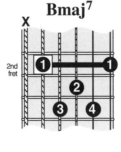 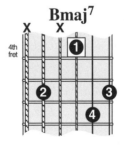 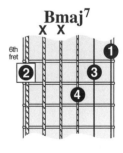

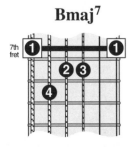 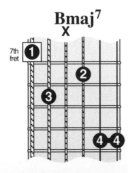 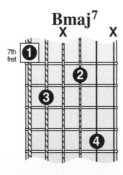 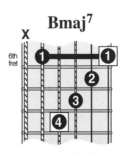 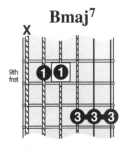

CHORD SYMBOL	MAJOR	CHORD FORMULA
maj⁷ or ∅		**1 3 5 7**

A good way to become familiar with a new chord type is to concentrate on two or three shapes at a time as shown below, using them to play a simple progression as shown in the following example. The progression alternates between two chords, but the same shape is not used every time the chord symbol appears. The shapes used on the recording are indicated above the notation.

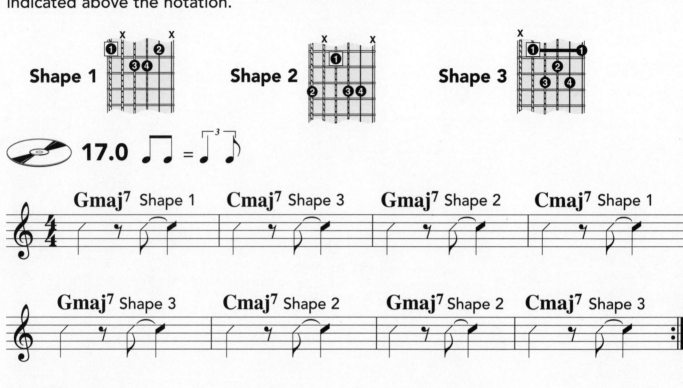

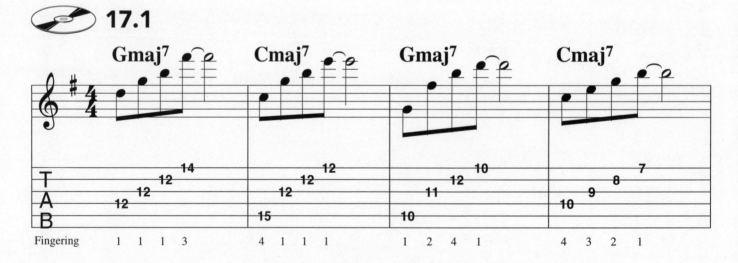

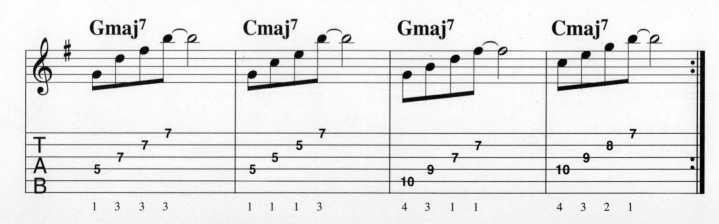

CHORD SYMBOL
7

SEVENTH

CHORD FORMULA
1   3   5   ♭7

A **dominant 7th** chord (usually just called a **7th chord**) is created by adding a **flattened 7th** degree to any major chord. E.g. a **C7** chord contains the notes **C, E, G** and **B♭** (**1, 3, 5** and ♭**7**). Shown below are some common open dominant 7th chord shapes.

OPEN CHORDS

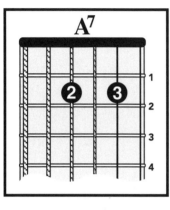
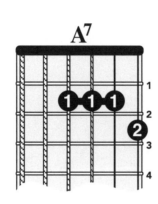
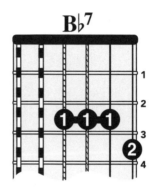
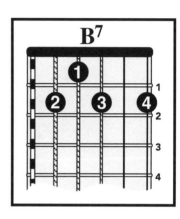

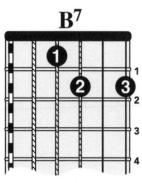
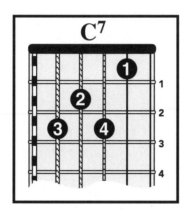
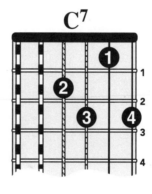
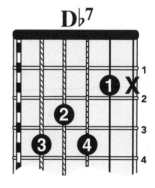

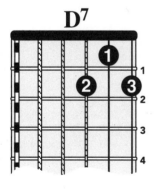
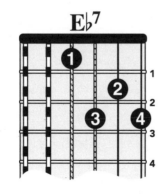
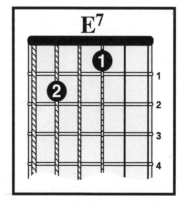

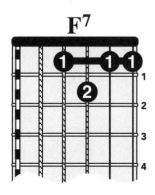
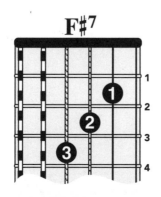
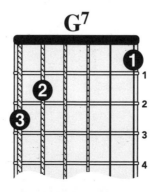
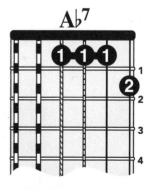

74

CHORD SYMBOL
7

SEVENTH

CHORD FORMULA
1 3 5 ♭7

MOVEABLE CHORDS

Here are some moveable fingerings for **dominant 7th** chords, shown here as **D♭7**. The fingerings on this page are all on groups of four adjacent strings - **top four**, **middle four** and **bottom four**. Once you are comfortable with each shape, transpose it to all keys.

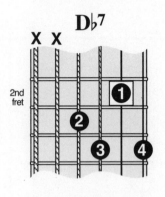
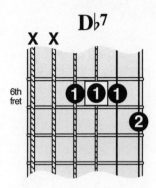
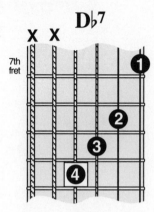
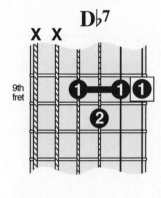
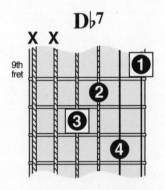
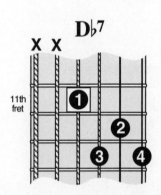
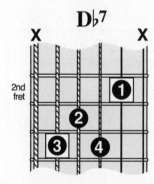
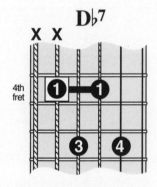
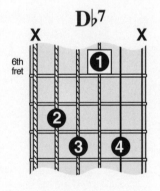
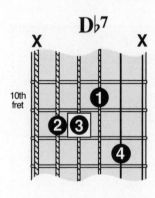
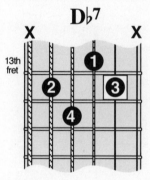
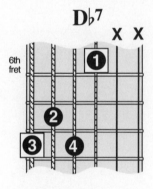
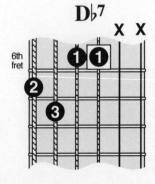
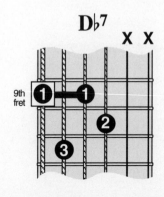
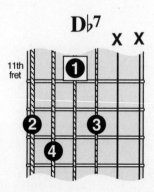
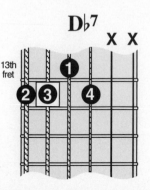

CHORD SYMBOL
7

SEVENTH

CHORD FORMULA
1 3 5 ♭7

MOVEABLE CHORDS

Here are some moveable dominant 7th chord shapes which are not on four adjacent strings. They all relate back to the five basic forms. Don't forget to transpose them to all keys.

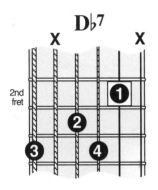
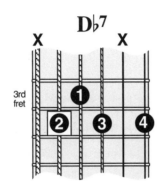
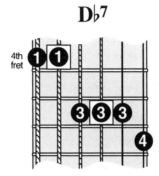
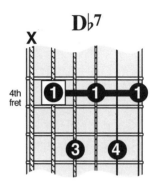

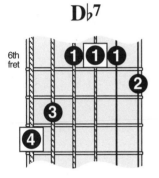
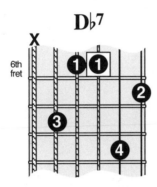
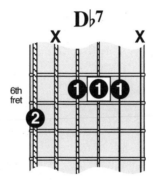
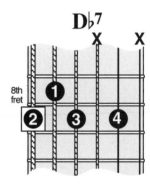

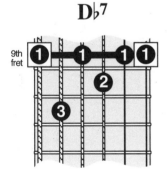
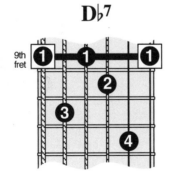
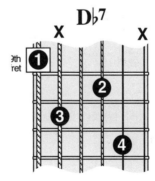
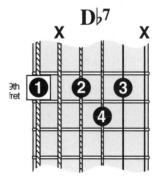

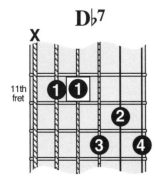
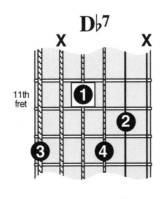
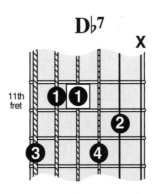
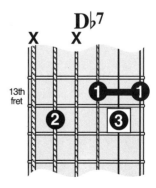

On the recording, this progression is played using only open chord shapes. Practice it with moveable shapes as well.

18.0 Open Chords

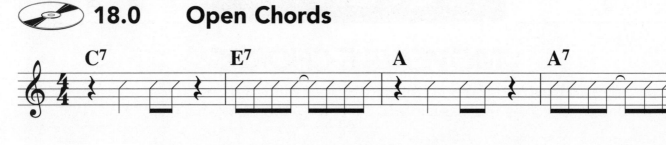

DOMINANT 7TH CHORDS AND THE BLUES

The 12 bar Blues is an excellent progression to use for practicing dominant 7th chords, since blues songs use them as the basis for any accompaniment. The following Blues is played with only one chord shape (shown below) which is moved up and down the fretboard to play the three chords in the progression. Try the same thing with other shapes.

18.1 One Shape Blues

18.2 Progression at 3rd Position

In this progression, all three chords are played at the 3rd fret. Try playing it in other positions using chord shapes which are close together on the fretboard.

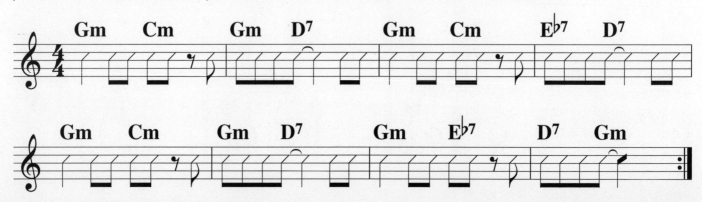

CHORD SYMBOL

m^7

MINOR

CHORD FORMULA

1 ♭3 5 ♭7

A **minor7th** chord is created by adding a **flattened 7th** degree to any minor chord. E.g. a **Cm7** chord contains the notes **C, E♭, G** and **B♭** (**1, ♭3, 5** and **♭7**). Shown below are some common open minor 7th chord shapes.

OPEN CHORDS

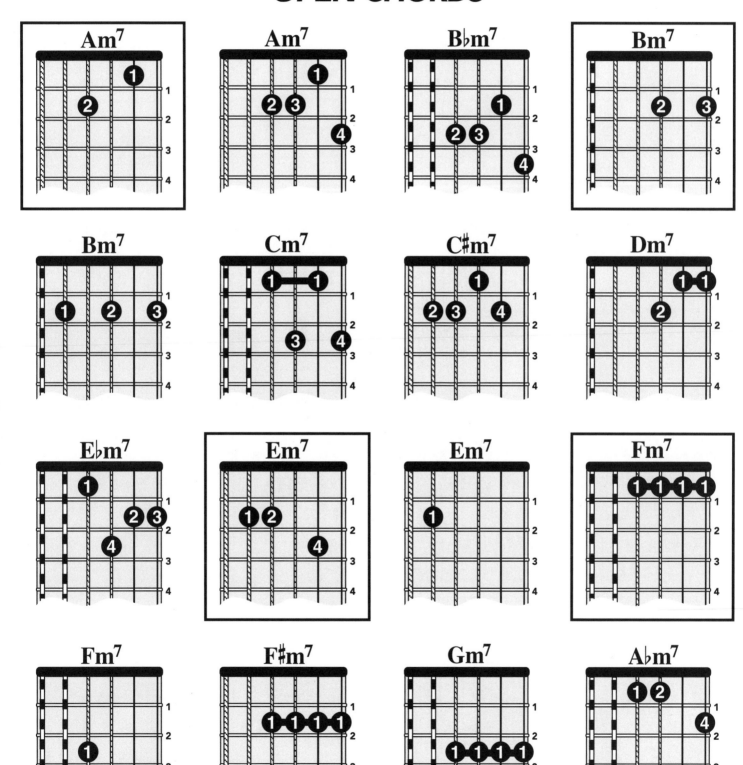

CHORD SYMBOL	MINOR	CHORD FORMULA
m⁷		**1 ♭3 5 ♭7**

MOVEABLE CHORDS

Here are some moveable fingerings for **minor 7th** chords, shown here as **E♭m7**. The first thirteen shapes are on groups of four adjacent strings. **As always, learn each shape and then transpose it to all keys.**

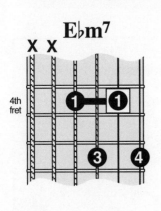 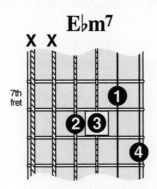 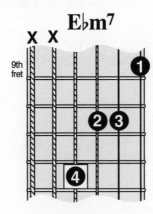 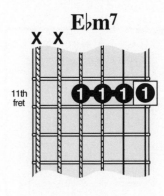

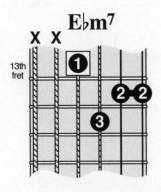 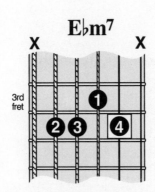 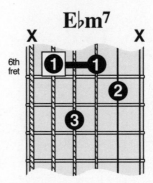 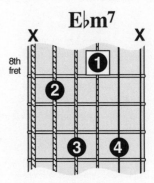

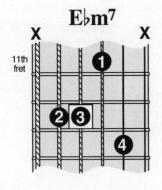 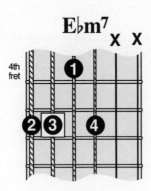 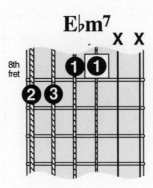 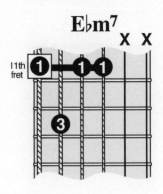

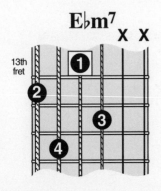 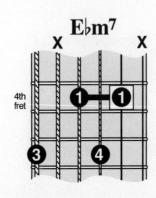 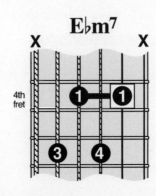 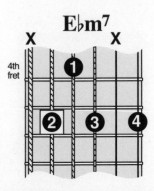

CHORD SYMBOL	MINOR	CHORD FORMULA
m⁷		**1 ♭3 5 ♭7**

MOVEABLE CHORDS

Here are some more moveable minor7th chord shapes which are not on four adjacent strings, but are commonly used and relate back to the five basic forms. Learn each one as **E♭m7** and then transpose it to all the other keys.

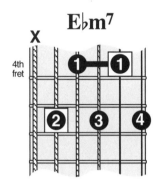

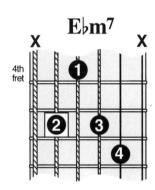

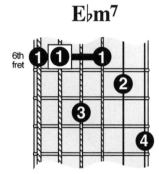

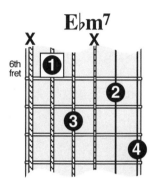

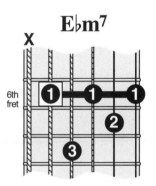

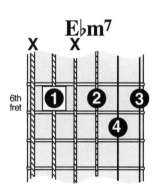

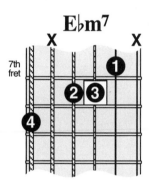

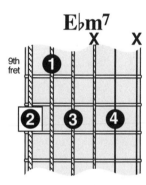

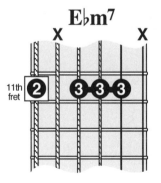

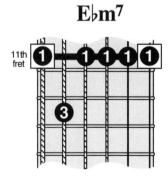

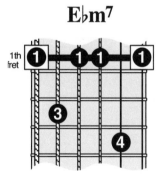

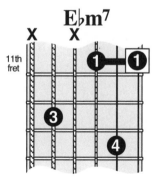

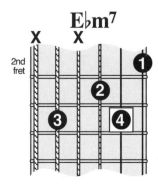

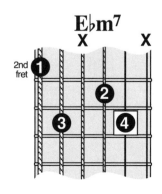

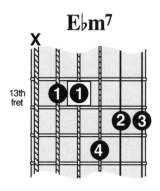

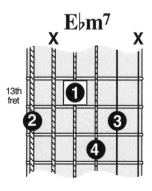

PROGRESSIONS USING MINOR 7TH CHORDS

The following example is a 12 bar Blues which features minor 7th chords. Try playing these chords as arpeggios, as well as experimenting with combinations of these and other chords you know.

 **19.0**

 **19.1**

Here is a guitar part which uses three note voicings of minor 7th chords. The flattened 3rd and 7th degrees are essential, but either the 5th or the root can be omitted. Try this approach with other four note chords.

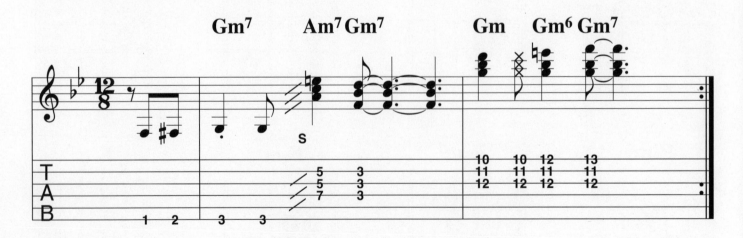

CHORD SYMBOL
m$^{(maj7)}$

MINOR

CHORD FORMULA
1 ♭3 5 7

A **minor major7th** chord is created by adding a **natural7th** degree to any minor chord. E.g. a **Cm$^{(maj7)}$** chord contains the notes **C, E♭, G** and **B** (**1, ♭3, 5** and **7**). Shown below are some common open minor major 7th chord shapes.

OPEN CHORDS

Am$^{(maj7)}$
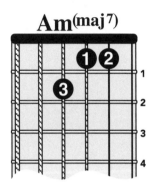

B♭m$^{(maj7)}$
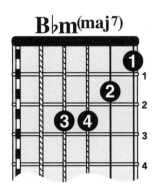

Bm$^{(maj7)}$
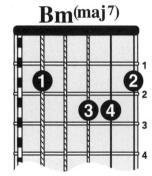

Cm$^{(maj7)}$
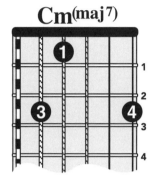

D♭m$^{(maj7)}$
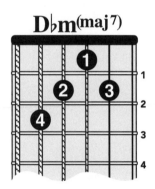

Dm$^{(maj7)}$
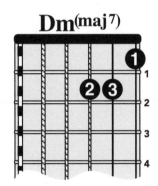

E♭m$^{(maj7)}$
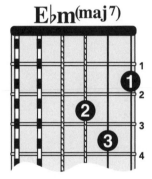

Em$^{(maj7)}$
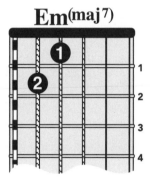

Fm$^{(maj7)}$
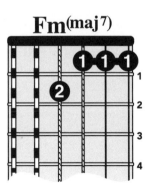

F♯m$^{(maj7)}$
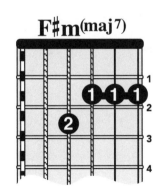

Gm$^{(maj7)}$
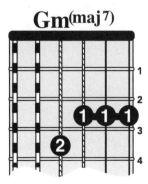

A♭m$^{(maj7)}$
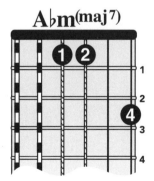

82

CHORD SYMBOL

$\mathbf{m^{(maj^7)}}$

MINOR

CHORD FORMULA

1 ♭3 5 7

MOVEABLE CHORDS

Here are some common moveable **minor** (**maj7th**) chord shapes, shown as **F♯m(maj7)**. This chord type is less common than the other 7th types, but by using the formula, you could go through the process of working out voicings on groups of four adjacent strings as well as the ones shown here which relate to the five basic forms.

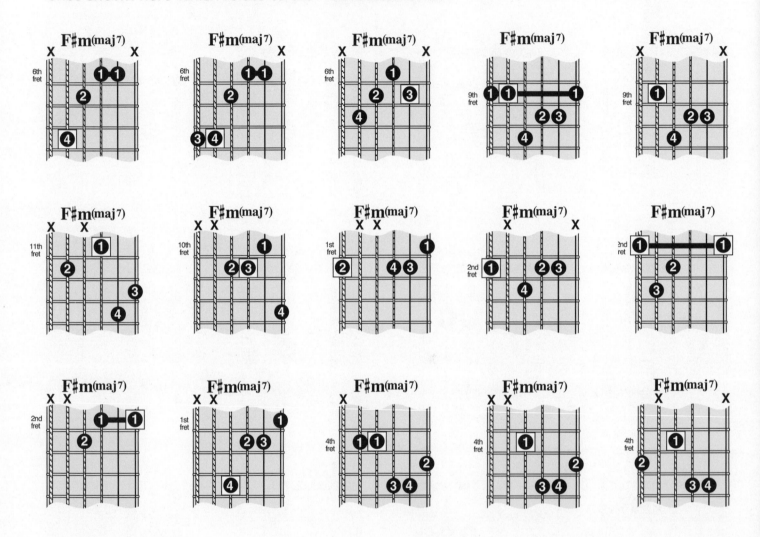

 **20.0**

This progression demonstrates a common way of using a **minor(maj7)** chord.

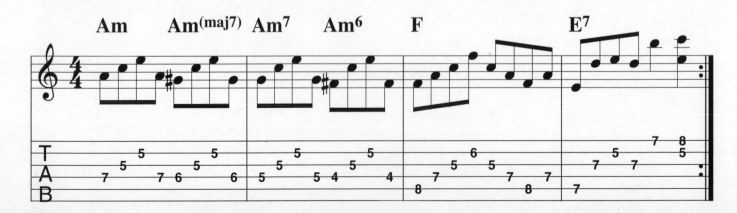

CHORD SYMBOL

m⁷♭5 or Ø

MINOR SEVENTH

CHORD FORMULA

1   ♭3   ♭5   ♭7

A **minor7th flat five** chord is created by **flattening the 5th** degree of any minor 7th chord. E.g. a **Cm7♭5** chord contains the notes **C, E♭, G♭** and **B♭** (**1, ♭3, ♭5** and **♭7**). Because of the flattened 5th degree, this chord is sometimes referred to as a **half diminished chord**. Shown below are some common open minor 7th flat five chord shapes.

OPEN CHORDS

Am⁷♭5
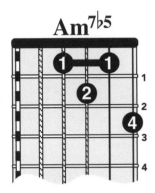

B♭m⁷♭5
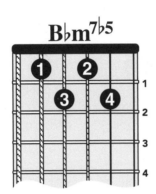

Bm⁷♭5
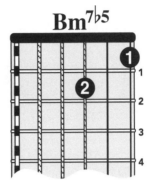

Cm⁷♭5
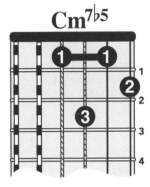

C#m⁷♭5

Dm⁷♭5
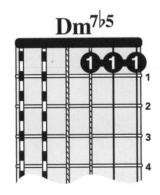

E♭m⁷♭5
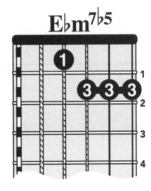

Em⁷♭5
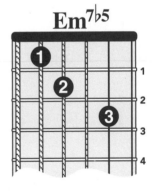

Fm⁷♭5
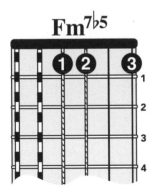

F#m⁷♭5
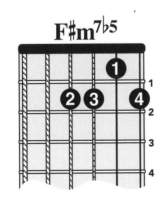

Gm⁷♭5
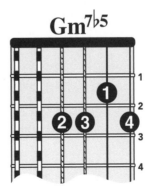

A♭m⁷♭5
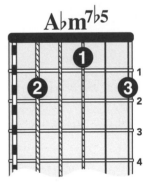

m⁷♭5 or Ø

MINOR SEVENTH

CHORD FORMULA

1 ♭3 ♭5 ♭7

MOVEABLE CHORDS

Here are some useful moveable **minor seventh flat five** chord shapes, shown as **Gm7♭5**. The fifteen shapes shown here are commonly used voicings made up of various string combinations, but you could use the formula to work out all possibilities on groups of four adjacent strings, as well as other possible fingerings. Experiment!

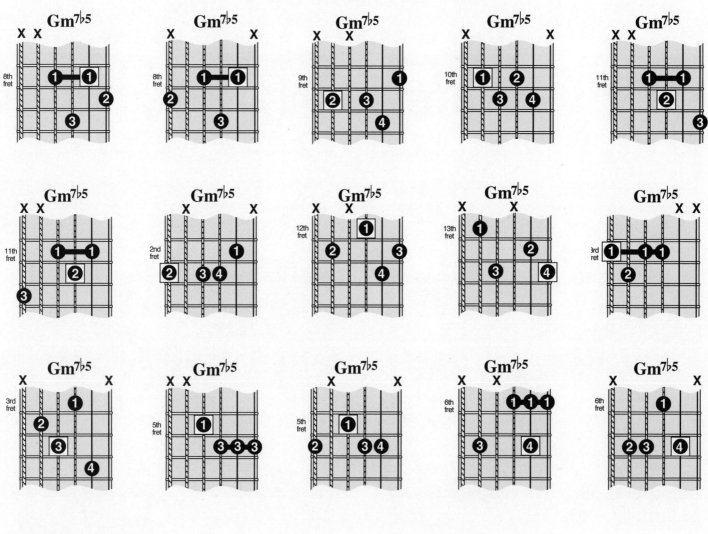

20.1

Minor 7♭5 chords are commonly used in minor keys as shown here.

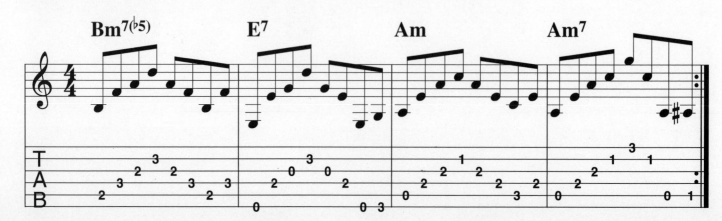

CHORD SYMBOL
º or º7 or dim

DIMINISHED

CHORD FORMULA
1 ♭3 ♭5 ♭♭7

A **diminished 7th** chord is created by **flattening the 7th** degree of any minor7 flat five chord. Because the 7th is already flattened, it becomes a **double flattened 7th**. E.g. a **C dim7** chord contains the notes **C, E♭, G♭** and **B♭♭ (1, ♭3, ♭5** and **♭♭7)**. A double flattened seventh is the same as a **6th** degree (e.g. **B♭♭ = A**). It is referred to as a double flat 7 because the chord is technically a type of 7th chord. Shown below are some common open diminished 7th chord shapes. Diminished 7ths are commonly just called **diminished** chords and are usually played instead of a diminished triad wherever a diminished chord symbol occurs.

OPEN CHORDS

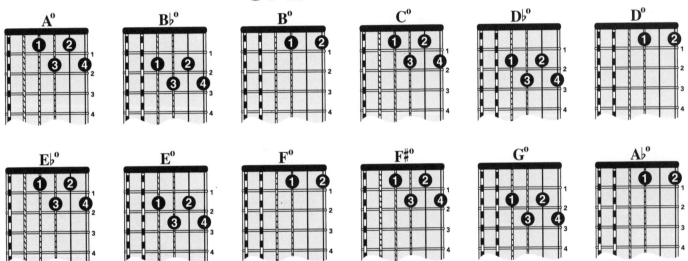

FOUR CHORDS IN ONE

If you look at the diagrams above, you will notice that only one shape is required to play all twelve possible augmented chords. Like augmented chords, the diminished 7th is a **symmetrical chord** which means that any of the notes in the chord can be the root note. Therefore, each diminished 7th chord has four possible names (or sometimes more counting enharmonic notes - e.g. **B♭ = A♯**). There are really only **three different** diminished chords, each one having at least four names. They can all be played by forming a diminished 7th chord and then moving the shape up the neck one fret at a time. After the third chord you get back to a repeat of the first one as demonstrated below.

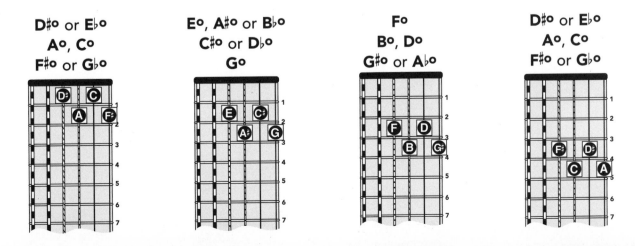

CHORD SYMBOL

o or o7 or dim

DIMINISHED

CHORD FORMULA

1 ♭3 ♭5 ♭♭7

Here are several more shapes for diminished 7th chords, each shown with all their names. Each shape can be played anywhere on the fretboard.

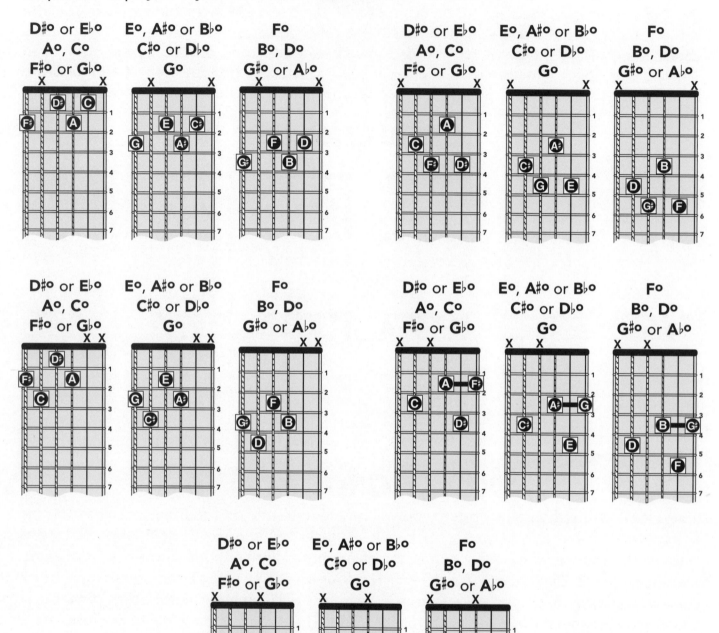

🔘 **20.2**

Diminished 7ths are commonly used as chromatic passing chords between scale tone chords. For more on passing chords, see *Progressive Complete Learn to Play Jazz Guitar Manual*.

CHORD SYMBOL

7sus or 7sus⁴

SEVENTH

CHORD FORMULA

| 1 | 4 | 5 | ♭7 |

A **suspended7th** chord is created by adding a **flattened 7th** degree to any suspended triad. E.g. a **C7sus** chord contains the notes **C, F, G** and **B♭** (**1, 4, 5** and **♭7**). Shown below are some common open7th suspended chord shapes.

OPEN CHORDS

A⁷sus
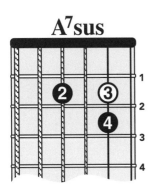

B♭⁷sus
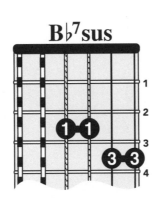

B⁷sus
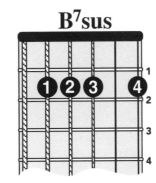

C⁷sus
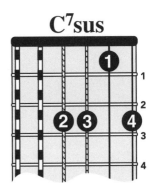

D♭⁷sus
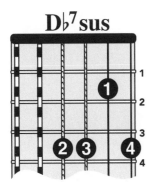

D⁷sus

E♭⁷sus
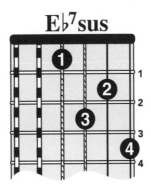

E⁷sus
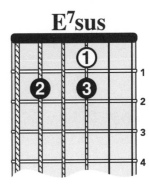

F⁷sus
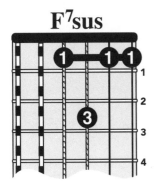

F#⁷sus
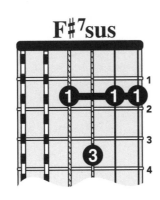

G⁷sus

A♭⁷sus
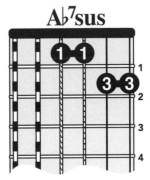

CHORD SYMBOL
7sus or 7sus⁴

SEVENTH

CHORD FORMULA
1   4   5   ♭7

MOVEABLE CHORDS

Here are some commonly used moveable **minor seventh suspended** chord shapes, shown as **A♭7sus**. The shapes shown here will work for any musical situation, but there are always more possibilities. As with previous chord types, use the formula shown above to come up with your own fingerings.

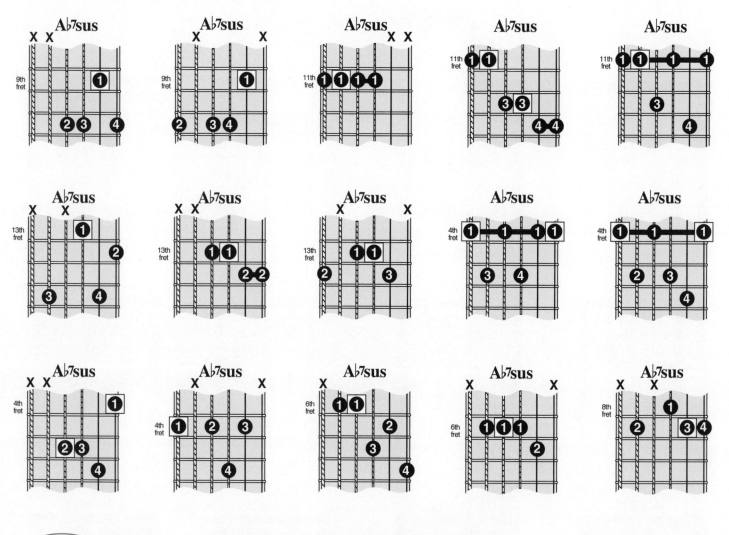

21.0   (all root 6 except E7sus bar)

Here is a progression demonstrating **7sus** chords. Notice how these chords often alternate with the dominant 7th chord of the same name. You can also create tension with these chords by **not** resolving back to the dominant 7th. Experiment!

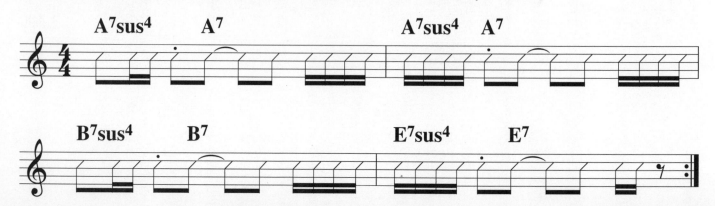

CHORD SYMBOL
7♯5 or +7

SEVENTH

CHORD FORMULA
1 3 ♯5 ♭7

A **7th sharp five** chord is created by **sharpening the 5th** degree of any dominant7th chord. E.g. a **C7♯5** chord contains the notes **C, E, G♯** and **B♭** (**1, 3, ♯5** and **♭7**). Because of the sharpened 5th degree, this chord is sometimes referred to as an **augmented 7th chord**. Shown below are some common open7th sharp five chord shapes.

OPEN CHORDS

A⁷♯⁵
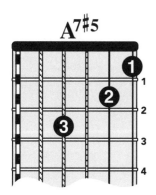

B♭⁷♯⁵
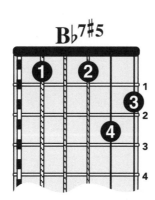

B⁷♯⁵
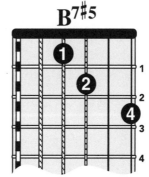

C⁷♯⁵
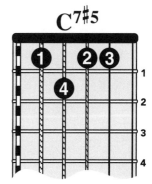

D♭⁷♯⁵
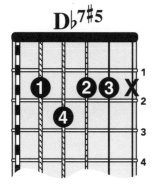

D⁷♯⁵
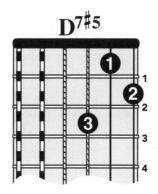

E♭⁷♯⁵
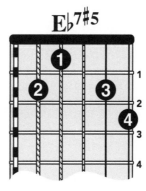

E⁷♯⁵
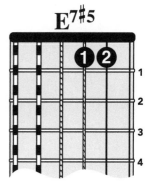

F⁷♯⁵
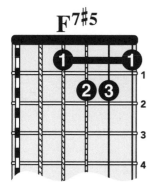

F♯⁷♯⁵
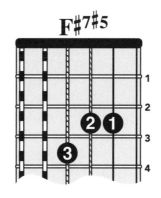

G⁷♯⁵
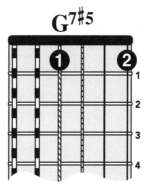

A♭⁷♯⁵
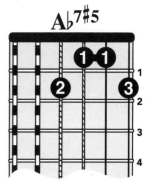

CHORD SYMBOL	SEVENTH	CHORD FORMULA
7 ♯5 or +7		1 3 ♯5 ♭7

MOVEABLE CHORDS

Here are some useful moveable **seven sharp five** chord shapes, shown as **C7♯5**. As mentioned previously, it is essential to transpose all chords to every key. A good way to do this is to use the **key cycle** as shown on page 143. Choose a shape and move it up and down the fretboard to every note on the key cycle until you have covered all 12 notes.

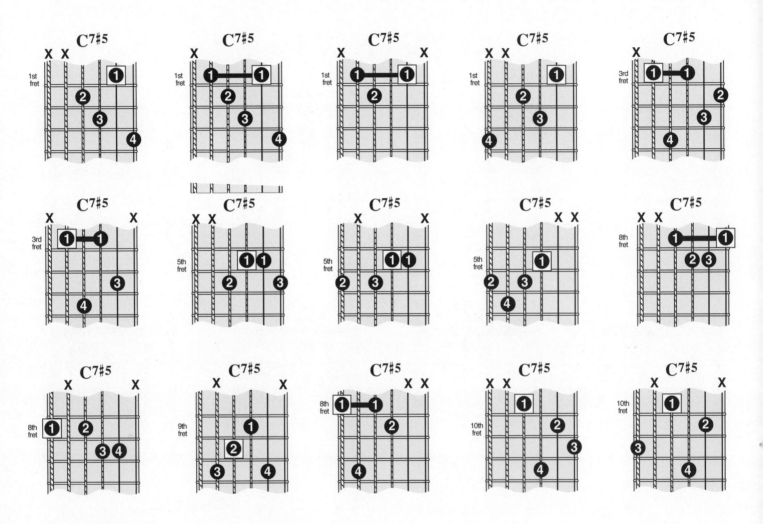

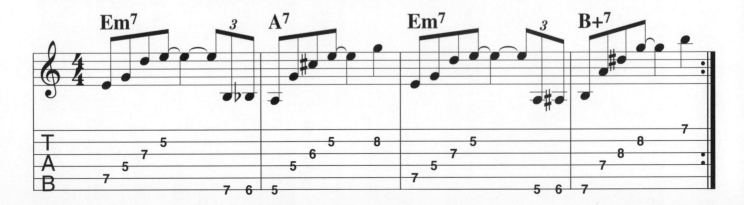

21.1

Listen to the tension created by the **B+7** chord in the 4th bar of this example. You can either resolve it or leave it hanging. Experiment with this in your own playing.

CHORD SYMBOL
7♭5

SEVENTH

CHORD FORMULA
1　3　♭5　♭7

A **7th flat five** chord is created by **flattening the 5th** degree of any dominant7th chord. E.g. a **C7♭5** chord contains the notes **C, E, G♭** and **B♭** (**1, 3, ♭5** and **♭7**). Shown below are some common open 7th flat five chord shapes.

OPEN CHORDS

A⁷♭5
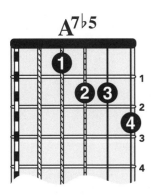

B♭⁷♭5
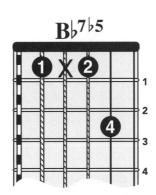

B⁷♭5
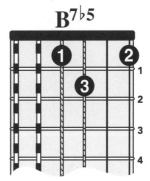

C⁷♭5
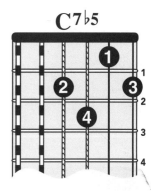

D♭⁷♭5
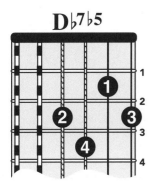

D⁷♭5
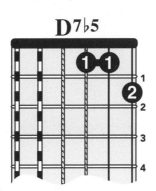

E♭⁷♭5
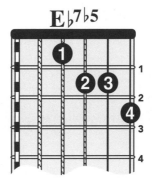

E⁷♭5
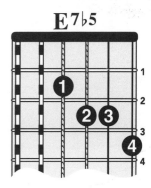

F⁷♭5
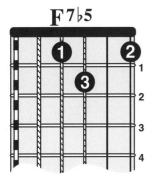

F♯⁷♭5
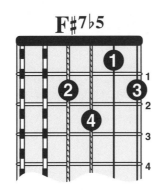

G⁷♭5
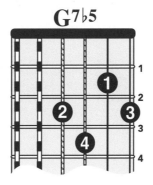

A♭⁷♭5
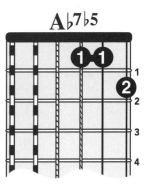

CHORD SYMBOL	SEVENTH	CHORD FORMULA
7♭5		1　3　♭5　♭7

MOVEABLE CHORDS

Like augmented triads and diminished sevenths, **seven flat five** chord shapes can have more than one root note. Each shape shown below has **two** possible names (or more if you include enharmonics). Each one can be played anywhere on the fretboard and the names will change each time it is moved. Analyze the notes in each of these shapes and then use the key cycle to learn them in all keys.

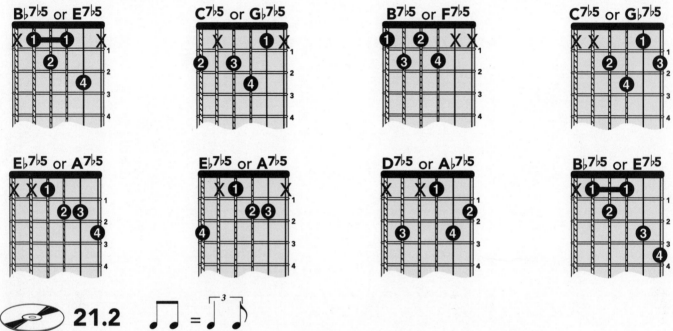

21.2

This progression uses **7♭5** chords along with other types of 7th chords.

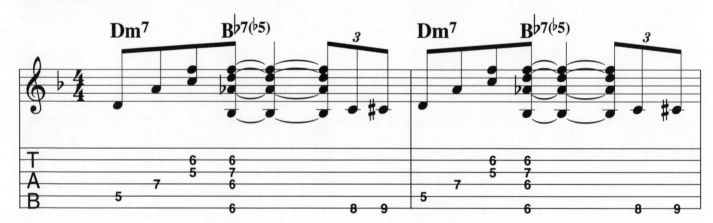

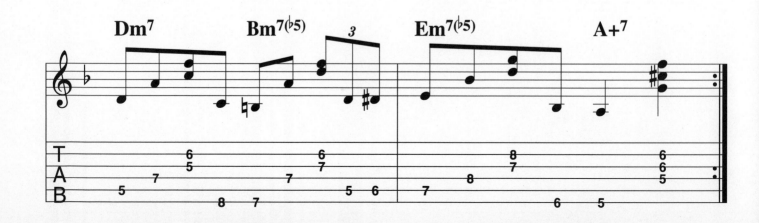

22. Jam-Along Track

The following progression is based on the Jazz standard **All the Things You Are** by Jerome Kern. It contains all the basic 7th chord types and has been recorded on the CD without a guitar part so you can jam along with the rhythm section. Use it to practice all the different voicings of the various chord types. As well as using Jam-along tracks, you should play with other musicians as often as possible. This will enable you to use your chords in a real musical context and help your playing develop much faster.

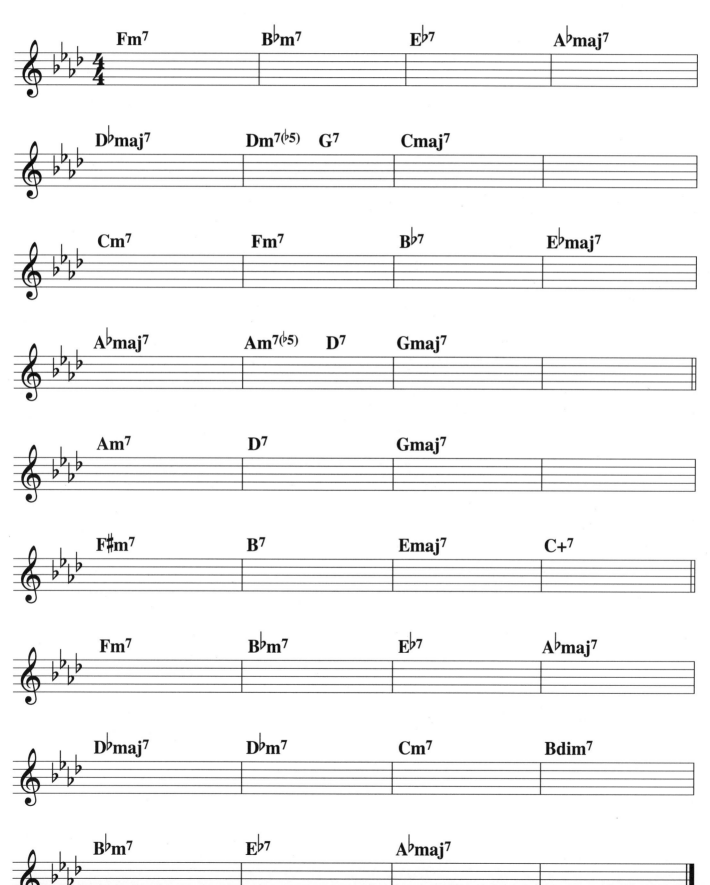

Section 3

Extended Chords, Altered Chords

The term **"extended chords"** refers to all the chord types which contain more than four notes, most notably **9ths**, **11ths** and **13ths**. They are all extensions of the basic chord types and can all be related back to the major scale. Shown below is the **C** major scale with degrees written under the notes up to a **13th**. These degrees are all used in chords in various combinations. These thirteen note degrees are all that is needed to create all chord types. Each chord type will have its own unique formula.

C MAJOR SCALE UP TO THE 13TH DEGREE

The term **"altered chords"** refers to the sharpening or flattening of degrees of a chord, usually the **5th** or the **9th**. This opens up many possible combinations and once you know the formula for any extended chord you can experiment with alterations to the degrees of the chord. The most common altered chords are dominants: e.g. you may see a symbol such as **E7♯9**. This refers to an **E7** chord with a sharpened **9th** degree added to it.

OMITTING NOTES FROM CHORDS

The more notes you add to chords, the more difficult they are to play and the more muddy they can sound. For this reason it is common to omit notes from extended chords, keeping only the notes which most clearly indicate the quality (sound) of the chord. The most frequently omitted note is the **5th**, although sometimes the 3rd or the root can be omitted. Usually the bass will be playing the root note anyway. With a dominant 7th chord, as long as the ♭7 degree is in the chord you still get the effect of a 7th chord. With a dominant 9th chord, as long as you have the 3rd, ♭7th and 9th, you have the effect of a 9th chord, etc. This is demonstrated below with an **E Ninth** chord.

Dominant Ninth Chord Formula

Chord Symbol

E9

$$1 \quad 3 \quad 5 \quad ♭7 \quad 9$$

Notes in Chord

E	G♯	B	D	F♯
1	3	5	♭7	9

Unless you have huge hands, it is very difficult to play this chord on the guitar with the notes in the order they are written according to the formula. All players rearrange and omit notes when playing extended chords. It is good to work out voicings for yourself, as this will improve your theoretical knowledge, your musical knowledge and your ear.

However, through the years certain voicings have become standard because they clearly indicate the chord type and they sound good. Shown below are are two commonly used **E9** chord shapes which have the 5th omitted. The formula for an **E9** chord is shown below the shapes, with arrows indicting the position of each degree. Play each each one first as a whole chord and then as an arpeggio and listen to the effect produced by each degree of the chord. The sound of a **9th** chord is clear and unambiguous. There is no necessity for the 5th degree in either voicing. This principle can be applied to all extended chords.

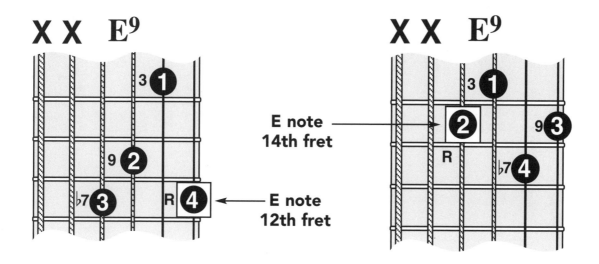

CHORD SYMBOL

6/9

SIXTH ADD NINE

CHORD FORMULA

1 3 5 6 9

A **sixth add9** chord is created by adding a **9th** degree to any major 6th chord. E.g. a **C6/9** chord contains the notes **C**, **E**, **G**, **A** and **D** (**1**, **3**, **5**, **6** and **9**). Shown below are some common open sixth add9 chord shapes.

OPEN CHORDS

A⁶ᐟ⁹
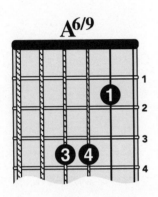

B♭⁶ᐟ⁹
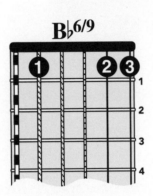

B⁶ᐟ⁹
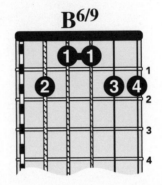

C⁶ᐟ⁹
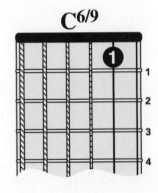

D♭⁶ᐟ⁹
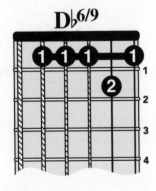

D⁶ᐟ⁹
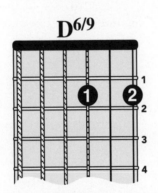

E♭⁶ᐟ⁹
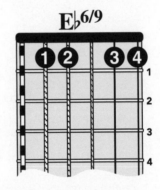

E⁶ᐟ⁹
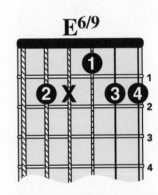

F⁶ᐟ⁹
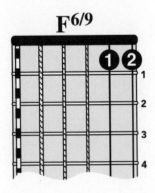

F♯⁶ᐟ⁹

G⁶ᐟ⁹
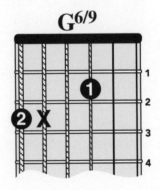

A♭⁶ᐟ⁹
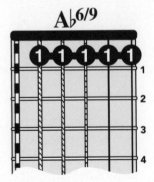

CHORD SYMBOL
6/9

SIXTH ADD NINE

CHORD FORMULA
1 3 5 6 9

MOVEABLE CHORDS

Here are some useful moveable **sixth add9** chord shapes. As chords become more complex and contain more notes and alterations, they can be harder to relate to other chords, so from here on, all moveable shapes will be shown in the first four frets. This makes it easier to compare chord types as they will all be in the same position on the fretboard. As mentioned previously, it is essential to transpose all chords to every key once you have memorized the fingering and position of the root note. If you find a shape difficult to play, move it further up the fretboard where there is less string tension until your fingers are comfortable with the shape.

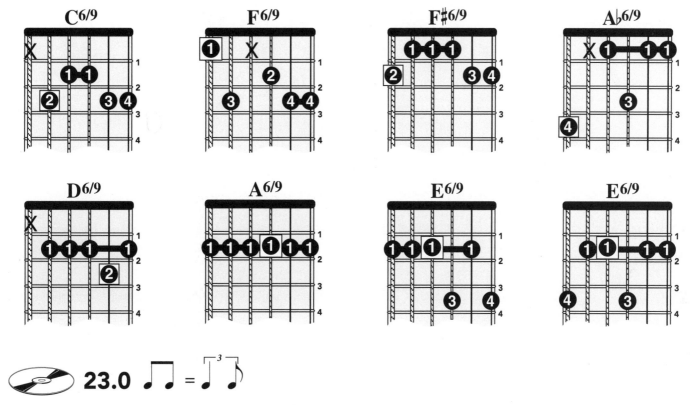

🔘 **23.0**

Here is a progression featuring the use of major 6 add9 chords.

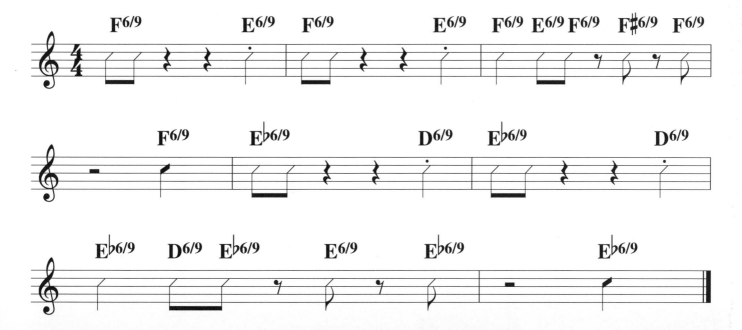

CHORD SYMBOL

m6/9

MINOR SIXTH

CHORD FORMULA

1 ♭3 5 6 9

A **minor sixth add9** chord is created by adding a **9th** degree to any minor 6th chord. E.g. a **Cm6/9** chord contains the notes **C**, **E♭**, **G**, **A** and **D** (**1**, **♭3**, **5**, **6** and **9**). Shown below are some common open minor sixth add9 chord shapes.

OPEN CHORDS

Am6/9
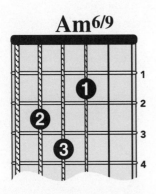

B♭m6/9
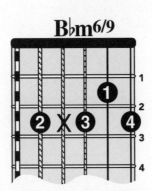

Bm6/9
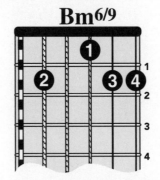

Cm6/9
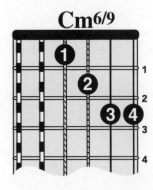

D♭m6/9
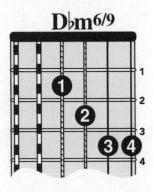

Dm6/9
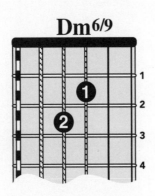

E♭m6/9
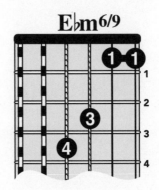

Em6/9
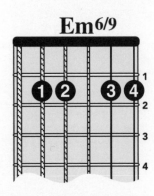

Fm6/9
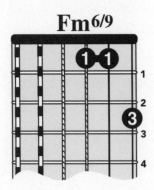

F#m6/9
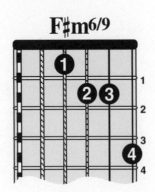

Gm6/9
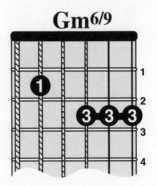

A♭m6/9
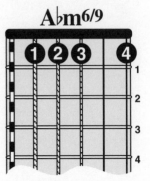

CHORD SYMBOL
m6/9

MINOR SIXTH

CHORD FORMULA
1 ♭3 5 6 9

MOVEABLE CHORDS

Here are some useful moveable **minor sixth add9** chord shapes shown in the first four frets. As with previous chord types, learn each shape and then transpose it to all keys.

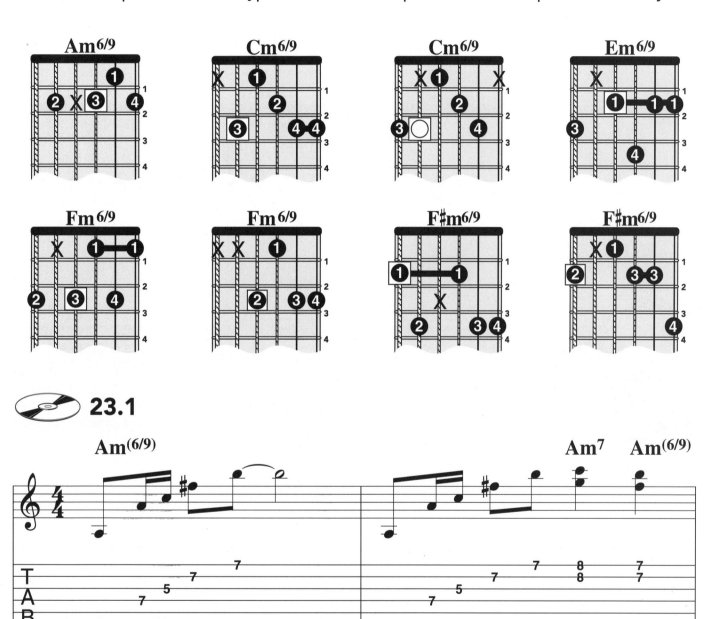

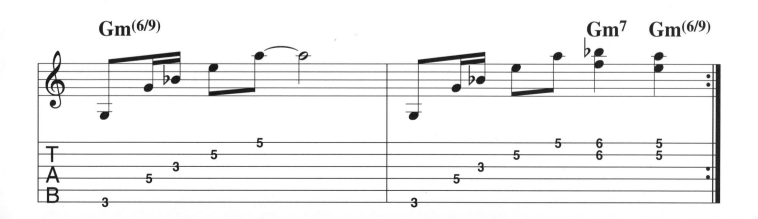

CHORD SYMBOL

maj⁹

MAJOR NINTH

CHORD FORMULA

1 3 5 7 9

A **major 9th** chord is created by adding a **9th** degree to any major 7th chord. E.g. a **Cmaj9** chord contains the notes **C**, **E**, **G**, **B** and **D** (**1**, **3**, **5**, **7** and **9**). Shown below are some common open maj9 chord shapes.

OPEN CHORDS

Amaj⁹
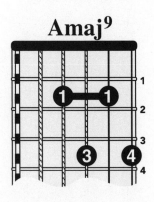

B♭maj⁹
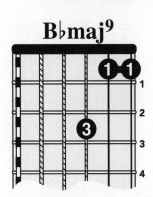

Bmaj⁹
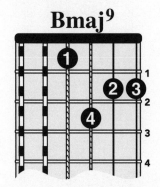

Cmaj⁹
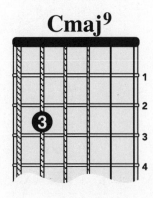

D♭maj⁹
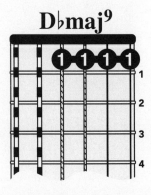

Dmaj⁹
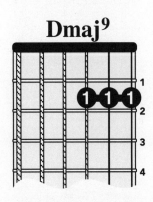

E♭maj⁹
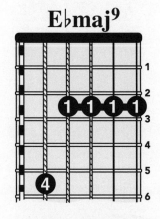

Emaj⁹
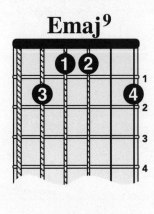

Fmaj⁹
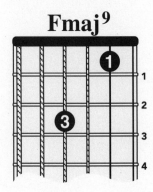

F♯maj⁹
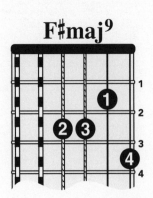

Gmaj⁹
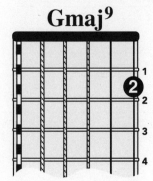

A♭maj⁹
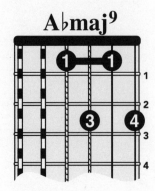

<table>
<tr><td>CHORD SYMBOL
maj⁹</td><td>MAJOR NINTH</td><td>CHORD FORMULA
1 3 5 7 9</td></tr>
</table>

CHORD SYMBOL

maj^9

MAJOR NINTH

CHORD FORMULA

1 3 5 7 9

MOVEABLE CHORDS

Here are some moveable **major 9th** chord shapes shown in the first four frets. As with previous chord types, learn each shape and then transpose it to all keys.

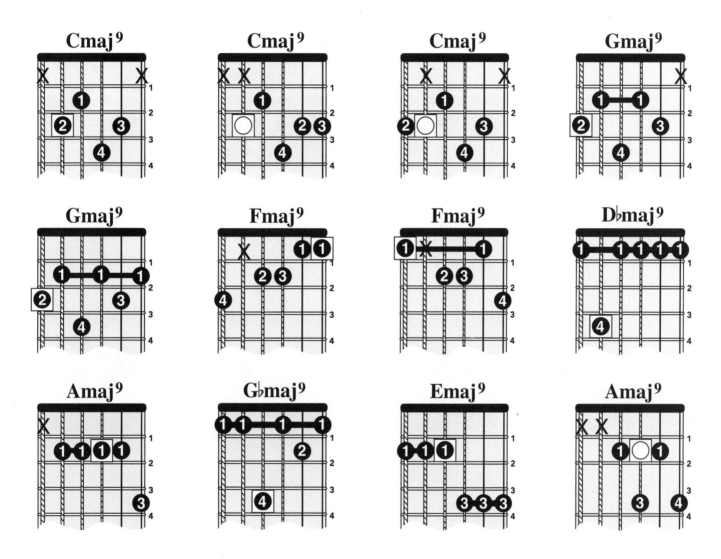

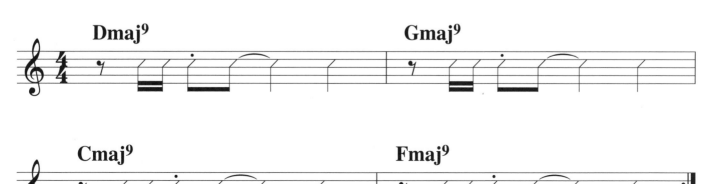

24.0

This progression can be played by moving one shape up and down the fretboard, or groups of two shapes, or four different shapes. Try each of these methods.

CHORD SYMBOL		CHORD FORMULA

CHORD SYMBOL

9

NINTH

CHORD FORMULA

1 3 5 ♭7 9

A **dominant 9th** chord (usually just called a **ninth chord**) is created by adding a **9th** degree to any dominant 7th chord. E.g. a **C9** chord contains the notes **C**, **E**, **G**, **B♭** and **D** (**1**, **3**, **5**, **♭7** and **9**). Shown below are some common open ninth chord shapes.

OPEN CHORDS

A⁹
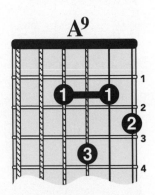

B♭⁹
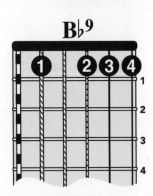

B⁹
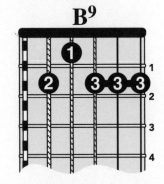

C⁹
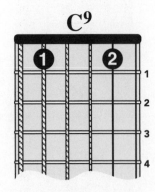

D♭⁹
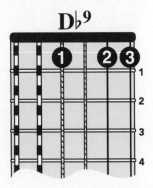

D⁹
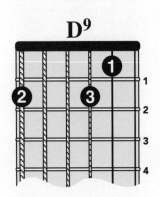

E♭⁹
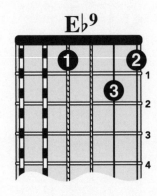

E⁹
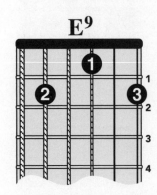

F⁹
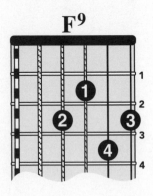

F♯⁹
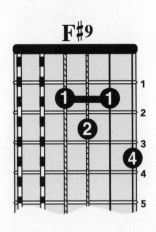

G⁹
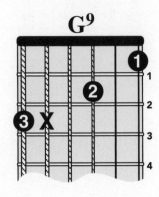

A♭⁹
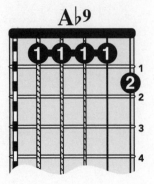

CHORD SYMBOL	NINTH	CHORD FORMULA
9		1 3 5 ♭7 9

MOVEABLE CHORDS

Here are some useful moveable **9th** chord shapes shown in the first four frets. As with previous chord types, learn each shape and then transpose it to all keys.

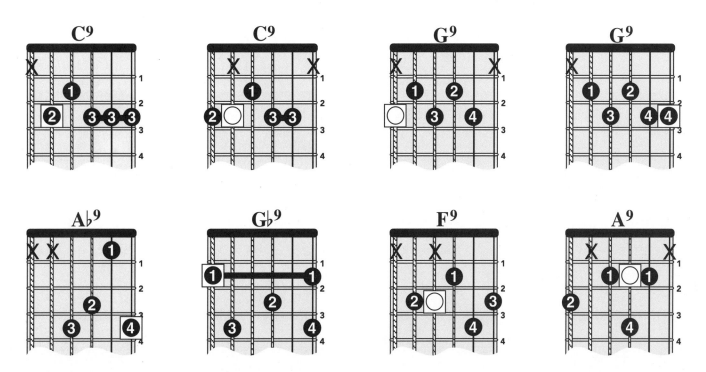

 **24.1**

This groove can be played using one shape, or a combination of shapes. On the recording two different shapes are used as indicated above the notation.

 **24.2**

This progression alternates between minor 7th and 9th chords.

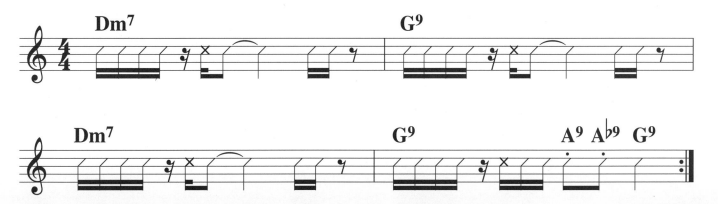

CHORD SYMBOL

m⁹

MINOR NINTH

CHORD FORMULA

1 ♭3 5 ♭7 9

A **minor9th** chord is created by adding a **9th** degree to any minor7th chord. E.g. a **Cm9** chord contains the notes **C, E♭, G, B♭** and **D** (**1, ♭3, 5, ♭7** and **9**). Shown below are some common open minor 9th chord shapes.

OPEN CHORDS

Am⁹
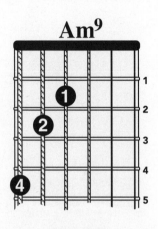

B♭m⁹
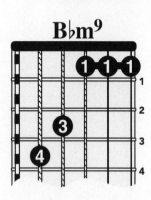

Bm⁹
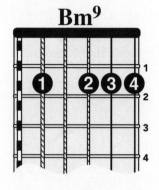

Cm⁹
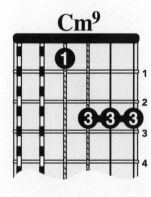

C♯m⁹

Dm⁹
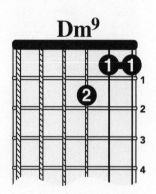

E♭m⁹
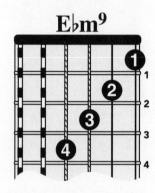

Em⁹
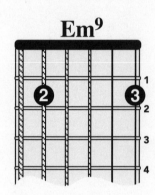

Fm⁹
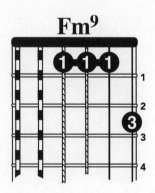

F♯m⁹
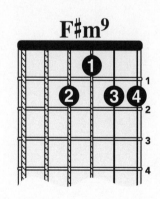

Gm⁹
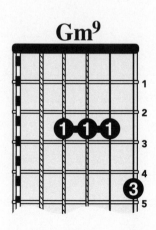

A♭m⁹
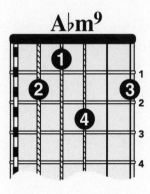

CHORD SYMBOL	MINOR NINTH	CHORD FORMULA
m⁹		1 ♭3 5 ♭7 9

(Chord symbol: m^9; Chord formula: $1\ \flat3\ 5\ \flat7\ 9$)

MOVEABLE CHORDS

Here are some useful moveable **minor 9th** chord shapes shown in the first four frets. As with all new chord types, learn each shape and then transpose it to all keys.

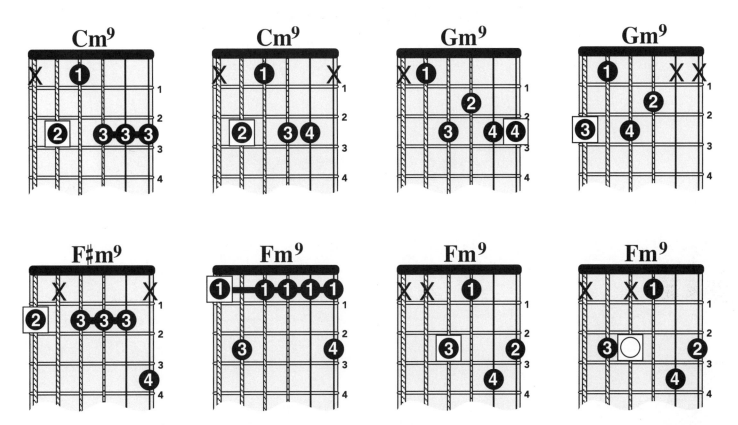

🔘 **24.3**

Here is a progression demonstrating minor 9th chords. Practice it with one shape and then with several different shapes. Each time you learn a progression using a new type of chord, practice it with several different shapes as well as transposing it to other keys. If you make a habit of this, you will find memorizing chord shapes easier because they make sense in a musical context rather than as abstract shapes.

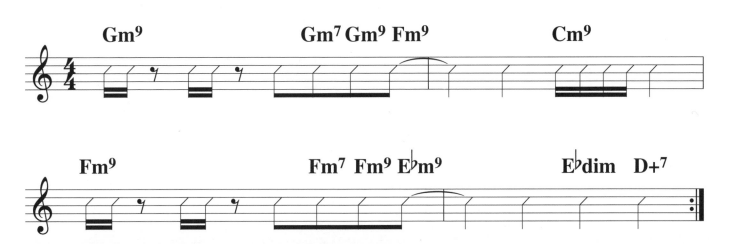

CHORD SYMBOL

7♯9

SEVENTH

CHORD FORMULA

1 3 5 ♭7 ♯9

A **seventh sharp nine** chord is created by adding a sharpened **9th** degree to any dominant 7th chord. E.g. a **C7♯9** chord contains the notes **C, E, G, B♭** and **D♯** (**1, 3, 5, ♭7** and **♯9**). Shown below are some common open seventh sharp 9 chord shapes.

THE HENDRIX CHORD

The seven sharp nine chord is often referred to as the "Hendrix chord' because it was a particular favorite of Jimi Hendrix, especially the voicing shown below as **B7♯9** and **C7♯9**. Hendrix often used it in the key of **E** by playing it in the 6th position

OPEN CHORDS

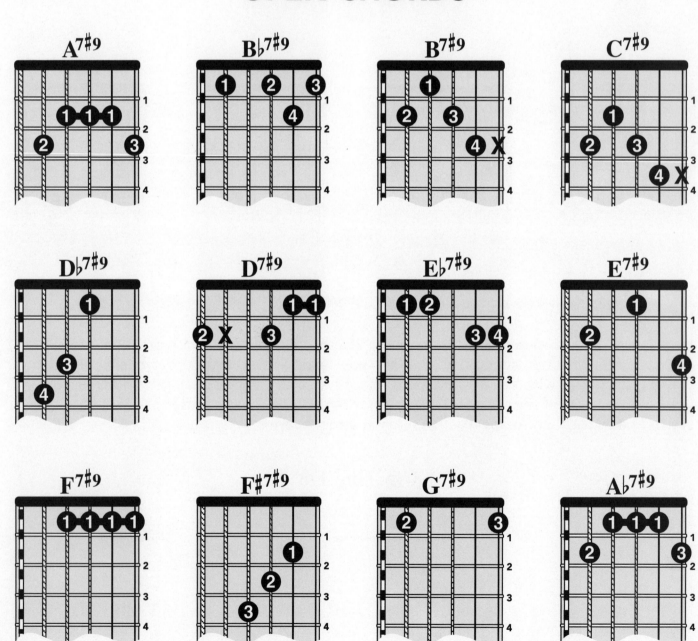

CHORD SYMBOL	SEVENTH	CHORD FORMULA
7♯9		1 3 5 ♭7 ♯9

MOVEABLE CHORDS

Here are some useful moveable **seven sharp nine** chord shapes shown in the first four frets. As with previous chord types, learn each shape and then transpose it to all keys.

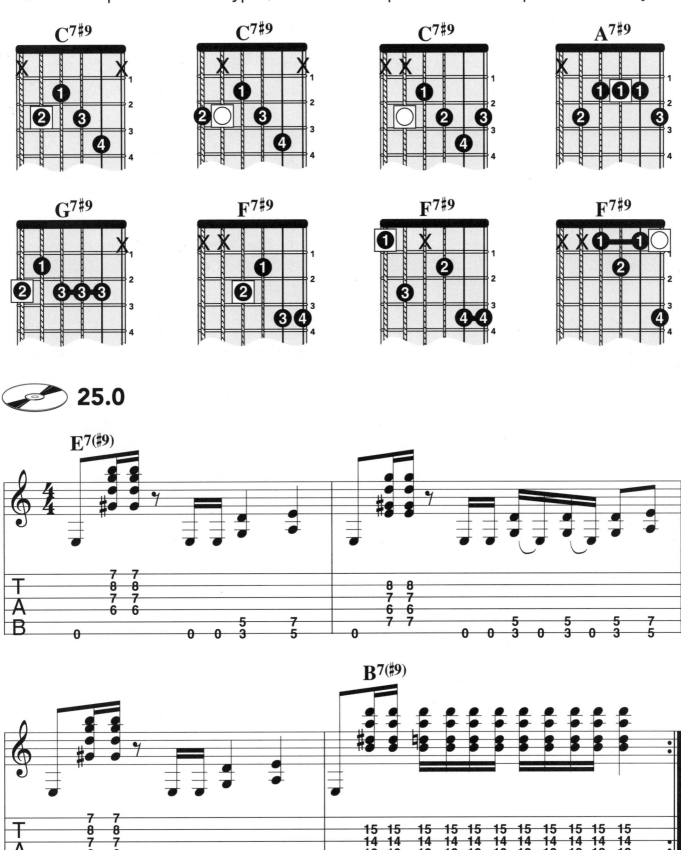

CHORD SYMBOL

$7\flat 9$

SEVENTH

CHORD FORMULA

$1 \quad 3 \quad 5 \quad \flat 7 \quad \flat 9$

A **seventh flat nine** chord is created by adding a flattened **9th** degree to any dominant 7th chord. E.g. a **C7♭9** chord contains the notes **C**, **E**, **G**, **B♭** and **D♭** (**1**, **3**, **5**, **♭7** and **♭9**). Shown below are some common open seventh flat 9 chord shapes.

OPEN CHORDS

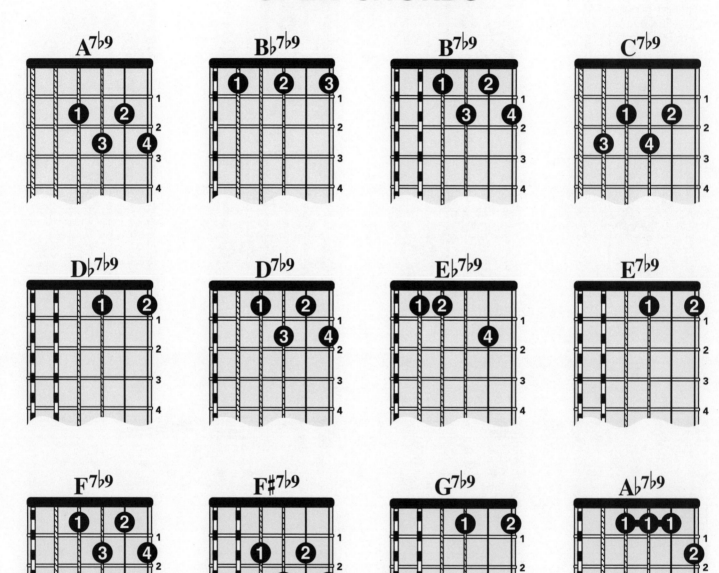

CHORD SYMBOL	SEVENTH	CHORD FORMULA
7♭9		1 3 5 ♭7 ♭9

MOVEABLE CHORDS

Here are some useful moveable **seven flat nine** chord shapes shown in the first four frets. As with previous chord types, learn each shape and then transpose it to all keys.

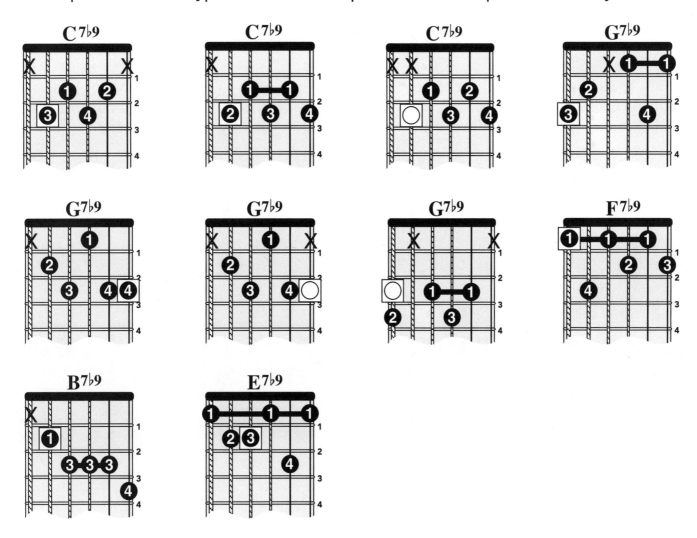

25.1

7♭9 chords are commonly substituted for dominant 7ths in Jazz songs as demonstrated here.

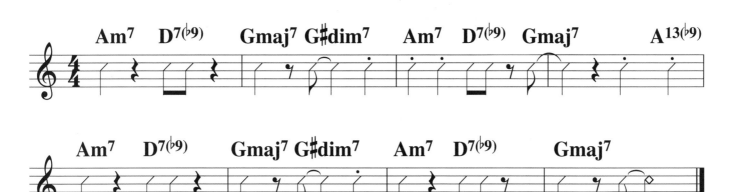

CHORD SYMBOL

7♯5♭9

SEVENTH SHARP

CHORD FORMULA

1 3 ♯5 ♭7 ♭9

A **Seventh sharp five flat nine** chord is created by adding a **flattened 9th** degree to any seventh sharp five chord. E.g. a **C7♯5♭9** chord contains the notes **C, E, G♯, B♭** and **D♭** (**1, 3, ♯5, ♭7** and **♭9**). Shown below are some common open **7♯5♭9** chord shapes.

OPEN CHORDS

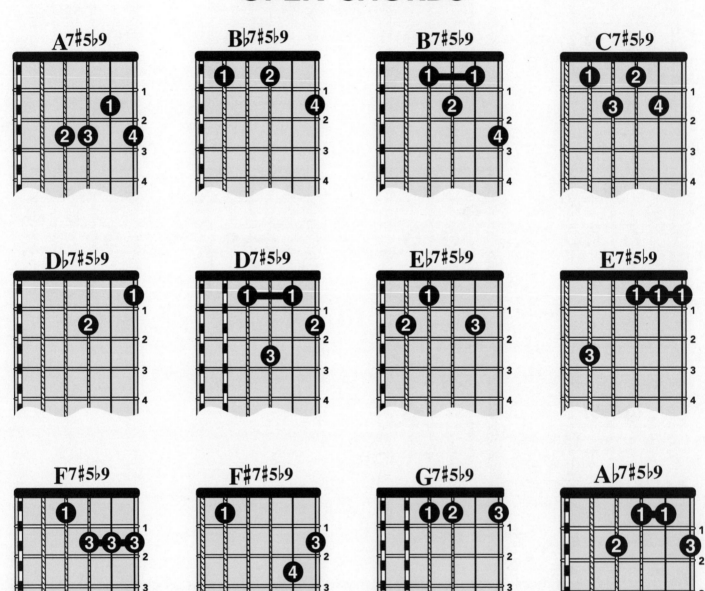

CHORD SYMBOL
$7^{\sharp5\flat9}$

SEVENTH SHARP

CHORD FORMULA
$1\quad 3\quad \sharp5\quad \flat7\quad \flat9$

MOVEABLE CHORDS

Here are some useful moveable **seven sharp five flat nine** chord shapes shown in the first four frets. As with previous chord types, learn each shape and then transpose it to all keys.

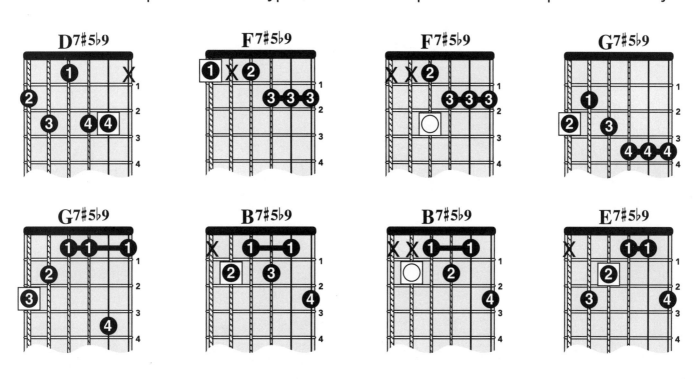

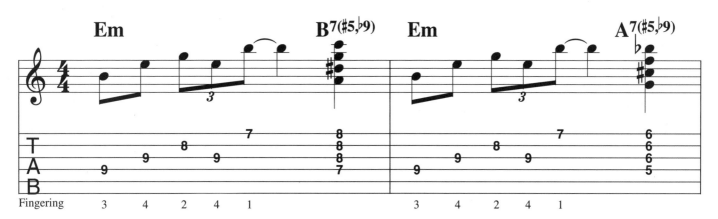

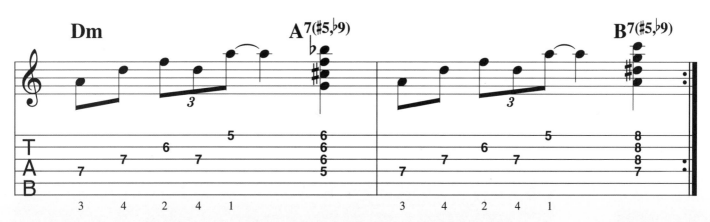

CHORD SYMBOL
9♯5

NINTH

CHORD FORMULA
1 3 ♯5 ♭7 9

A **Ninth sharp five** chord is created by **sharpening the 5th** degree of any ninth chord. E.g. a **C9♯5** chord contains the notes **C**, **E**, **G♯**, **B♭** and **D** (**1**, **3**, **♯5**, **♭7** and **9**). Shown below are some common open **9♯5** chord shapes.

OPEN CHORDS

A⁹♯⁵
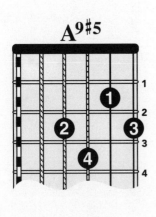

B♭⁹♯⁵
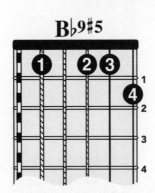

B⁹♯⁵
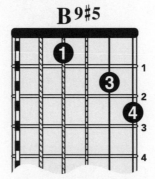

C⁹♯⁵
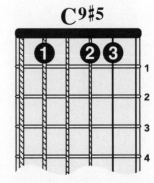

D♭⁹♯⁵
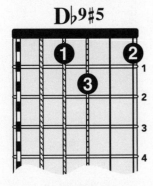

D⁹♯⁵
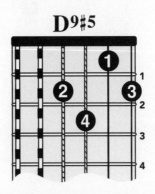

E♭⁹♯⁵
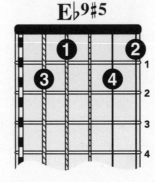

E⁹♯⁵
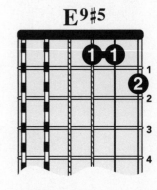

F⁹♯⁵
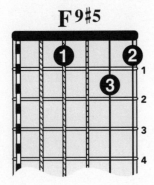

F♯⁹♯⁵
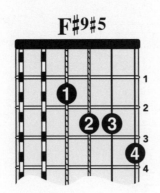

G⁹♯⁵
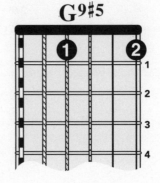

A♭⁹♯⁵
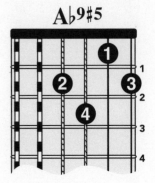

CHORD SYMBOL	NINTH	CHORD FORMULA
9♯5		1 3 ♯5 ♭7 9

MOVEABLE CHORDS

Here are some useful nine sharp five chord shapes shown in the first four frets. As with previous chord types, learn each shape and then transpose it to all keys.

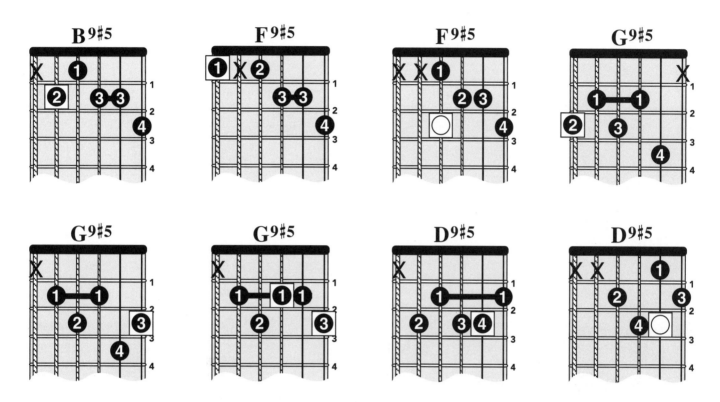

 26.0

As with many altered chords, the **9♯5** is used here to create tension before moving back to a dominant seventh which contains less tension. Tension and release is an essential element in all styles of music.

CHORD SYMBOL

9♭5

NINTH

CHORD FORMULA

1 3 ♭5 ♭7 9

A **Ninth flat five** chord is created by **flattening the 5th** degree of any ninth chord. E.g. a **C9♭5** chord contains the notes **C, E, G♭, B♭** and **D** (**1, 3, ♭5, ♭7** and **9**). Shown below are some common open **9♭5** chord shapes.

OPEN CHORDS

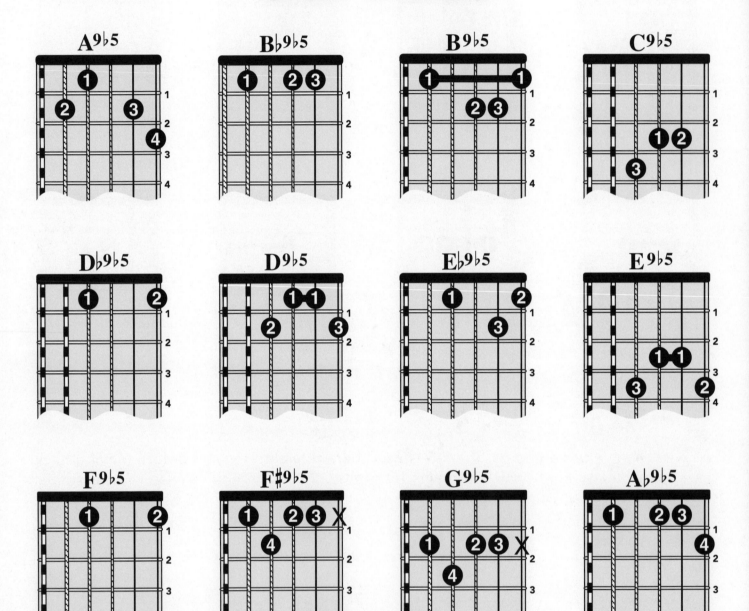

CHORD SYMBOL	NINTH	CHORD FORMULA
9♭5		1 3 ♭5 ♭7 9

MOVEABLE CHORDS

Here are some useful moveable **nine flat five** chord shapes shown in the first four frets. As with previous chord types, learn each shape and then transpose it to all keys.

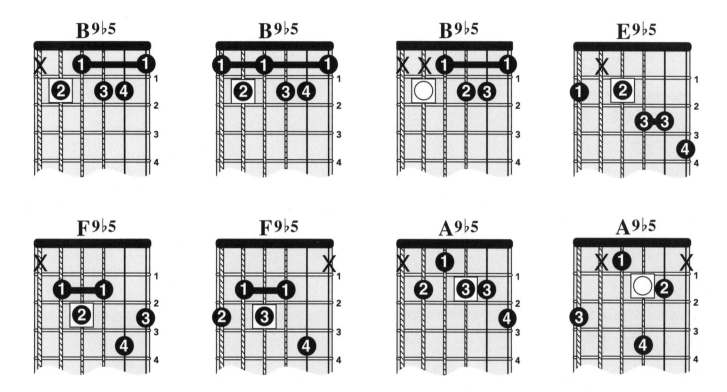

 **26.1**

Here is a progression demonstrating the use of nine flat five chords with an arpeggio picking pattern. Remember to experiment with different ways of playing any new chord type you learn.

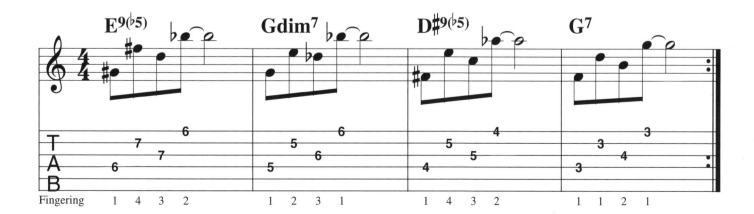

CHORD SYMBOL

m9maj7

MINOR NINE

CHORD FORMULA

1 ♭3 5 7 9

A **minor9 major7** chord is created by adding a **9th** degree to any minor (major7th) chord. E.g. a **Cm9(maj7)** chord contains the notes **C, E♭, G, B** and **D** (**1, ♭3, 5, 7** and **9**). Shown below are some common open m9th(maj7) chord shapes.

OPEN CHORDS

Am9(maj7)
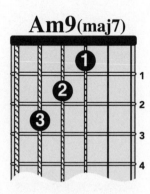

B♭m9(maj7)
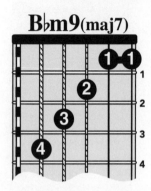

Bm9(maj7)
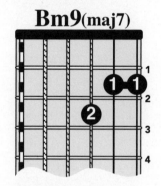

Cm9(maj7)
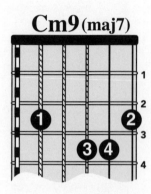

C♯m9(maj7)
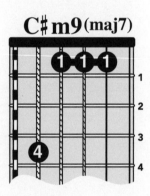

Dm9(maj7)
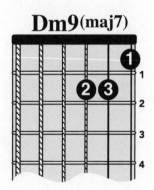

E♭m9(maj7)
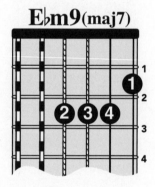

Em9(maj7)
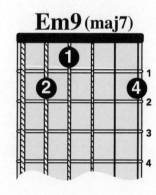

Fm9(maj7)
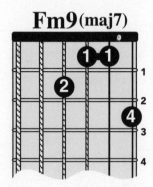

F♯m9(maj7)
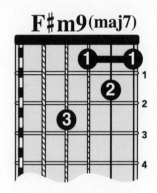

Gm9(maj7)

A♭m9(maj7)
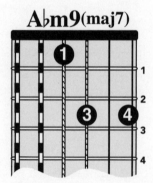

CHORD SYMBOL
m9maj7

MINOR NINE

CHORD FORMULA
1 ♭3 5 7 9

MOVEABLE CHORDS

Here are some useful moveable **minor 9(maj7)** chord shapes shown in the first four frets. As with previous chord types, learn each shape and then transpose it to all keys.

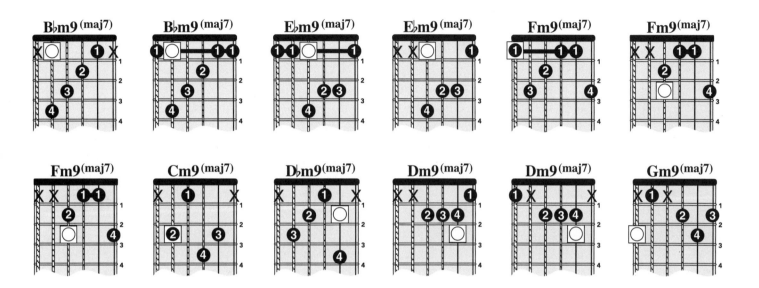

 **26.2**

This progression demonstrates a typical use of a **minor 9(maj7)** chord. It is largely the use of this chord that gives the intro to the song **Stairway to Heaven** its distinctive sound.

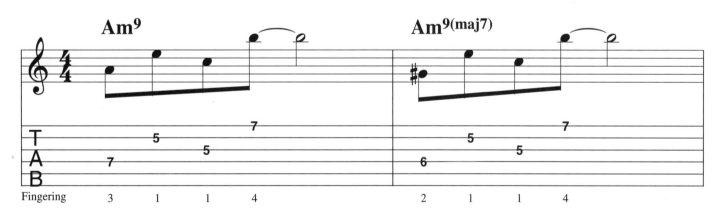

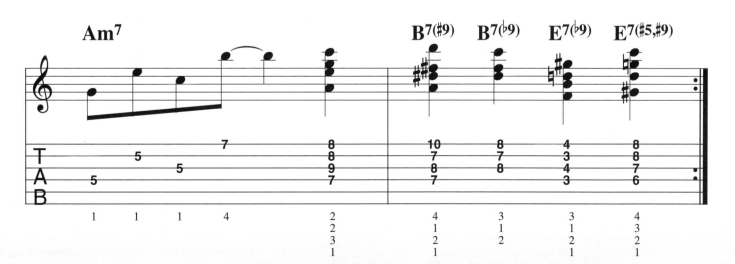

CHORD SYMBOL	ELEVENTH	CHORD FORMULA
11		**1 (3) 5 ♭7 9 11**

An **eleventh** chord is created by adding an 11th degree to any dominant 9th chord. E.g. a **C11** chord contains the notes **C, E, G, B♭, D** and **F** (**1, 3, 5, ♭7, 9** and **11**). The **3rd** degree is usually omitted because of its clash with the 11th degree. Shown below are some common open 11th chord shapes.

OPEN CHORDS

A¹¹
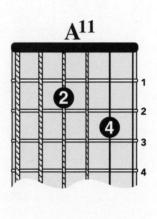

B♭¹¹
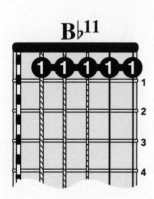

B¹¹
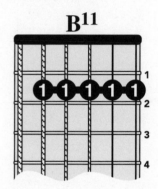

C¹¹
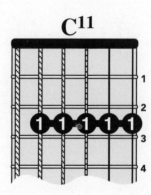

D♭¹¹
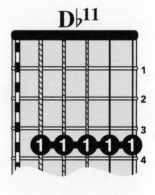

D¹¹
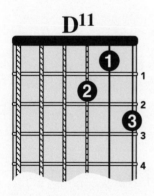

E♭¹¹
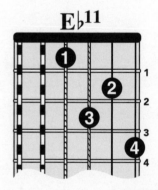

E¹¹
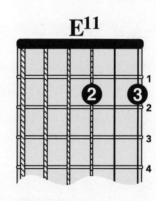

F¹¹
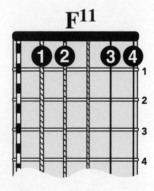

F#¹¹
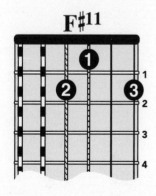

G¹¹
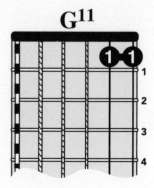

A♭¹¹
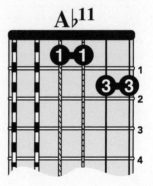

CHORD SYMBOL
11

ELEVENTH

CHORD FORMULA
1 (3) 5 ♭7 9 11

MOVEABLE CHORDS

Here are some useful eleventh chord shapes shown in the first four frets. As with previous chord types, learn each shape and then transpose it to all keys.

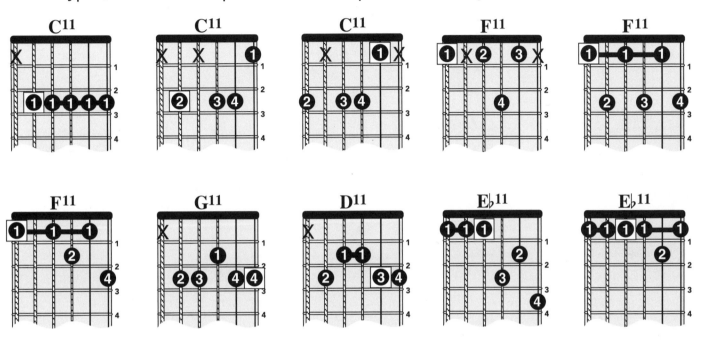

🔘 **27.0**

When the notes of an **11th** chord are picked separately, it can sound good to include the 3rd of the chord as shown here. However, when all the notes are played together, the 3rd is usually omitted, or if the 3rd is essential, a sharp 11 degree is used.

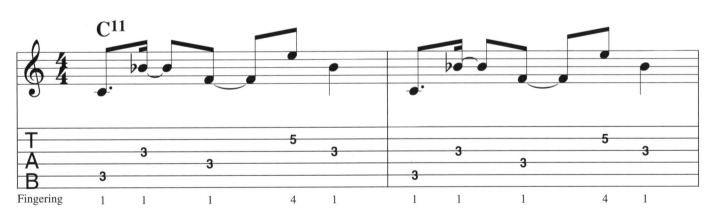

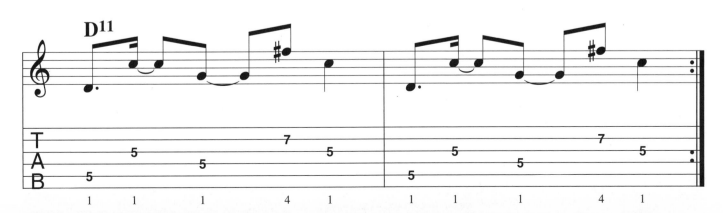

CHORD SYMBOL

m^{11}

MINOR

CHORD FORMULA

$1\flat3\ 5\flat7\ 9\ 11$

A **minor eleventh** chord is created by adding an 11th degree to any minor 9th chord. E.g. a **Cm11** chord contains the notes **C, E♭, G, B♭, D** and **F** (**1, ♭3, 5, ♭7, 9** and **11**). Shown below are some common open minor 11th chord shapes.

OPEN CHORDS

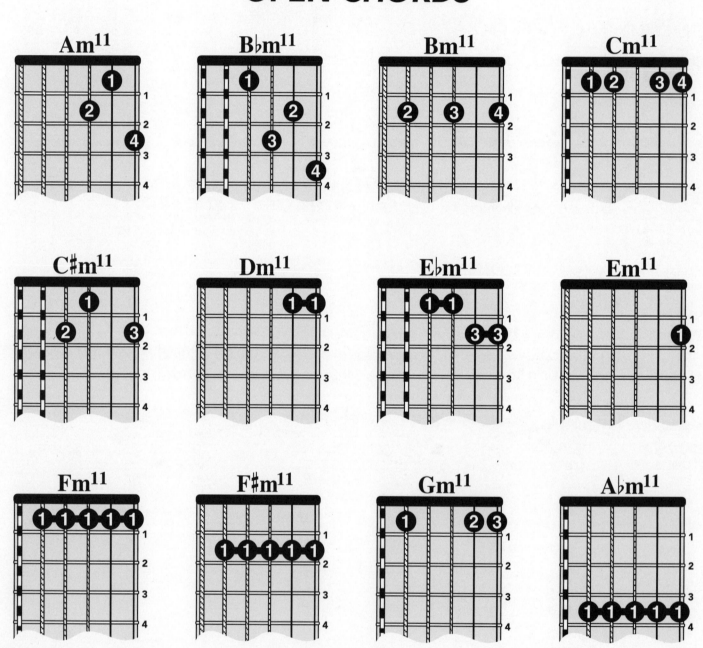

CHORD SYMBOL	MINOR	CHORD FORMULA
m^{11}		1 ♭3 5 ♭7 9 11

MOVEABLE CHORDS

Here are some useful moveable **minor 11th** chord shapes shown in the first four frets. As with previous chord types, learn each shape and then transpose it to all keys.

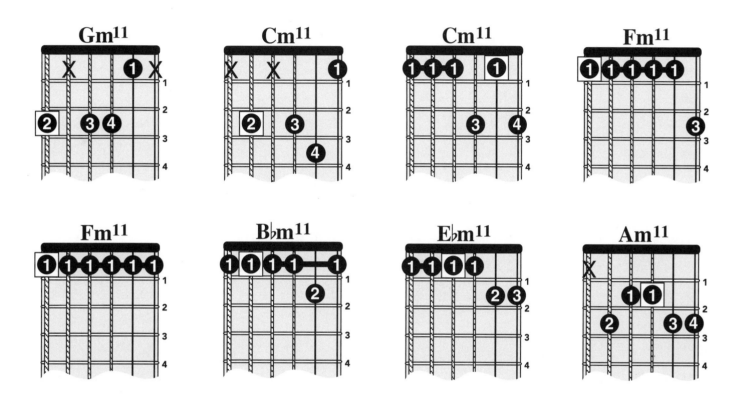

Chords with names like 9ths, 11ths and 13ths may seem complex, but they can often be played with simple fingerings. This example uses one finger moved up and down a distance of two frets to play both **minor 11th** chords.

 **27.1**

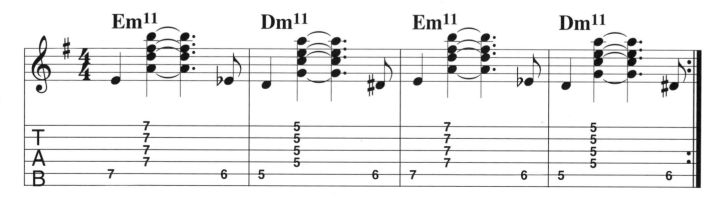

CHORD SYMBOL
Maj7 11

MAJOR SEVENTH

CHORD FORMULA
1 3 5 7 9 #11

Here are some common **major 7 sharp 11** chord shapes shown in the first four frets. As with previous chord types, learn each shape and then transpose it to all keys. Use the formula to work out other fingerings. It may help to remember that the **11** degree is the same as a **flattened 5th**. The spelling used depends on the musical context.

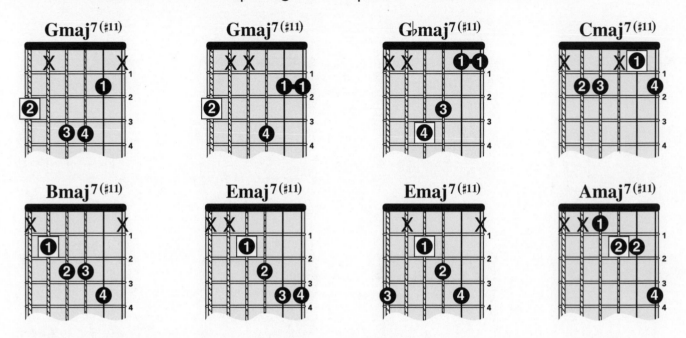

Sharp eleven chords are often used along with the **lydian mode**, which is common in Fusion and modern Jazz. This sound is demonstrated in the following example. To learn more about sharp 11 chords, modes and related topics, see *Progressive Complete Learn to Play Jazz Guitar Manual*.

28.0

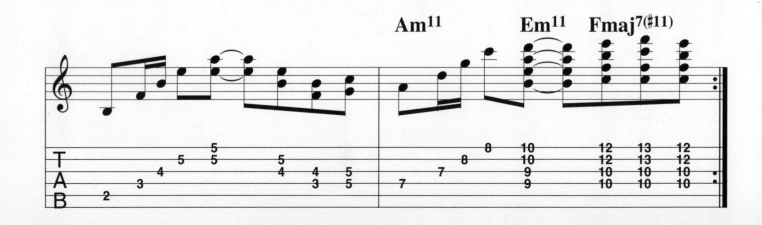

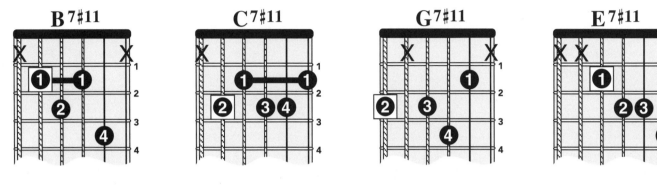

CHORD SYMBOL	SEVENTH	CHORD FORMULA
7 #11		1 3 5 ♭7 9 #11

Here are some common **dominant 7 sharp 11** chord shapes shown in the first four frets. As with previous chord types, learn each shape and then transpose it to all keys. There are many other possibilities. Use the formula to work out some more fingerings.

28.1

Here is a progression demonstrating the use of dominant **711** chords. There are many other ways of using these chords and in some tunes they are the basis of the whole tonality.

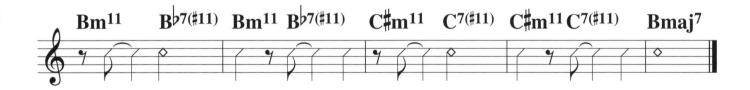

EXTENDED SHARP ELEVEN CHORDS

The **sharp 11** degree can also be added to all the various **9th** and **13th** chords. Shown below are some examples of dominant **911** and **1311** chords. To learn more about these types of chords, see *Progressive Complete Learn to Play Jazz Guitar Manual*.

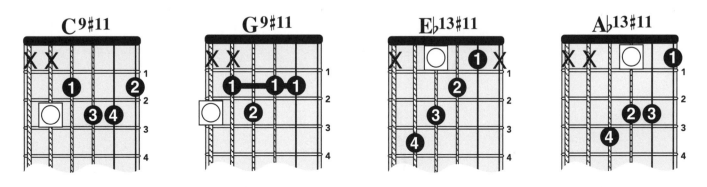

CHORD SYMBOL
Maj13

MAJOR

CHORD FORMULA
1 3 5 7 9 (11) 13

(When playing **thirteenth** chords
the **11th** is usually omitted)

A **major thirteenth** chord is created by adding a 13th degree to any major 11th chord. E.g. a **Cmaj13** chord contains the notes **C, E, G, B, D, F** and **A** (**1, 3, 5, 7, 9, 11** and **13**). The **11th** degree is usually omitted because of its clash with the 13rd degree. Shown below are some common open **Maj13th** chord shapes.

OPEN CHORDS

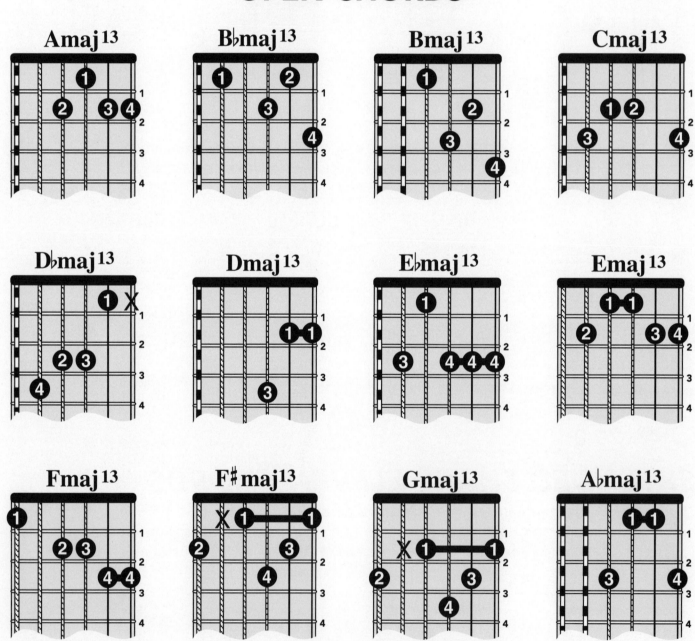

CHORD SYMBOL	MAJOR	CHORD FORMULA
Maj13		1 3 5 7 9 (11) 13

MOVEABLE CHORDS

Here are some useful moveable **major 13th** chord shapes shown in the first four frets. As with previous chord types, learn each shape and then transpose it to all keys. Don't forget to experiment with the formula to create your own fingerings. Make a habit of this with every new chord type you learn.

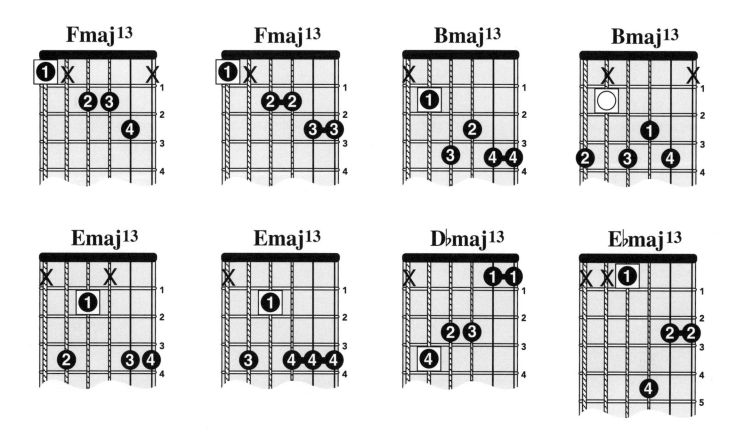

 **29.0**

Here is a rhythmic part using an **Amaj13** chord. It can be played either with one shape or several different shapes. Try it both ways as well as transposing it to other keys.

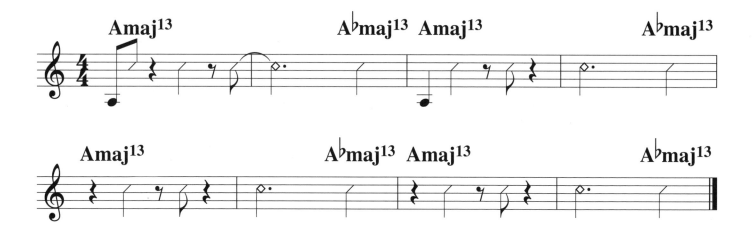

CHORD SYMBOL
13

THIRTEENTH

CHORD FORMULA
1 3 5 ♭7 9 (11) 13

(When playing **thirteenth** chords the **11th** is usually omitted)

A **thirteenth** chord is created by adding a 13th degree to any dominant 11th chord. E.g. a **C13** chord contains the notes **C, E, G, B♭, D, F** and **A** (**1, 3, 5, ♭7, 9, 11** and **13**). The **11th** degree is usually omitted because of its clash with the 13rd degree. Shown below are some common open 13th chord shapes.

OPEN CHORDS

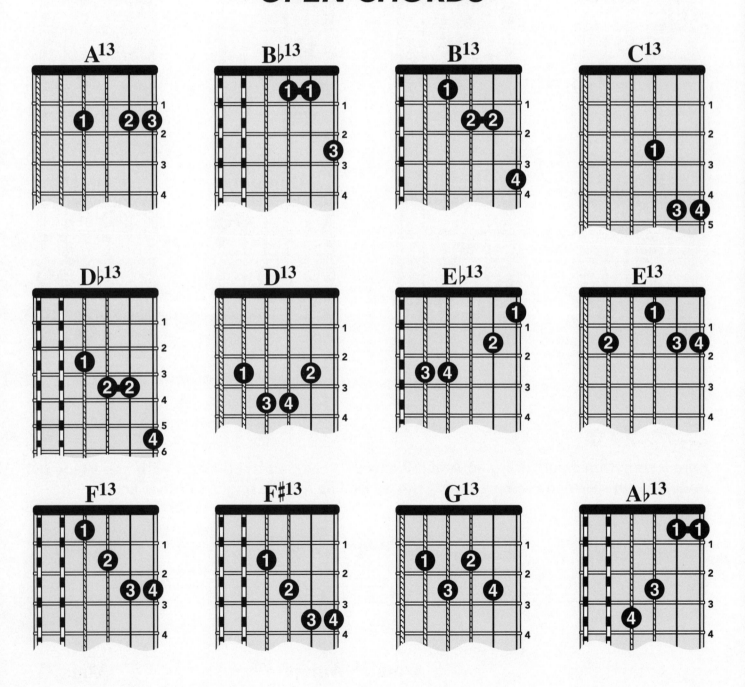

CHORD SYMBOL		CHORD FORMULA
13	# THIRTEEN	1 3 5 ♭7 9 (11) 13

MOVEABLE CHORDS

Here are some useful moveable **13th** chord shapes shown in the first four frets. As with previous chord types, learn each shape and then transpose it to all keys.

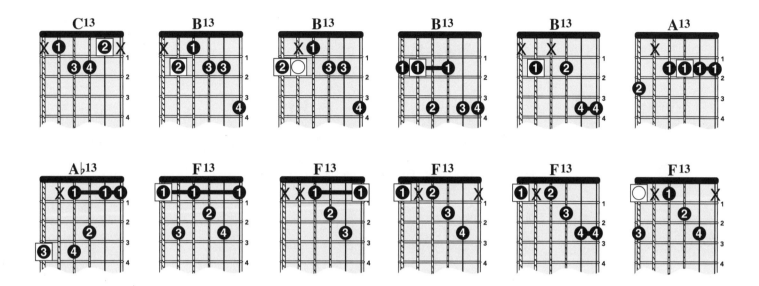

The following Jazz Blues is played almost exclusively with thirteenth chords. Once again you could use several different shapes, or stick with one shape and move it up and down the fretboard to find the various chords. Practice both approaches with the voicings shown in the diagrams above.

29.1   Jazz Blues using 13th Chords

CHORD SYMBOL

m13

MINOR

CHORD FORMULA

1 ♭3 5 ♭7 9 (11) 13

A **minor thirteenth** chord is created by adding a 13th degree to any minor11th chord. E.g. a **Cm13** chord contains the notes **C, E♭, G, B♭, D, F** and **A** (**1, ♭3, 5, ♭7, 9, 11** and **13**). Shown below are some common open **min13th** chord shapes.

OPEN CHORDS

Amin¹³
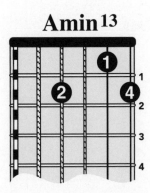

B♭min¹³
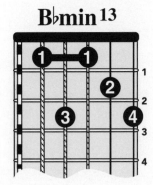

Bmin¹³
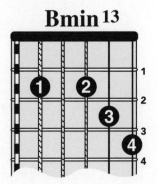

Cmin¹³
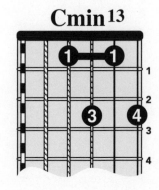

C♯min¹³
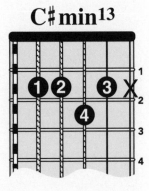

Dmin¹³
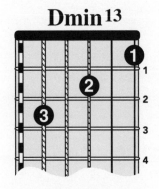

E♭min¹³
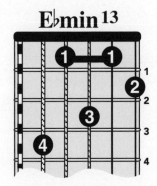

Emin¹³
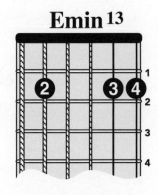

Fmin¹³
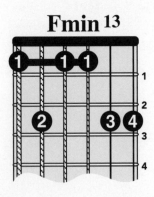

F♯min¹³
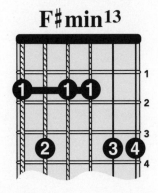

Gmin¹³
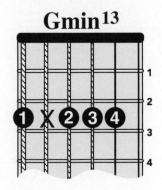

A♭min¹³
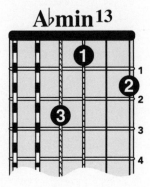

CHORD SYMBOL	MINOR	CHORD FORMULA
m13		1 ♭3 5 ♭7 9 (11) 13

MOVEABLE CHORDS

Here are some moveable **minor13th** chord shapes shown in the first four frets. As with previous chord types, learn each shape and then transpose it to all keys. Don't forget to experiment with the formula to create your own fingerings.

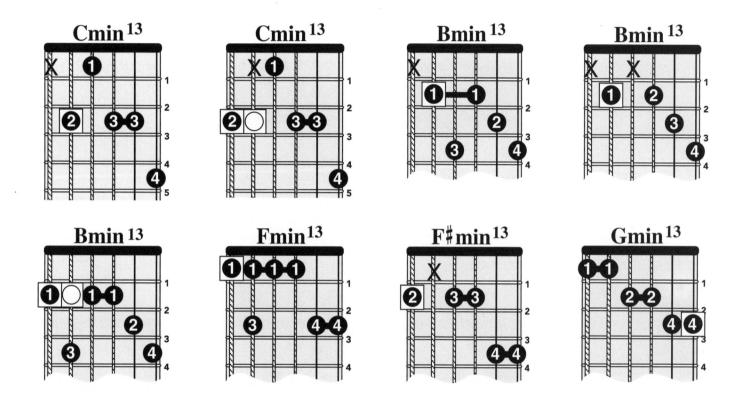

Here is a guitar part using an **minor 13th** chords. It can be played either with one shape or several different shapes. Practice it both ways as well as transposing it to other keys.

 **29.2**

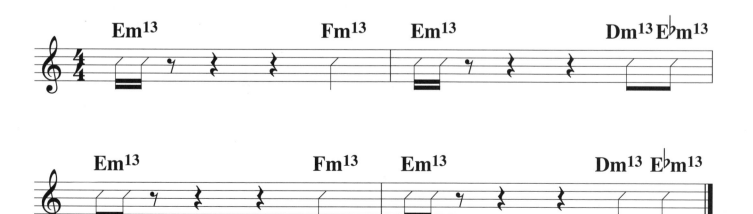

ALTERED THIRTEENTH CHORDS

Chord names don't go any higher than a **13th**. If you add another 3rd interval above the 13th degree, it takes you back to the root note of the chord. You can create many more variations on 13th chords and other extended chords by using various combinations of alterations to the **5ths** and **9ths** of the chords. Now you know how to create all the various chord types, it is recommended that you make a habit of experimenting with alterations every time you practice. When and where they work best depends on the musical context.

Two of most common altered thirteenth chords are the **13♯9** and the **13♭9**. These are demonstrated below and on the following page.

CHORD SYMBOL	THIRTEENTH	CHORD FORMULA
13♯9		1 3 5 ♭7 ♯9 (11) 13

Shown below is a **13♯9** chord shape which has two names. The first two diagrams show how it works as an **F13♯9** and the third and fourth diagrams demonstrate the same shape as a **B13♯9**. Practice moving it around the key cycle (up and down the fretboard) visualizing the root note on the **1st** string, and then on the **5th** string. Soon you will be able to quickly find it in any key without having to move more than a couple of frets. This should be your eventual aim with all chord types.

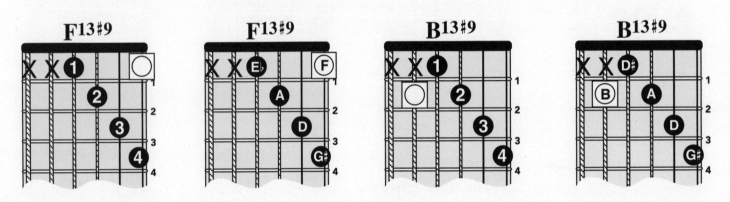

30.0

Experiment with various fret positions when playing this progression. There are several different ways it can be played. Experiment with the formula to find other voicings as well.

CHORD SYMBOL	THIRTEENTH	CHORD FORMULA
13♭9		**1 3 5 ♭7 ♭9 (11) 13**

Here are some common voicings for **13♭9** chords. None of these voicings contains the root note, but it can be added to each of them if you wish. Experiment with the formula to come up with your own voicings.

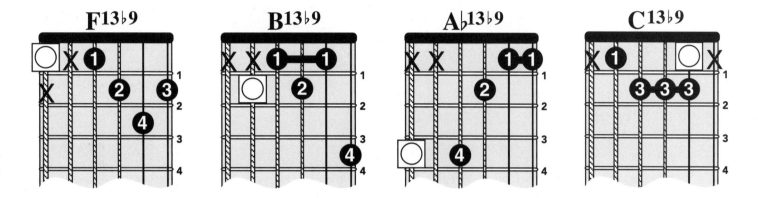

Remember that any chord can be played as an arpeggio, thus opening up other fingering possibilities. You can move around between the notes of a chord in any order or using any rhythm that sounds good in whatever musical context you are playing in. Some of the greatest recorded guitar parts are based on a simple repeating rhythm pattern applied to one or two chords. The following example demonstrates this concept applied to an **E13♭9** chord.

 **30.1**

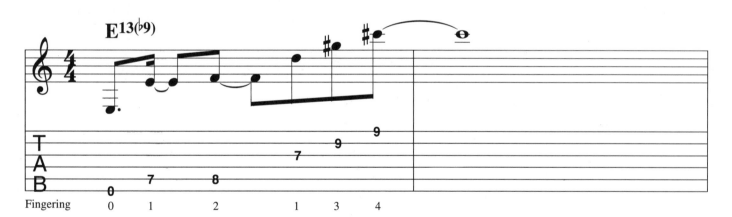

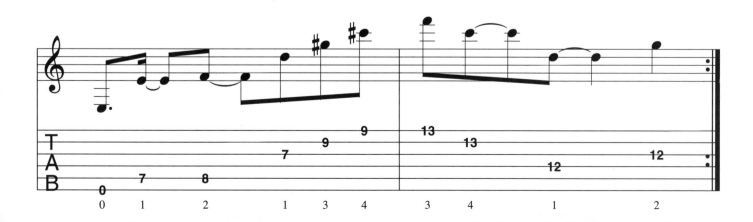

CREATING YOUR OWN CHORDS

As mentioned previously, once you know the formula for a chord, you can play the notes in any order, play them together or as an arpeggio, or random pattern, omit some of them, alter some of them, etc. You can also create your own chords by working out a formula even if you don't know any shapes for the chord. Just say you want to experiment with altering 13th chords, for a start you could alter the **5th**, or the **9th**, or both. Shown below is the formula for a **13♭5♭9** chord along with a voicing built from a **C** root note.

CHORD SYMBOL	THIRTEENTH FLAT FIVE, FLAT NINE	CHORD FORMULA
13 ♭5 ♭9		1 3 5 ♭7 ♭9 (11) 13

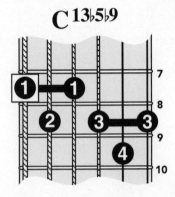

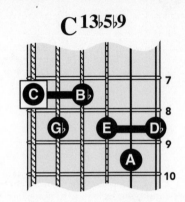

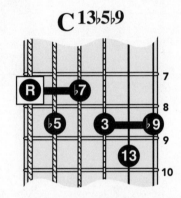

You could create a part from this by simply playing the notes of the chord and leaving a space before repeating the sequence. This is demonstrated in the following example.

 **30.2**

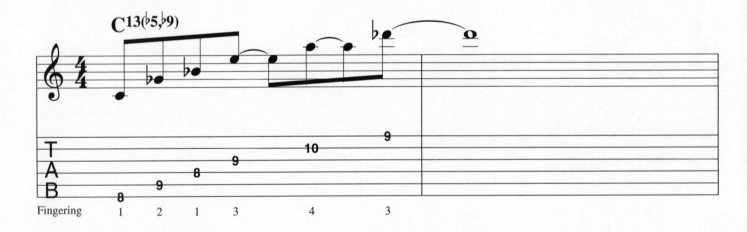

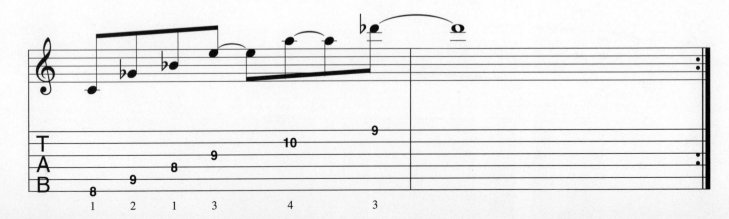

Another possibility would be to flatten the **5th**, but sharpen the **9th, as shown in the following example**. You don't even have to hold down a chord shape. as long as you play notes from the chord formula, you will get the effect of the chord (in this case **C13♭5♯9**).

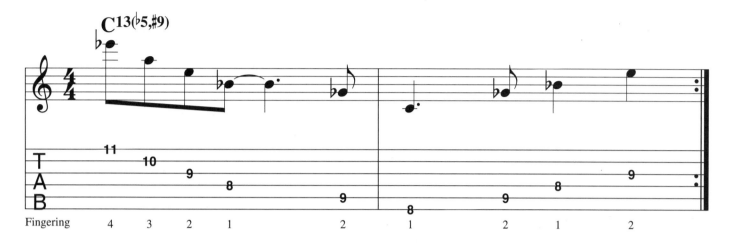

You don't have to use an extended chord formula to come up with your own chords. Another good thing to experiment with is to take a basic major or minor chord and add other notes to it. You can add any note to any chord if you think it sounds good. There are no rules in music, only concepts. Some are tried and true, others are experimental. Everyone has their own ears and their own opinion.

Shown below is a chord which could be described as **E add ♭5** or **E add ♯11**. It is simply an E major triad with an added ♭5 degree along with its natural 5th degree. You won't find it in most music textbooks, but it is commonly used by Funk players, and it is great for creating tension. The example below demonstrates this chord in a musical context.

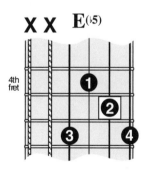

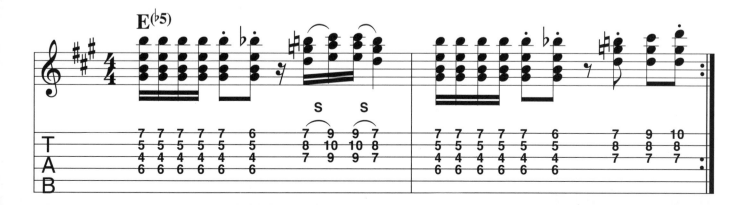

MOVING CHORDS OVER ONE SYMBOL

In many charts for Funk, Jazz or Rock tunes, you may see one chord symbol for an extended period, yet when you listen to a recording of the tune, you can hear the guitarist moving between several chords. As long as you stick to the chord family (e.g. minor, or dominant) you can move freely between chords which have the same root as the basic chord symbol. The following guitar part could be played in a Funk tune over an **Em** chord symbol.

 32.0   Em Groove

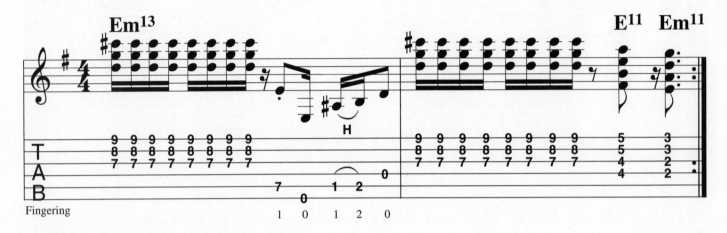

 32.1   E7 Groove

Here is an example of what a Funk player might do over an **E7** chord symbol. This approach is best learned by a combination of experimenting, listening, transcribing parts, and playing with other musicians as often as possible. The more you do it, the easier it gets.

Section 4

How Chords Relate to Scales and Keys

THE MAJOR SCALE

The **major scale** is a series of **8** notes in alphabetical order that has the familiar sound:

Do   Re   Mi   Fa   So   La   Ti   Do

Thus the **C major scale** contains the following notes.

The distance between each note is two frets except for **EF** and **BC** where the distance is only one fret.
A distance of two frets is called a **tone**, indicated by **T**.
A distance of one fret is called a **semitone**, indicated by **ST**.

THE OCTAVE

An **octave** is the range of **8 notes** of a major scale. The first note and last note of a major scale always have the same name. In the **C major** scale the distance from the first **C** to the **C** note above it is one octave (8 notes). The following example is one octave of the C major scale.

C MAJOR SCALE

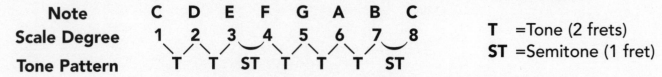

Each of the 8 notes in the major scale is given a **scale number**, or **scale degree**.

Note	C	D	E	F	G	A	B	C
Scale Degree	1	2	3	4	5	6	7	8
Tone Pattern		T	T	ST	T	T	T	ST

T =Tone (2 frets)
ST =Semitone (1 fret)

The distance between any two notes is called an **interval**. In any major scale the interval between the 3rd and 4th notes, and the 7th and 8th notes of the scale is one semitone apart; i.e. they are one fret apart. All other notes are one tone (2 frets) apart.

SHARPS AND FLATS

A sharp (♯) raises the pitch of a note by one semitone. A flat (♭) lowers the pitch of a note by one semitone. In music notation the ♯ and ♭ signs (called accidentals) are always placed before the note heads.

 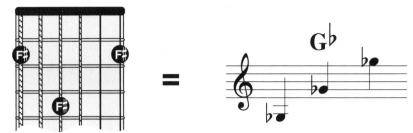

This example illustrates that the same note has two different names (i.e. F♯ and G♭ have the same position on the fretboard). These are referred to as **enharmonic** notes. Other examples of enharmonic notes are: **A♯/B♭, C♯/D♭, D♯/E♭, F♯/G♭, G♯/A♭** . (This principle also applies to the naming of chords e.g. **A♯ Majo**r = **B♭ Major**, **C♯m7** = **D♭ m7** etc.)

A natural (♮) cancels the effect of a sharp or flat. A sharp or flat, when placed before a note, affects the same not if it recurs in the remainder of that bar. It does not, however, affect notes in the next bar, e.g.:

With the inclusion of sharps and flats, there are 12 different notes within one octave, e.g.:

A A♯/B♭ **B C** C♯/D♭ **D** D♯/E♭ **E F** F♯/G♭ **G** G♯/A♭ **A**

Note that there are not sharps or flats between **B** and **C**, or **E** and **F**.

THE CHROMATIC SCALE

The chromatic scale is based upon a sequence of **semitones** only and thus includes every possible note within one octave. Here is the **C** chromatic scale:

C C♯ D D♯ E F F♯ G G♯ A A♯ B C

The same scale could be written out using flats, however it is more common to do this when descending, as such:

C B B♭ A A♭ G G♭ F E E♭ D D♭ C

Because each chromatic scale contains every possible note within one octave, once yOu have learnt one you have basically learnt them all. As an example, the A chromatic scale (written below) contains exactly the same notes as the C chromatic scale, the only difference between them being the note upon which they commence. This starting note, in all scales, is referred to as the **root** or **key note**.

A Chromatic scale: **A A♯ B C C♯ D D♯ E F F♯ G G♯ A**

MORE ABOUT MAJOR SCALES

Once you know the pattern of tones and semitones used to create the C major scale, you can build a major scale on any of the twelve notes used in music. It is important to memorize this pattern, which is shown below.

Tone   Tone   Semitone   Tone   Tone   Tone   Semitone

The **semitones** are always found between the **3rd and 4th**, and **7th and 8th degrees** (notes) of the scale. All the other notes are a tone apart.

To demonstrate how the major scale pattern works starting on any note, here is the **G major scale**. Notice that the 7th degree is F sharp (**F#**) instead of F. This is done to maintain the correct pattern of tones and semitones and thus retain the sound of the major scale (**do re mi fa so la ti do**).

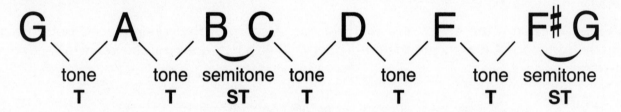

This example shows two octaves of the G Major scale.

THE F MAJOR SCALE

The **F major** scale starts and ends on the note F and contains a B flat (**B♭**) note. Written below are two octaves of the **F major** scale. In the **F major** scale, a **B♭** note must be used instead of a B note in order to keep the correct pattern of tones and semitones for the major scale.

As you will have noticed with the scales of G major and F major, major scales starting on different notes are simply higher or lower versions of the same sequence of sounds. This is because they always use the same pattern of tones and semitones. It is important to memorize this pattern, which is shown below.

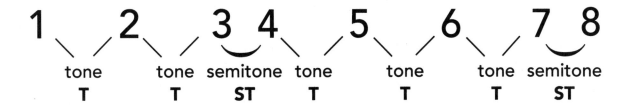

The **semitones** are always found between the **3rd and 4th**, and **7th and 8th** degrees of the scale. All the other notes are a tone apart. By simply following the pattern of tones and semitones, it is possible to construct a major scale starting on any note. The scale will be named by the note it starts on. The following example demonstrates three more major scales.

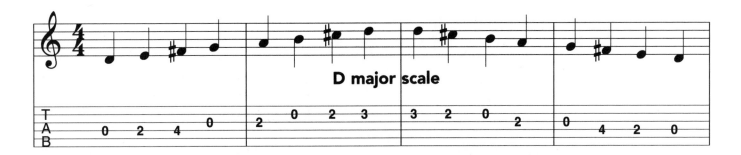

KEYS AND KEY SIGNATURES

The **key** describes the note around which a piece of music is built. When a song consists of notes from a particular scale, it is said to be written in the **key** which has the same notes as that scale. For example, if a song contains mostly notes from the **C major scale**, it is said to be in the **key of C major**. If a song contains mostly notes from the **F major scale**, it is said to be in the **key of F major**. If a song contains mostly notes from the **G major scale**, it is said to be in the **key of G major**. When playing in any major key other than C, the key will contain at least one sharp or flat, and possibly as many as six. Instead of writing these sharps or flats before each note as they occur, they are usually written at the beginning of the song just before the time signature. These sharps or flats are called a **key signature**. The sharps or flats in the key signature are the same as the sharps or flats in the corresponding major scale. The major scales and key signatures for the keys of **F** and **G** are shown below. Without sharps and flats, these scales would not contain the correct pattern of tones and semitones and would therefore not sound like a major scale.

G Major Scale

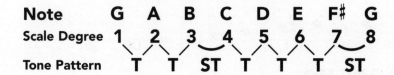

Key Signature of G Major

The **G major** scale contains one sharp, F#, therefore the key signature for the key of **G major** contains one sharp, F#.

F Major Scale

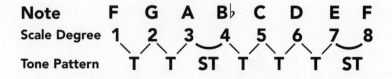

Key Signature of F Major

The **F major** scale contains one flat, B♭, therefore the key signature for the key of **F major** contains one flat, B♭.

The reason some scales contain sharps while others contain flats is that there has to be a separate letter name for each note in the scale. E.g. the G major scale contains F# instead of G♭ even though these two notes are identical in sound. However, if G♭ was used, the scale would contain two notes with the letter name G and no note with the letter name F. This is the reason for choosing to call the note F# in this key. In the key of F major, the note B♭ is chosen instead of A# for the same reason. If A# was used, the scale would contain two notes with the letter name A and no note with the letter name B. The note each major scale starts on will determine how many sharps or flats are found in each key signature because of the necessity for the scale to have the correct pattern of tones and semitones in order to sound right. The charts on the following page contain the key signatures of all the major scales used in music, along with the number of sharps or flats contained in each key. Because there are 12 notes used in music, this means there are 12 possible starting notes for major scales (including sharps and flats). Therefore some of the keys will have sharps or flats in their name, e.g. F# major, B♭ major, E♭ major, etc. Keys which contain sharps are called sharp keys and keys which contain flats are called flat keys.

The key signatures for all the major scales that contain sharps are:

The sharp key signatures are summarised in the table below.

*The new sharp **key** is a fifth interval * higher*

Key	Number of Sharps	Sharp Notes
G	1	F♯
D	2	F♯, C♯
A	3	F♯, C♯, G♯
E	4	F♯, C♯, G♯, D♯
B	5	F♯, C♯, G♯, D♯, A♯,
F♯	6	F♯, C♯, G♯, D♯, A♯, E♯

*The new sharp **note** is a fifth interval higher*

Written below are the key signatures for all the major scales that contain flats.

The flat key signatures are summarised in the table below.

*The new flat **key** is a fourth interval higher*

Key	Number of Flats	Flat Notes
F	1	B♭
B♭	2	B♭, E♭
E♭	3	B♭, E♭, A♭
A♭	4	B♭, E♭, A♭, D♭
D♭	5	B♭, E♭, A♭, D♭, G♭,
G♭	6	B♭, E♭, A♭, D♭, G♭, C♭

*The new flat **note** is a fourth interval higher*

* An **interval** is the distance between two notes. Intervals are named by the number of letters they are apart, e.g. C to G is a fifth. Intervals are discussed in detail on pages 145 to 152.

THE KEY CYCLE

There are many reasons why you need to be able to play equally well in every key. Bands often have to play in keys that suit their singer. That could be **F#** or **Db** for example. Keyboard players tend to like the keys of **C**, **F** and **G**, while **E** and **A** are fairly common keys for guitar. Horn players like flat keys such as **F**, **Bb** and **Eb**. Apart from this, Jazz tunes often contain many key changes in themselves. For these reasons, you need to learn how keys relate to each other so you can move quickly between them.

One way to do this is to use the **key cycle** (also called the **cycle of 5ths** or **cycle of 4ths**). It contains the names of all the keys and is fairly easy to memorize.

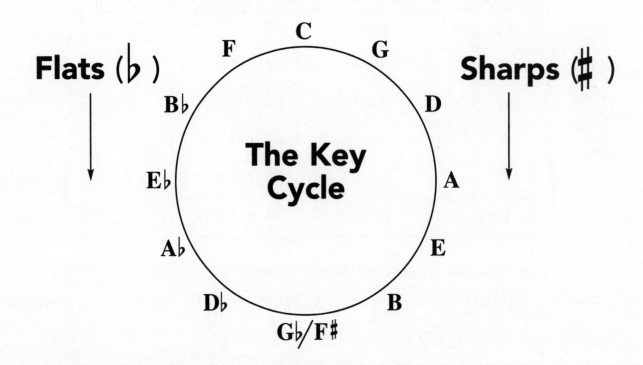

Think of the key cycle like a clock. Just as there are 12 points on the clock, there are also 12 keys. **C** is at the top and contains no sharps or flats. Moving around clockwise you will find the next key is **G**, which contains one sharp (**F#**). The next key is **D**, which contains two sharps (**F#** and **C#**). Progressing further through the sharp keys each key contains an extra sharp, with the new sharp being the 7th note of the new key, and the others being any which were contained in the previous key. Therefore the key of A would automatically contain **F#** and **C#** which were in the key of D, plus **G#** which is the 7th note of the A major scale. When you get to **F#** (at 6 o'clock), the new sharp is called **E#** which is enharmonically the same as **F**. Remember that **enharmonic** means two different ways of writing the same note. Another example of enharmonic spelling would be **F#** and **Gb**. This means that **Gb** could become the name of the key of **F#**. The key of **F#** contains six sharps, while the key of **Gb** contains six flats–all of which are exactly the same notes.

If you start at **C** again at the top of the cycle and go anti-clockwise you will progress through the flat keys. The key of **F** contains one flat (**Bb**), which then becomes the name of the next key around the cycle. In flat keys, the new flat is always the 4th degree of the new key. Continuing around the cycle, the key of **Bb** contains two flats (**Bb** and **Eb**) and so on. **Practice playing all the notes around the cycle both clockwise and anticlockwise.** Once you can do this, play chords around the cycle as demonstrated on the following page.

USING THE KEY CYCLE

A good way to learn a new chord in all keys is to play it from each note of the key cycle, moving clockwise until you get back to the starting point. Then reverse the order and go anticlockwise. This is a quick way of covering all keys and also gets you used to moving between keys in an order that occurs frequently in songs. The following examples demonstrate this process with several chord types. You can use one shape and move it up and down the fretboard to each new key, or you can use different shapes close together on the fretboard. It is recommended that you use both methods.

33.0   Minor 7ths Clockwise

33.1   Dominant 9ths Anticlockwise

33.2   Major Triads Anticlockwise

MAJOR SCALES IN ALL KEYS

The following example demonstrates one octave of the major scale ascending and descending in every key, moving anticlockwise around the key cycle. The scales are shown here **without tablature** to help improve your music reading. There is a vast amount of written music which does not contain tablature. If you can't read notation, it means a large proportion of the music in the world is unavailable to you. However, if you can read music well, it is easy to learn a new style or music written for **any** instrument, not just guitar.

You already know all the notes contained in these scales and they can all be played in the open position or first position. Knowledge of the notes in these scales is essential for constructing chords in all the keys. Chords are commonly built on all seven notes of each of these scales and used as the basis for chord progressions within each key (see page 153). The better you know the scales, the quicker you will be able to work out chords for songs in any key as well as transposing chord progressions from one key to another.

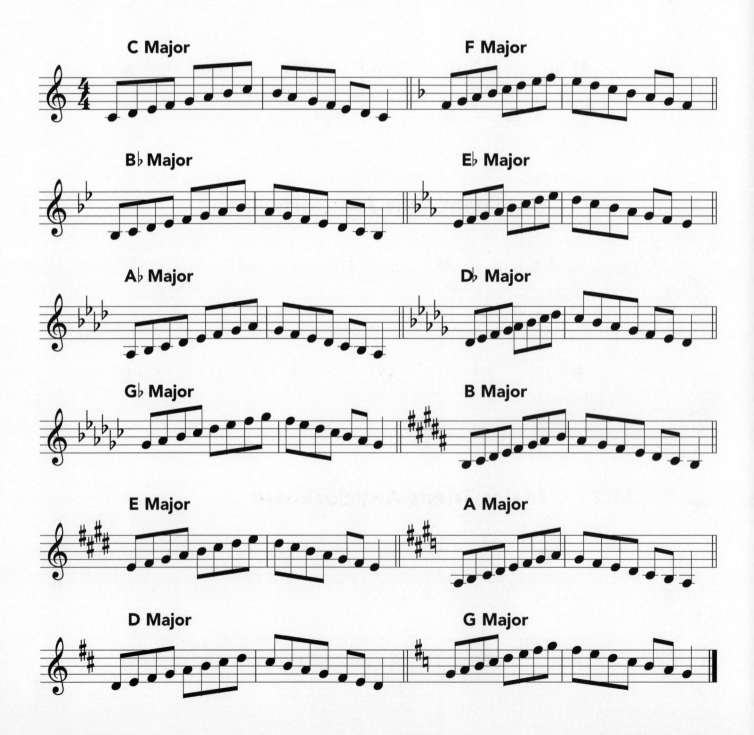

INTERVALS

An **interval** is the distance between two musical notes. **All melodies and chords are made up of a series of intervals.** Intervals are measured in numbers, and are calculated by counting the number of letter names (**A B C D E F G A**) between and including the notes being measured. Within an octave, intervals are: **Unison** (two notes of the same pitch played or sung together or consecutively), **2nd**, **3rd**, **4th**, **5th**, **6th**, **7th** and **Octave** (two notes an octave apart). Thus **A** to **B** is a **2nd** interval, as is B to C, C to D etc. **A** to **C** is a **3rd** interval, **A** to **D** is a **4th**, **A** to **E** is a **5th**, **A** to **F** is a **6th**, **A** to **G** is a **7th** and **A** to the next **A** is an **octave**.

Intervals may be **melodic** (two notes played consecutively) or **harmonic** (two notes played at the same time). Hence two people singing at the same time are said to be singing in harmony.

INTERVAL QUALITIES

Different intervals have different qualities, as shown below:

Quality	Can be applied to
Perfect	Unisons, 4ths, 5ths and Octaves
Major	2nds, 3rds, 6ths and 7ths
Minor	2nds, 3rds, 6ths and 7ths
Augmented	All intervals
Diminished	All intervals

Interval qualities can be best explained with the aid of a chromatic scale. If you look at the one below, it is easy to see that since **intervals are measured in semitones**, they may begin or end on a sharp or flat rather than a natural note.

Perfect intervals are **4ths**, **5ths** and **octaves**. If you **widen** a perfect interval by a semitone it becomes **augmented** (added to). E.g. if you add a semitone to the perfect 4th interval **C** to **F**, it becomes the **augmented 4th interval C** to **F♯**. Notice that the letter name remains the same–it is not referred to as C to G♭.

If you **narrow** a perfect interval by a semitone it becomes **diminished** (lessened). E.g. if you lessen the perfect 5th interval **D** to **A** by a semitone, it becomes the **diminished 5th interval D to A♭**. Again, the letter name remains the same–it is not referred to as D to G♯.

Major intervals (2nds, 3rds, 6ths and 7ths) become minor if narrowed by a semitone and **minor** intervals become major if widened by a semitone. A **diminished** interval can be created by narrowing a perfect or minor interval by a semitone. An **augmented** interval can be created by widening a perfect or major interval by a semitone.

INTERVAL DISTANCES

In summary, here is a list of the distances of all common intervals up to an octave, measured in semitones. Each new interval is one semitone further apart than the previous one. Notice that the interval of an octave is exactly twelve semitones. This is because there are twelve different notes in the chromatic scale. Notice also that the interval which has a distance of six semitones can be called either an augmented 4th or a diminished5th. This interval is also often called a **tritone** (6 semitones = 3 tones).

Minor 2nd - One semitone

Major 2nd - Two semitones

Minor 3rd - Three semitones

Major 3rd - Four semitones

Perfect 4th - Five semitones

Augmented 4th or Diminished 5th - Six semitones

Perfect 5th - Seven semitones

Minor 6th - Eight semitones

Major 6th - Nine semitones

Minor 7th - Ten semitones

Major 7th - Eleven semitones

Perfect Octave - Twelve semitones

Shown below are all of the common intervals ascending within one octave, starting and ending on the note **C**.

FINDING INTERVALS ON THE FRETBOARD

A good musician can instantly play any interval from any note either harmonically (at the same time) or in ascending or descending order. The diagrams below show the most common ways of playing intervals on the guitar. Learn them one at a time and listen carefully to the sound of each interval as you play it.

Minor 2nd
(One Semitone)

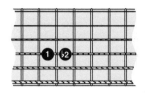 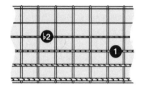 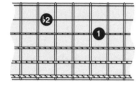

Major 2nd
(Two Semitones)

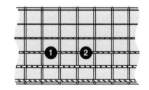 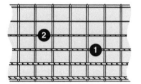 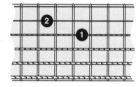

Minor 3rd
(Three Semitones)

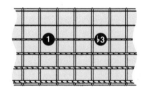 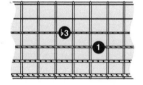 

Major 3rd
(Four Semitones)

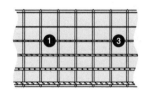 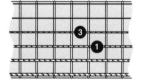 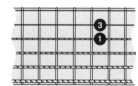

Perfect 4th
(Five Semitones)

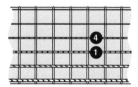 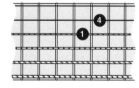

Tritone -Aug 4th or Dim 5th
(Six Semitones)

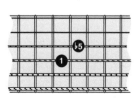 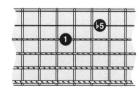

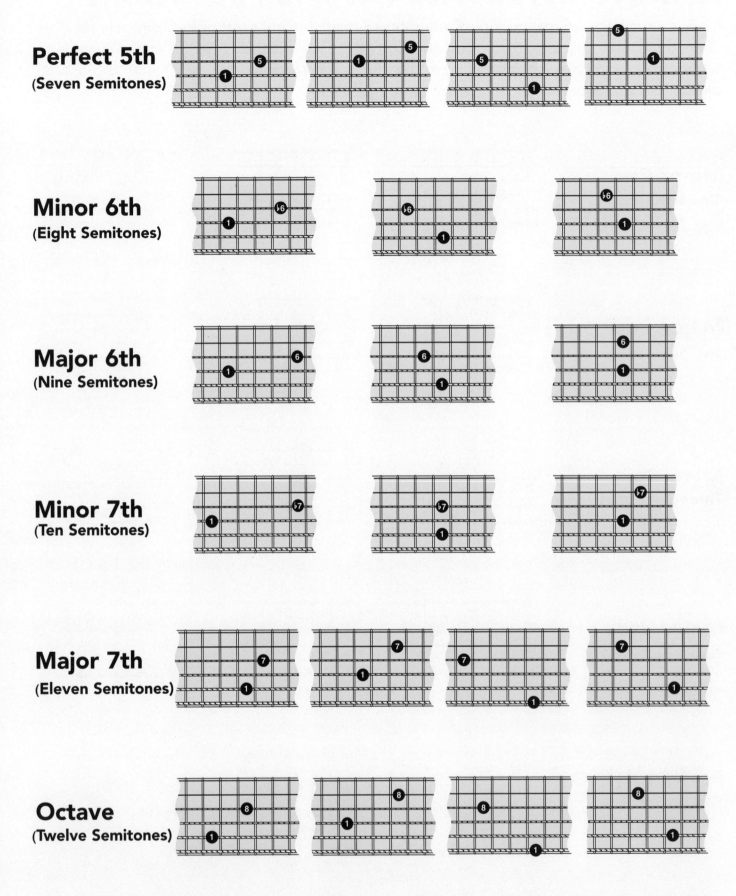

Perfect 5th
(Seven Semitones)

Minor 6th
(Eight Semitones)

Major 6th
(Nine Semitones)

Minor 7th
(Ten Semitones)

Major 7th
(Eleven Semitones)

Octave
(Twelve Semitones)

These diagrams show only the most common ways of playing intervals on the guitar, but they are not the only patterns. You should also work on playing every possible interval on each individual string. This is easier than it sounds. All you have to do is work out how many frets apart the interval is: e.g. a perfect 4th is five frets apart, a minor 6th is eight frets apart, etc.

IDENTIFYING INTERVALS BY EAR

Since all melodies are made up of a series of intervals, it is essential to learn to identify intervals by ear and be able to reproduce them at will, both with your voice and on your instrument. If you can sing something accurately, it means you are hearing it accurately. Here are some ways of developing your ability to identify and reproduce intervals. The example used in the first two exercises is a minor 3rd, but it is essential to go through these processes with **all** intervals.

1.   Choose an interval you wish to work on (e.g. minor 3rds). Play a starting note (e.g. C) and sing it. Then sing a minor 3rd up from that note (E♭). Hold the note with your voice while you test its accuracy on your instrument. Then choose another starting note and repeat the process. Keep doing this until you are accurate every time. The next step is to sing the interval (in this case a minor 3rd) downwards from your starting note. Again, do this repeatedly until you are accurate every time.

2.   Sing the same interval consecutively upwards and then downwards several times. E.g. start on C and sing a minor 3rd up from it (E♭). Then sing a minor 3rd up from E♭ (G♭). Then another minor third up from G♭ (B♭♭ - which is enharmonically the same as A). Then up another minor 3rd (C an octave higher than the starting note). Once you can do this, reverse the process (Start on C and sing a minor 3rd down to A, then another minor 3rd down and then another, etc).

3.   Play and sing a starting note (e.g. C) and then think of it as the first degree of the chromatic scale - sing "one". Now sing the flattened second degree of the scale - sing "flat two". This note is a minor 2nd up from your C note (a D♭ note). Then sing the C again ("one"). Then sing the second degree of the scale (a D note - sing "two"). Next, sing your C Note again ("one"). Continue in this manner all the way up the chromatic scale until you reach C an octave above. The entire sequence goes: 1, ♭2, 1, 2, 1, ♭3, 1, 3, 1, 4, 1, ♭5, 1, 5, 1, ♭6, 1, 6, 1, ♭7, 1, 7, 1, 8, 1. As with the previous exercises, once you can do this accurately (check your pitches on your instrument), reverse the process and sing downwards from the top of the scale, working your way down the chromatic scale again. The downward sequence goes 1(8), 7, 1, ♭7, 1, 6, 1, ♭6, 1, 5, 1,♭ 5, 1, 4, 1, 3, 1, ♭3, 1, 2, 1, ♭2, 1, 1, 1(8).

4.   As well as hearing intervals melodically (one note at a time), it is important to be able to hear them harmonically (two notes played together). A good way to develop this is to have a friend play random harmonic intervals on either guitar or keyboard while you identify them. Keep your back to your friend while you do this, so that you cannot identify the intervals by sight.

Don't get frustrated if you can't hear intervals accurately at first. Most people have trouble with this. If you work at it regularly for several months, you will see a dramatic improvement in your musical hearing, and you will be able to improvise much more freely, as well as being able to work out parts off CDs more easily.

POWER CHORDS

A **power chord** is actually an interval of a **perfect 5th**. This forms the root and fifth of a chord and when used with distortion produces a distinctive sound which is commonly used in Rock and Metal. The notes can also be inverted (creating a **4th**) as demonstrated in example 34.1.

 34.0   **Power Chords**

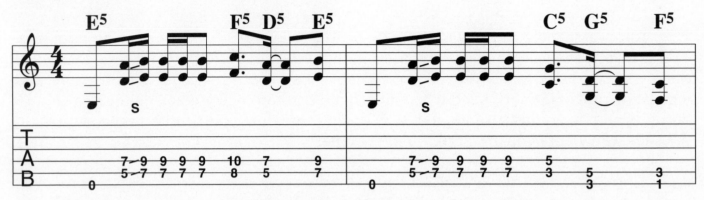

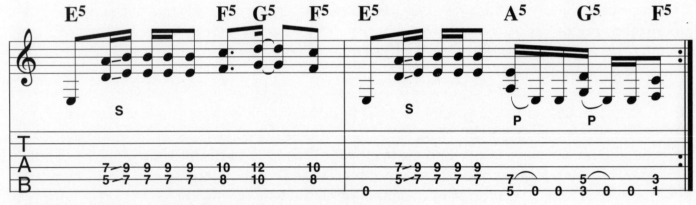

 34.1 Inverted Power Chords

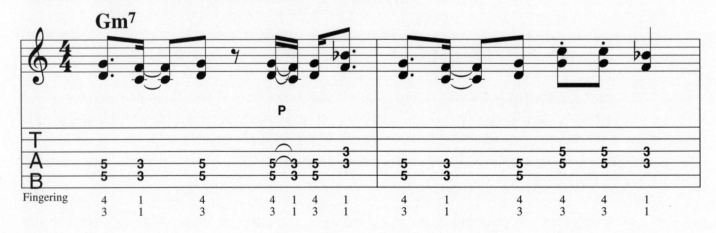

CHORDS USING 4THS

It is possible to construct whole chords using 4ths. In the chords shown below, **one shape** is used but the **name** of the chord changes depending on the **position of the root note**. There are many chords with more than one name. This topic is discussed on page 177.

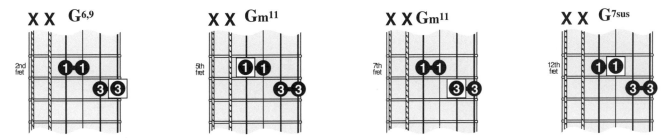

It is possible to harmonize an entire scale with these chords. The example below shows the **G Blues scale** harmonized from below with chords voiced in 4ths. For more information on the Blues scale, see *Progressive Complete Learn to Play Blues Guitar.*

35.0

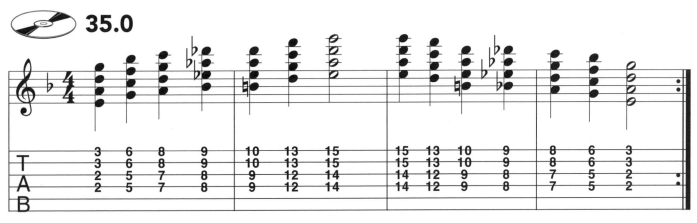

35.1

Here is an example of how these chords can be used over a **G minor** Funk groove. You can move freely between these chords because they all relate to the **Gm** chord symbol.

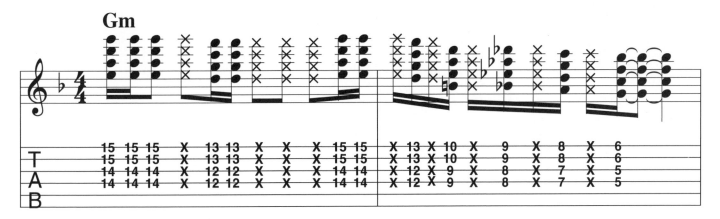

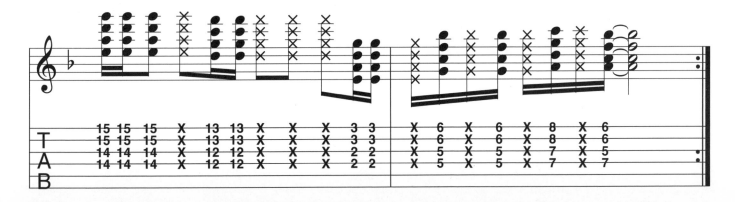

CHORD CONSTRUCTION USING INTERVALS

Chords are usually made up of combinations of major and minor third intervals. As mentioned previously, the simplest chords are made up of three notes. These are called **triads**. There are **four** basic types of triads: **major**, **minor**, **augmented** and **diminished**. Examples of each of these are shown below along with the formula for each one.

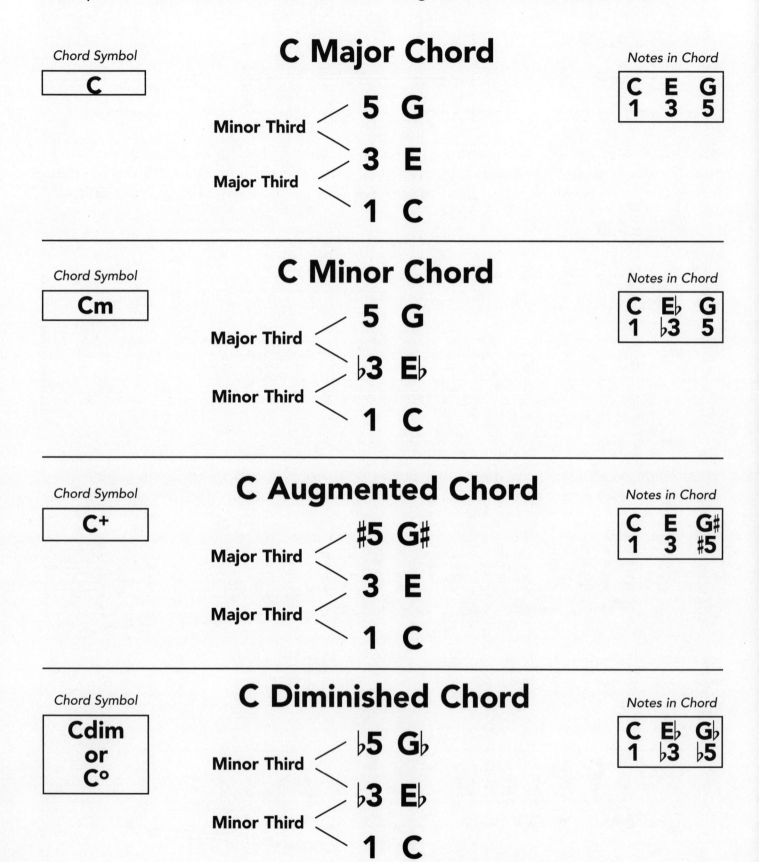

SCALE TONE CHORDS

In any key it is possible to build chords on each note of a scale. This means that for every major scale there are **seven** possible chords which can be used for creating guitar parts and harmonising melodies. These seven chords are called **scale tone chords**. It is common practice to describe all the chords within a key with **roman numerals**. The example below which demonstrates the seven scale tone triads (three note chords) in the key of C major.

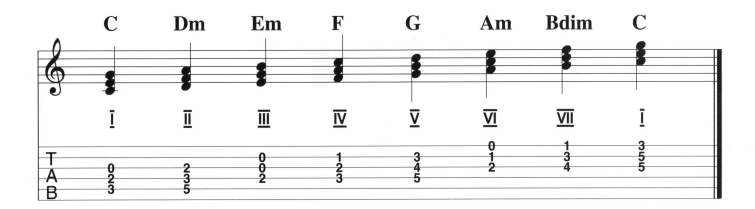

Once you know the notes for any of these chords, you can use any fingering you know to play them. This may involve re-arranging the order of the notes or doubling some of the notes, but as long as the chord shape you are playing contains only the three note names of that particular chord, you are still playing the right chord.

The example below demonstrates a common progression in the key of C. This progression would be described as I III IV V III VI II V. On the CD it is played using open chords. You could also play this (or any) progression as arpeggios, or using bar chords, or other moveable shapes. Experiment!

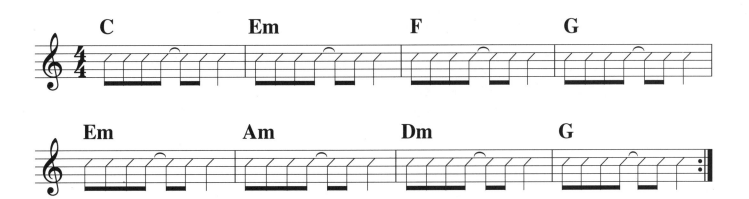

MAJOR KEY TRIAD PATTERN

If you go through all the scale tone chords in the key of C major you come up with the following pattern:

I̱	**Major**	**(C Major)**
I̱I̱	**Minor**	**(D Minor)**
I̱I̱I̱	**Minor**	**(E Minor)**
I̱V̱	**Major**	**(F Major)**
V̱	**Major**	**(G Major)**
V̱I̱	**Minor**	**(A Minor)**
V̱I̱I̱	**Diminished**	**(B Diminished)**

This pattern remains the same regardless of the key. For **any major key**, Chord I̱ is **always** major, chord I̱I̱ is always minor, chord I̱I̱I̱ is always minor, etc. The only thing that changes from one key to the next is the letter names of the chords. This can be demonstrated by looking at the scale tone triads for the key of **G major** which are shown below.

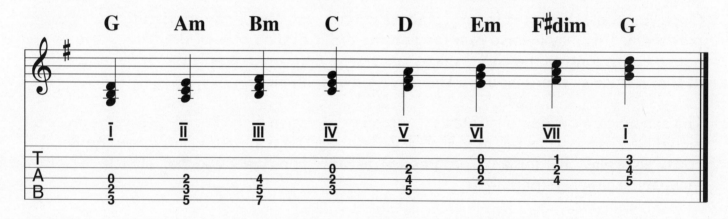

TRANSPOSING CHORD PROGRESSIONS

As mentioned earlier in the book, **transposing** means changing the key of a piece of music. By simply following the roman numerals and remembering which chords are major, minor, etc, it is easy to transpose chords from one key to another. Here is the progression from the previous page transposed to the key of **G**.

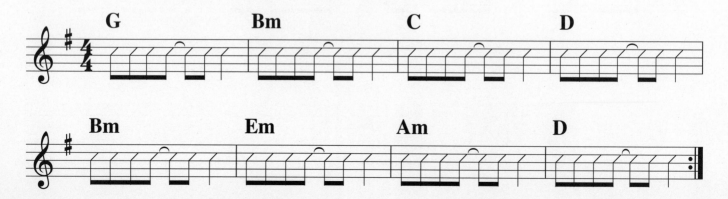

SCALE TONE CHORDS ALONG THE STRINGS

A useful way to practice scale tone chords is to practice them along a particular group of strings, keeping the same inversion for each chord. The following example demonstrates the C major scale tone triads played in root position along the 3rd, 4th and 5th strings.

 36.0

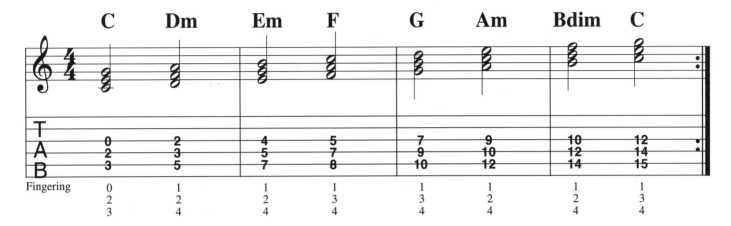

 36.1

Here are the same chords as arpeggios played up an octave on the 1st, 2nd and 3rd strings.

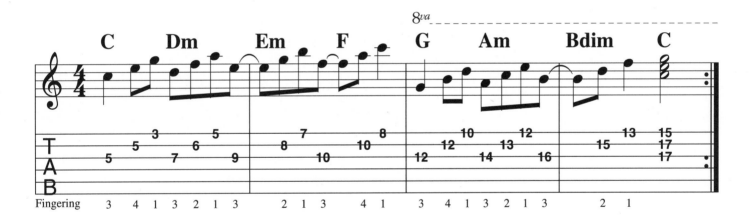

 36.2

This time the chords are in first inversion on the 2nd, 3rd and 4th strings. The inversion you choose largely depends on which note you want at the top of the chord.

PRIMARY CHORDS

In any key there are some chords which are more commonly used than others. The three most common chords are I̱, I̱V̱ and V̱. These are called the **primary chords**. With these three chords, it is possible to harmonize (accompany with chords) any melody in the key, because between them they contain every note of the scale, as shown below in the key of **C**.

C Major Scale C D E F G A B C

Primary Triads

G	C	D
E	A	B
C	F	G
I̱	I̱V̱	V̱

HARMONIZING MELODIES

To harmonize a melody, you simply play a chord which contains a note from that melody on the **first beat of each bar**. In time, you could also add another chord on the **third** beat of the bar. There is always more than one chord which could be used, but some sound better than others. The more songs you learn and analyze, the easier it becomes to find the right chords to play. If you look at the scale and chords above, you will notice that the notes **C** and **G** appear in more than one of the chords. This means that if you were harmonizing a melody in the **key of C**, you could try both chords wherever one of these notes appear on the first beat of a bar. The following example shows a melody in C major harmonized with chords I̱, I̱V̱ and V̱. Learn it and then transpose it to all the other keys.

The table below shows the primary chords in all twelve major keys.

PRIMARY TRIADS IN ALL MAJOR KEYS

KEY	I̱	I̱V̱	V̱	KEY	I̱	I̱V̱	V̱
C	C	F	G	F	F	B♭	C
G	G	C	D	B♭	B♭	E♭	F
D	D	G	A	E♭	E♭	A♭	B♭
A	A	D	E	A♭	A♭	D♭	E♭
E	E	A	B	D♭	D♭	G♭	A♭
B	B	E	F♯	G♭	G♭	C♭	D♭
F♯	F♯	B	C♯				

Although most melodies can be harmonized using only chords $\bar{I}$, $\overline{IV}$ and $\bar{V}$, it is also common to use one or more of the remaining chords ($\overline{II}$, $\overline{III}$, $\overline{VI}$ and $\overline{VII}$) to create a different feeling. These other chords are called **secondary chords**. As with primary chords, the secondary chord chosen for the harmony in any given bar should contain the melody note which occurs on the first or third beat of that bar (wherever the chord changes). Here is the melody from the previous example harmonized with both primary and secondary chords. Once again, learn it and then transpose both the melody and the chords to all the other keys.

COMMON PROGRESSIONS

One of the best ways to become familiar with chords in all keys is to take a simple progression and transpose it to all of the keys. This may be slow at first, but the more you do it, the easier it gets. Here are some common progressions to learn and transpose. Remember to practice them in different ways, e.g. as strummed chords and fingerpicked as arpeggios.

$\bar{I}$ $\overline{IV}$ $\bar{V}$ $\bar{I}$ $\bar{I}$ $\overline{VI}$ $\overline{IV}$ $\bar{V}$ $\overline{II}$ $\bar{V}$ $\bar{I}$ $\bar{I}$ $\overline{VI}$ $\overline{II}$ $\bar{V}$ $\bar{I}$ $\overline{IV}$ $\overline{VII}$ $\overline{III}$ $\overline{VI}$ $\overline{II}$ $\bar{V}$

SCALE TONE TRIADS IN ALL MAJOR KEYS

Scale Note:	$\bar{I}$	$\overline{II}$	$\overline{III}$	$\overline{IV}$	$\bar{V}$	$\overline{VI}$	$\overline{VII}$	$\overline{VIII}$ ($\bar{I}$)
Chord Constructed:	major	minor	minor	major	major	minor	dim	major
C Scale	C	Dm	Em	F	G	Am	B°	C
G Scale	G	Am	Bm	C	D	Em	F#°	G
D Scale	D	Em	F#m	G	A	Bm	C#°	D
A Scale	A	Bm	C#m	D	E	F#m	G#°	A
E Scale	E	F#m	G#m	A	B	C#m	D#°	E
B Scale	B	C#m	D#m	E	F#	G#m	A#°	B
F# Scale	F#	G#m	A#m	B	C#	D#m	E#° (F°)	F#
F Scale	F	Gm	Am	B♭	C	Dm	E°	F
B♭ Scale	B♭	Cm	Dm	E♭	F	Gm	A°	B♭
E♭ Scale	E♭	Fm	Gm	A♭	B♭	Cm	D°	E♭
A♭ Scale	A♭	B♭m	Cm	D♭	E♭	Fm	G°	A♭
D♭ Scale	D♭	E♭m	Fm	G♭	A♭	B♭m	C°	D♭
G♭ Scale	G♭	A♭m(G#m)	B♭m	C♭ (B)	D♭	E♭m	F°	G♭

SCALE TONE 7TH CHORDS

The scale tone chords studied so far involve the placement of two notes (separated by an interval of a third) above a root note. This method of building scale tone chords can be extended by adding another note of a third interval, illustrated in the following table:

	7	B	C	D	E	F	G	A	B	
	5	G	A	B	C	D	E	F	G	} *Third Interval*
	3	E	F	G	A	B	C	D	E	} *Third Interval*
C Scale:	1	C	D	E	F	G	A	B	C	} *Third Interval*
Chord Constructed:		Cmaj7	Dm7	Em7	Fmaj7	G7	Am7	Bm7♭5*	Cmaj7	
Chord Numeral:		Imaj7	IIm7	IIIm7	IVmaj7	V7	VIm7	VIIm7♭5	Imaj7	

 37

Here are the scale tone 7ths in C major played in root position.

| Cmaj⁷ | Dm⁷ | Em⁷ | Fmaj⁷ | G⁷ | Am⁷ | Bm⁷⁽♭⁵⁾ | Cmaj⁷ |

```
       Cmaj7    Dm7     Em7    Fmaj7    G7      Am7    Bm7(b5)  Cmaj7

         I       II      III     IV       V       VI      VII       I
T      0       1       3       5       1       3       5       7
A      0       2       4       5       3       5       6       8
B      2       3       5       5       4       5       7       9
       3       5       7       8       5       7       9      10
```

The following example contains all seven scale tone 7ths in C major. The progression is Ī ĪV V̄II ĪII V̄I ĪI V̄ Ī. The shapes used here are all close together on the fretboard. This makes them easy to play and results in a smoother sound than moving up and down one string to find the root notes of the chords.

 **42.1**

| Cmaj⁷ | Fmaj⁷ | Bm⁷⁽♭⁵⁾ | Em⁷ |

𝄞 $\frac{4}{4}$

| Am⁷ | Dm⁷ | G⁷ | Cmaj⁷ |

SCALE TONE 7TH PATTERN

Like triads, the pattern of scale tone 7th chord types remains the same for every key. The pattern is summarized below, followed by the progression from the previous example transposed to the key of **F**. Use the chart below to transpose it to all the other keys.

I	II	III	IV	V	VI	VII	VIII
major7	m7	m7	maj7	7	m7	m7♭5 or (∅7)	maj7

$$Fmaj^7 \quad B\flat maj^7 \quad Em^{7(\flat 5)} \quad Am^7 \quad Dm^7 \quad Gm^7 \quad C^7 \quad Fmaj^7$$

The following chart shows scale tone 7th chords in all keys. If you intend to play Jazz, or any kind of Fusion music, it is essential to memorize all these chords. Work through each key and then take a simple progression and play it in every key. Then try a longer progression, then a song containing the various 7th chord types. The more you do this, the easier it gets.

Scale Tone Seventh Chords in all Keys

I	II	III	IV	V	VI	VII	VIII
Major7	**Minor7**	**Minor7**	**Major7**	**7**	**Minor7**	**Minor7♭5**	**Major7**
Cmaj7	Dm7	Em7	Fmaj7	G7	Am7	Bm7♭5	Cmaj7
Gmaj7	Am7	Bm7	Cmaj7	D7	Em7	F♯m7♭5	Gmaj7
Dmaj7	Em7	F♯m7	Gmaj7	A7	Bm7	C♯m7♭5	Dmaj7
Amaj7	Bm7	C♯m7	Dmaj7	E7	F♯m7	G♯m7♭5	Amaj7
Emaj7	F♯m7	G♯m7	Amaj7	B7	C♯m7	D♯m7♭5	Emaj7
Bmaj7	C♯m7	D♯m7	Emaj7	F♯7	G♯m7	A♯m7♭5	Bmaj7
F♯maj7	G♯m7	A♯m7	Bmaj7	C♯7	D♯m7	E♯(F)m7♭5	F♯maj7
Fmaj7	Gm7	Am7	B♭maj7	C7	Dm7	Em7♭5	Fmaj7
B♭maj7	Cm7	Dm7	E♭maj7	F7	Gm7	Am7♭5	B♭maj7
E♭maj7	Fm7	Gm7	A♭maj7	B♭7	Cm7	Dm7♭5	E♭maj7
A♭maj7	B♭m7	Cm7	D♭maj7	E♭7	Fm7	Gm7♭5	A♭maj7
D♭maj7	E♭m7	Fm7	G♭maj7	A♭7	B♭m7	Cm7♭5	D♭maj7
G♭maj7	A♭m7	B♭m7	C♭(B) maj7	D♭7	E♭m7	Fm7♭5	G♭maj7

EXTENDED SCALE TONE CHORDS

Higher extensions (9ths, 11ths and 13ths) can added to all the scale tone chords in a key, simply by adding more 3rd intervals above the top note of each chord. Shown below are the scale tone 9th chords for the key of C major.

D	E	F	G	A	B	C
B	C	D	E	F	G	A
G	A	B	C	D	E	F
C	D	E	F	G	A	B
I	II	III	IV	V	VI	VII
CMaj9	Dm9	Em9	FMaj9	G9	Am9	Bm9♭5

 38.0

Upper extensions can be added to all the chords in a progression. Here is a II V I progression in C major using scale tone 9th chords.

Dm^9 G^9 $Cmaj^9$

 38.1

Here is another II V I progression in C major using 11th chords. Notice that the 11th is sharpened in the two chords that contain a major 3rd degree, in order to avoid a clash.

Dm^{11} $G^{7(\sharp11)}$ $Cmaj^{7(\sharp11)}$

 38.2

This time 13ths are used for all the chords. Notice how adding different extensions changes the flavor even though the basic progression is still II V I in the key of C. Experiment with adding upper extensions to other progressions.

Dm^{13} G^{13} $Cmaj^{13}$

VOICE LEADING

When you move between two chords, the change will sound smoother if the chords are close together on the fretboard, particularly if both chords are on the same group of strings. The way each note of a chord moves to the closest note of the next chord is called **voice leading**.

The following example demonstrates a simple progression played two different ways. In the first two bars, the chords are changed by moving a first inversion chord up and down the fretboard. In the third and fourth bars, different inversions are used for each chord in order to find voicings which are closer together. This produces a smoother sound and would generally be considered better voice leading.

 39.0

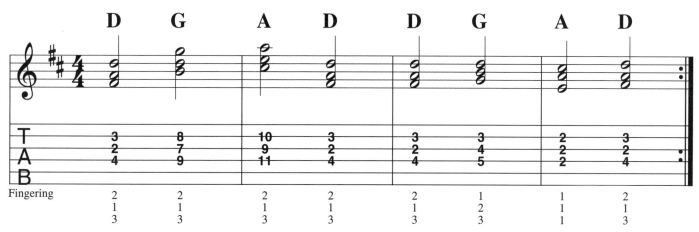

 39.1

Here is another voice leading example using broken chords. Notice how the notes of each chord progress smoothly and logically to the closest note of the next chord.

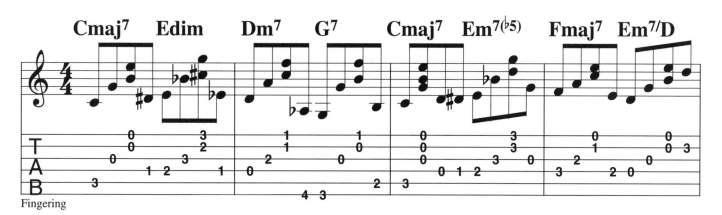

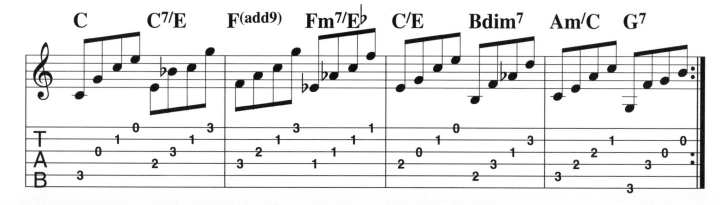

GUIDE TONES

In any chord, there are certain notes which tell you exactly what the chord is. In major and minor triads it is the 3rd (the 5th is the same in both chords) and in seventh chords, it is the 3rd and the 7th. These notes are called **guide tones**. Shown below are various chords built on a **C** root note, with the guide tones indicated. Notice that these are the notes which change from one chord type to another, while the root and the 5th remain the same.

Guide Tones (7ths)			B	B♭	B♭
	G	G	G	G	G
Guide Tones (3rds) →	E	E♭	E	E	E♭
	C	C	C	C	C
	C	**Cm**	**Cmaj7**	**C7**	**Cm7**

Play the following example and listen to the way the **E (natural 3rd)** and **E♭** (flattened 3rd) determine whether the chord is C major or C minor.

 **40.0**

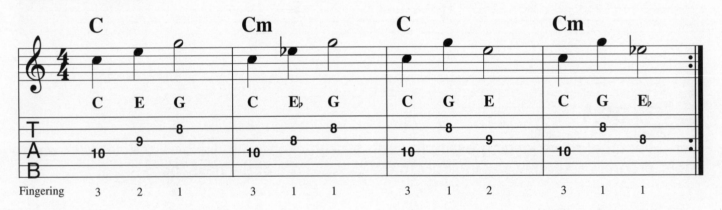

 **40.1**

In this example, both the 3rd and the 7th are necessary to indicate the chord types.

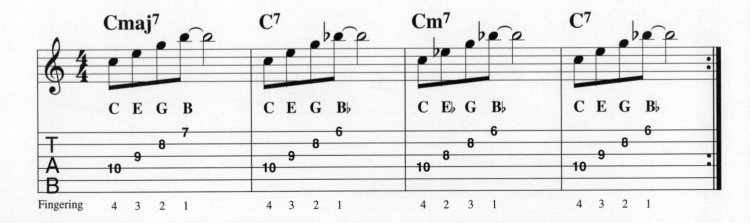

USING GUIDE TONES

Guide tones are extremely useful when writing a song arrangement, as they make for economical writing. E..g. the bass will usually play the root of a chord, so there is no need for a two part horn section to repeat that note. The 5th doesn't indicate major, minor or dominant chord quality, so it can also be left out. By using only the guide tones, you leave space in the music for other instruments, and the music becomes more precise. In general, the bigger the band, the less notes in each musician's part.

The following example is a two part Funk part the guide tones of the chords **C7** (**E** and **B♭**), **F7** (**E♭** and **A**), and **G7** (**F** and **B**). These are chords Ī, ĪV and V̄ in the **key of C** played as dominants – as in a Blues. The part is created by simply playing the guide tones and adding a rhythm which works in the musical context.

 **41.0**

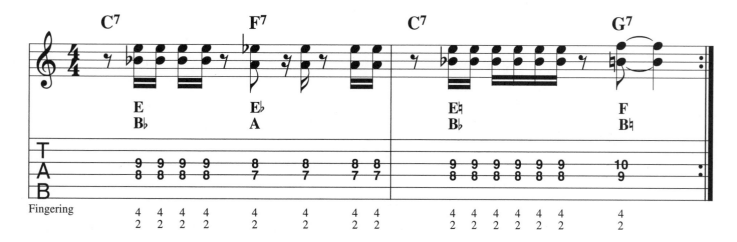

 **41.1**

An effective way of varying a guide tone based part (or a full chord) is to approach it from a semitone below or to deviate from the chord temporarily by a semitone in either direction before returning to the chord tones. This is called **side-slipping**. Here is an example based on the previous part.

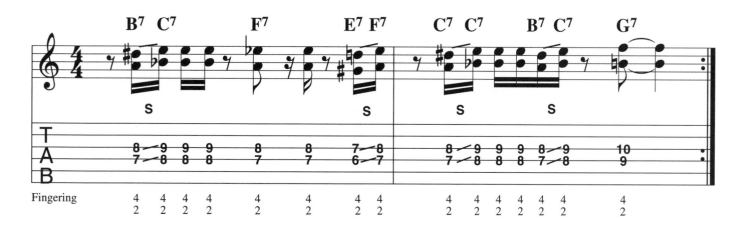

The following example shows two guide tone lines for II̲ V̲ I̲ progressions. Notice how the 3rd of one chord becomes the 7th of the next chord and vice versa. In the first half, the 7th is above the 3rd, while in the second half, they are reversed. The choice of which note is on top is up to the player, depending on the musical context.

 **42.0**

Using guide tones makes it possible to create smooth chord progressions. The 3rd of one chord often progresses to the 7th of the next chord and vice versa as shown below. In the case of a **m7b5** chord and a **dim7** chord, the 5th can also be a guide tone, but in major, minor and dominant 7ths, the 5th can be omitted.

 **42.1**

OTHER GUIDE TONES

Although the 3rd and 7th of a chord are the most common guide tones, there are other notes in various types of chords which can be important in indicating the particular chord type. In triads, this can be the **5th**, which can indicate a diminished or augmented chord when combined with the 3rd of the chord. In **6th chords**, the **6th degree** is a guide tone as demonstrated in the following example.

 **43.0**

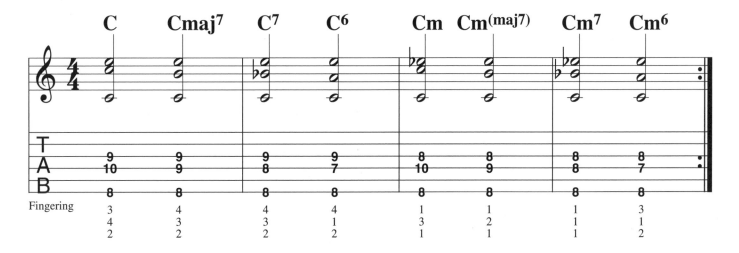

All the upper extensions of a chord (9ths, 11ths and 13ths) can also be used as guide tones. The 13th degree is the same as the 6th. This means that the 7th of the chord is also necessary to distinguish a 13th chord from a 6th chord.

The more notes there are in a chord, the more possible guide tones it contains. In a seventh chord, there are two but anything higher contains three. The fact that there are more guide tones can make it easier to create a smooth line between chord changes. In the following example, the note **G** becomes a different degree in each new chord, as shown between the notation and the TAB. The better you know the degrees of all chord types in all keys, the more creative you can be with chord progressions.

 **43.1**

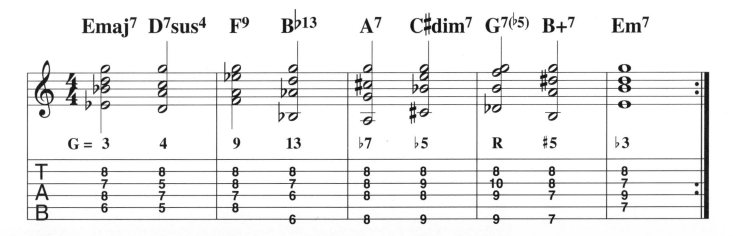

MINOR KEYS AND SCALES

Apart from major keys, the other basic tonality used in western music is a **minor key**. Minor keys are often said to have a sadder or darker sound than major keys. Songs in a minor key use notes taken from a **minor scale**. There are three types of minor scale — the **natural minor scale**, the **harmonic minor scale** and the **melodic minor scale**. Written below is the **A natural minor** scale.

THE NATURAL MINOR SCALE

The A natural minor contains exactly the same notes as the C major scale. The difference is that it starts and finishes on an **A** note instead of a C note. The A note then becomes the key note. To highlight the difference, the degrees of the scale as they would relate to the A major scale are written under the note names. Notice the **flattened 3rd, 6th and 7th**.

THE HARMONIC MINOR SCALE

The harmonic minor is often described as having an "Eastern" sound. It has a distance of 1½ tones (instead of one) between the **6th** and **7th** degrees. The raised 7th degree is the only difference between the harmonic minor and the natural minor scale.

THE MELODIC MINOR SCALE

In Classical music, a **melodic minor** scale has the **6th** and **7th** notes sharpened when ascending and returned to natural when descending. However, in Jazz and other more modern styles, the melodic minor descends the same way it ascends. An easy way to think of the ascending melodic minor is as a major scale with a flattened third degree.

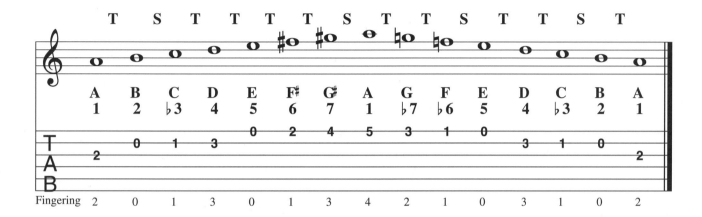

TABLE OF MINOR SCALES

This table shows the notes of the **melodic minor** scale in all twelve keys. Remember that the **descending melodic minor is the same as the natural minor**. To work out the notes for the **harmonic minor**, simply **flatten the 6th** degree of the ascending melodic minor.

	T	S	T	T	T	T	S	T	T	S	T	T	S	T
A MELODIC MINOR*	A	B	C	D	E	F#	G#	A	G♮	F♮	E	D	C	B	A
E MELODIC MINOR*	E	F#	G	A	B	C#	D#	E	D♮	C♮	B	A	G	F#	E
B MELODIC MINOR*	B	C#	D	E	F#	G#	A#	B	A♮	G♮	F#	E	D	C#	B
F# MELODIC MINOR*	F#	G#	A	B	C#	D#	E#	F#	E♮	D♮	C#	B	A	G#	F#
C# MELODIC MINOR*	C#	D#	E	F#	G#	A#	B#	C#	B♮	A♮	G#	F#	E	D#	C#
G# MELODIC MINOR	G#	A#	B	C#	D#	E#	G	G#	F#	E♮	D#	C#	B	A#	G#
D# MELODIC MINOR	D#	E#	F#	G#	A#	B#	D	D#	C#	B♮	A#	G#	F#	E#	D#
D MELODIC MINOR*	D	E	F	G	A	B♮	C#	D	C♮	B♭	A	G	F	E	D
G MELODIC MINOR*	G	A	B♭	C	D	E♮	F#	G	F♮	E♭	D	C	B♭	A	G
C MELODIC MINOR	C	D	E♭	F	G	A♮	B♮	C	B♭	A♭	G	F	E♭	D	C
F MELODIC MINOR	F	G	A♭	B♭	C	D♮	E♮	F	E♭	D♭	C	B♭	A♭	G	F
B♭ MELODIC MINOR	B♭	C	D♭	E♭	F	G♮	A♮	B	A♭	G♭	F	E♭	D♭	C	B♭
E♭ MELODIC MINOR	E♭	F	G♭	A♭	B♭	C♮	D♮	E♭	D♭	C♭	B♭	A♭	G♭	F♭	E♭
ROMAN NUMERALS	Ⅰ	Ⅱ	Ⅲ	Ⅳ	Ⅴ	Ⅵ	Ⅶ	Ⅷ	Ⅶ	Ⅵ	Ⅴ	Ⅳ	Ⅲ	Ⅱ	Ⅰ

MINOR KEY SCALE TONE TRIADS

The example below shows the scale tone triads for the key of **A minor**, the chords derived from the **natural minor** scale. As you will see, the chords are exactly the same as those contained in the key of C major. This is because C major and A minor are **relative keys** (see page 175). The only difference is the starting and finishing point – because the minor scale starts on **A**, A minor will now be chord I̲ instead of V̲I̲.

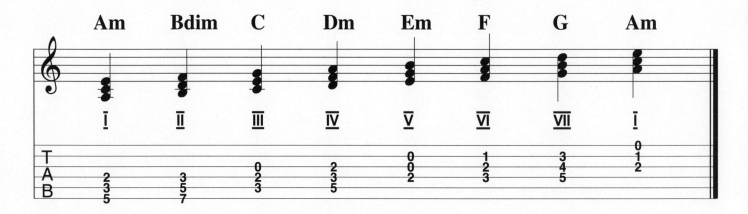

Like major key scale tone chords, it is important to be able to play the chords in minor keys anywhere on the fretboard, particularly inversions along sets of strings. This will prepare you for any musical situation as well as increase your choices for chord substitution. Take one inversion at a time and move it through all the chords in the key along a particular string group.

MINOR KEY CHORD PROGRESSIONS

The following progression could be described in two possible ways. It could be written as V̲I̲ I̲ V̲ V̲I̲ I̲V̲ V̲ V̲I̲ I̲ V̲ I̲V̲ V̲ V̲I̲ in **C major** or I̲ I̲I̲I̲ V̲I̲I̲ I̲ V̲I̲ V̲I̲I̲ I̲ I̲I̲I̲ V̲I̲I̲ V̲I̲ V̲I̲I̲ I̲ in **A minor**. Because the progression has an obvious minor tonality (sound), musicians would use the second description. Experiment with other chord combinations in the key of **A minor**.

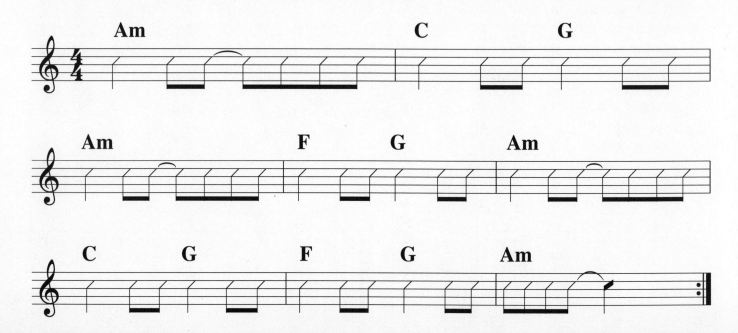

CHORDS IN OTHER MINOR KEYS

Written below are the scale tone chords for the key of **E natural minor** which is the relative minor of G major. Once again, the chords will be the same as those of its relative, but the starting note is E instead of G so **Em** will be chord Ī.

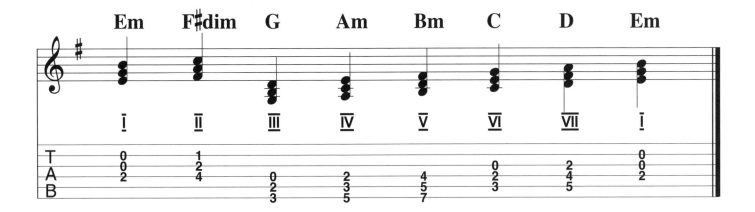

TRANSPOSING IN MINOR KEYS

Like music written in major keys, anything in a minor key can be transposed to other keys. The following example shows the progression from the previous page transposed to the key of **E minor**. Once you have learned the progression in this key, write out the scale tone chords in the remaining eleven minor keys and transpose the progression to those keys as well.

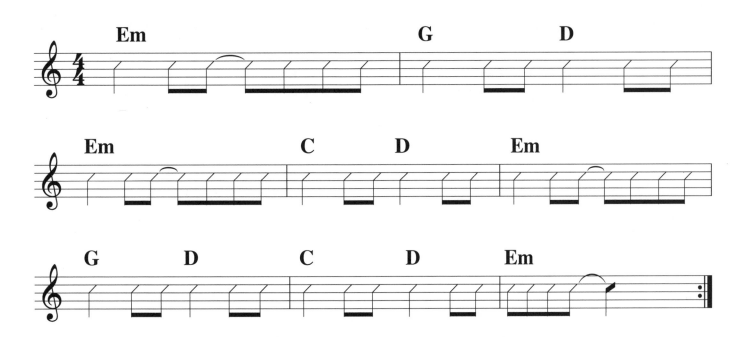

HARMONIC MINOR SCALE TONE CHORDS

Because there are three different minor scales, it is possible to come up with different sets of chords for a minor key by building chords on the notes of each different minor scale. Each variation to the notes of the scale alters the type of chords built on the scale. The letter names of the chords remain the same, but the chord type may change. E.g. shown below are scale tone chords derived from the **A harmonic minor scale**. Notice that chord **III** is now **augmented** instead of major, and also that chord **V** is **major** instead of minor and chord **VII** is **diminished** instead of major. These changes are all brought about by the raising of the 7th degree of the scale from **G** to **G♯**.

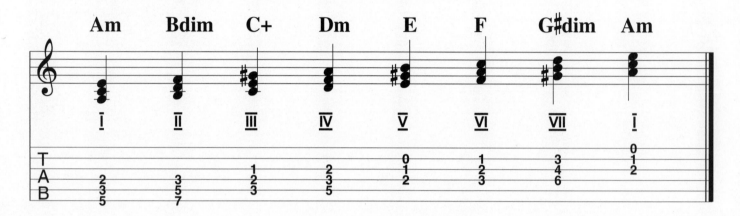

 **44.**

This arpeggio based part uses chords derived from the **A harmonic minor** scale. Experiment with other ways of playing these chords and make up other progressions from them.

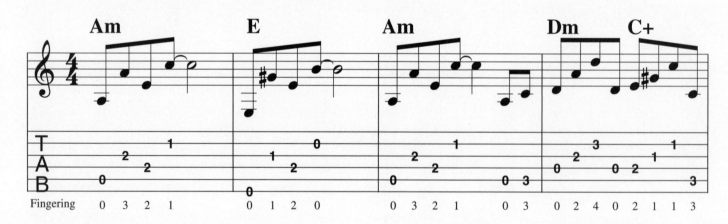

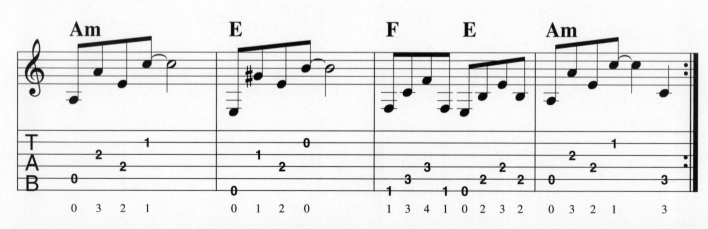

MELODIC MINOR SCALE TONE CHORDS

The scale tone chords derived from the **A melodic minor scale** are shown below. Because of the sharpened 6th degree, there will be more changes to the types of chords derived from this scale. Chord Ⅱ is now **minor** instead of major, chord Ⅳ is **major** instead of minor and chord Ⅵ is **diminished** instead of major. These changes are all brought about by the raising of the 6th degree of the scale from **F** to **F♯**.

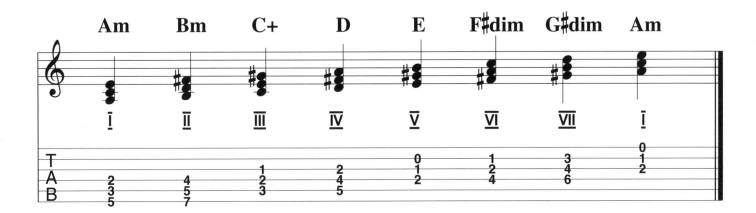

 **45.**

The following example is derived from the **A melodic minor** scale tone chords shown above. It also contains one chromatic note (**A♯** or **B♭**) as part of a repeating bass run.

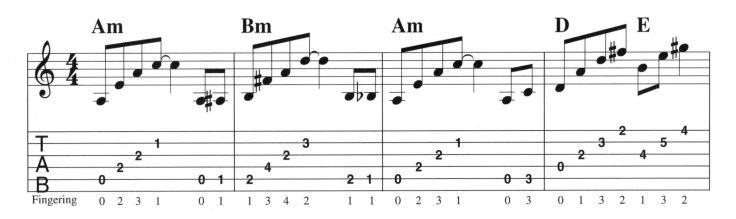

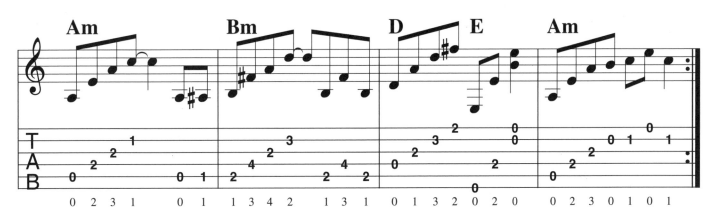

SCALE TONE 7THS IN MINOR KEYS

Shown below is an A natural minor scale harmonized as 7th chords. Remember that the chords will be exactly the same as those contained in the key of C major (the relative major key). The only difference is the starting and finishing point. Because the minor scale starts on A, **Am7** will now be chord Ī instead of V̄Ī.

	Ī	ĪĪ	ĪĪĪ	ĪV̄	V̄	V̄Ī	V̄ĪĪ
Natural Minor	G E C A	A F D B	B G E C	C A F D	D B G E	E C A F	F D B G
	Am7	Bm7♭5	Cmaj7	Dm7	Em7	Fmaj7	G7

If you harmonize the harmonic or melodic minor scale, the chords will **not** be identical to those of the relative major. Shown below is the A harmonic minor harmonized as 7th chords. The raised 7th degree results in different chord types for chords Ī (a minor chord with a major 7th: **m/maj7**), ĪĪĪ, (a major 7th chord with a raised 5th: **maj7♯5**), V̄ (a dominant 7th chord) and V̄ĪĪ (a diminished 7th chord).

	Ī	ĪĪ	ĪĪĪ	ĪV̄	V̄	V̄Ī	V̄ĪĪ
Harmonic Minor	G♯ E C A	A F D B	B G♯ E C	C A F D	D B G♯ E	E C A F	F D B G♯
	Am/maj7	Bm7♭5	Cmaj7♯5	Dm7	E7	Fmaj7	G♯°7

By harmonizing the ascending melodic minor scale, even more of the chords are altered. As you can see from the table below, none of the chords here are the same as those derived from the natural minor. The fact that there are three different minor scales gives you many chord options for harmonizing a melody in a minor key. This is discussed on the following page.

	Ī	ĪĪ	ĪĪĪ	ĪV̄	V̄	V̄Ī	V̄ĪĪ
Melodic Minor	G♯ E C A	A F♯ D B	B G♯ E C	C A F♯ D	D B G♯ E	E C A F♯	F♯ D B G♯
	Am/maj7	Bm7	Cmaj7♯5	D7	E7	F♯m7♭5	G♯m7♭5

As mentioned earlier, it is common to find chords derived from all three minor scales in the one progression. Here is an example using minor key scale tone 7ths.

Am⁷	Bm⁷	Cmaj⁷	Bm⁷	Am⁽maj7⁾	G♯m⁷⁽♭5⁾/B

Fmaj⁷	E⁷	Cmaj⁷	G♯m⁷⁽♭5⁾	Cmaj⁷⁽⁺5⁾	Fmaj⁷

Bm⁷⁽♭5⁾	E⁷	Am	Am⁽maj7⁾	Am⁷	E⁷

HIGHER EXTENSIONS IN MINOR KEYS

Like major scale tone chords, it is possible to add 9ths, 11ths and 13ths to chords built on the notes of minor scales. Shown below are scale tone 9th chords built on an A harmonic minor scale. Notice that some of the chords are no longer straight minor, dominant or major 9ths, but have more complex names because of the alterations caused by the raised 7th degree of the harmonic minor scale (in this case, a **G♯** note). These chords may seem confusing at first and may take a while to learn, but in the long run it is well worth it, as knowledge of these chords will help you improvise better and more easily in minor keys.

	I	II	III	IV	V	VI	VII
	B	C	D	E	F	G♯	A
	G♯	A	B	C	D	E	F
	E	F	G♯	A	B	C	D
Harmonic Minor	C	D	E	F	G♯	A	B
	A	B	C	D	E	F	G♯
	$\underline{\text{I}}$	$\underline{\text{II}}$	$\underline{\text{III}}$	$\underline{\text{IV}}$	$\underline{\text{V}}$	$\underline{\text{VI}}$	$\underline{\text{VII}}$
	Am9/maj7	Bm7♭5♭9	Cmaj9♯5	Dm9	E7♭9	Fmaj7♯9	G♯m6/9♭5

When harmonizing melodies in minor keys, some of the higher extensions are more commonly used than others. The most common are the use of the ♭9 **and/or** ♯9 in chord $\underline{\text{V}}$ and the upper extensions of chord $\underline{\text{I}}$ as demonstrated in the following example.

Bm⁷⁽♭5⁾	E⁷⁽♯9⁾	E⁷⁽♭9⁾	Am⁷	Am⁶	Am¹¹	Am⁹⁽maj7⁾

RELATIVE KEYS

if you compare the **A natural minor** scale with the **C major** scale you will notice that they contain the same notes; the only difference is that they start on a different note. Because of this, these two scales are referred to as "relatives"; **A minor** is the **relative minor** of **C major** and vice versa.

Major Scale: C Major

Relative Minor Scale: A Natural Minor

The harmonic and melodic minor scale variations are also relatives of the same major scale, e.g. the **A harmonic** and **A melodic minor** scales are all relatives of **C major**.
For every major scale (and ever major chord) there is a relative minor scale which is based upon the **6th note** of the major scale. This is outlined in the table below.

MAJOR KEY (I)	C	D♭	D	E♭	E	F	F♯	G♭	G	A♭	A	B♭	B
RELATIVE MINOR KEY (VI)	Am	B♭m	Bm	Cm	C♯m	Dm	D♯m	E♭m	Em	Fm	F♯m	Gm	G♯m

Both the major and the relative minor share the same key signature, as illustrated below.

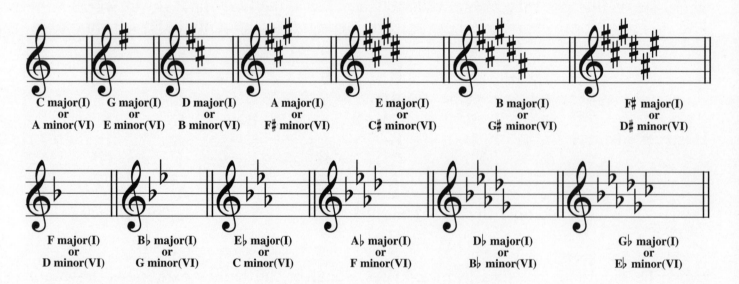

To determine whether a song is in a major key or the relative minor key, look at the last note or chord of the song. Songs often finish on the root note or the root chord which indicates the key. E.g., if the key signature contained one sharp, and the last chord of the song was **Em**, the key would probably be **E minor**, not **G major**. Minor key signatures are always based on the natural minor scale. The sharpened 6th and 7th degrees from the harmonic and melodic minor scales are not indicated in the key signature. This usually means there are accidentals (temporary sharps, flats or naturals) in melodies created from these scales.

SLASH CHORDS

Sometimes a composer or songwriter wants a specific bass note played under a chord. This is indicated by the use of **slash chords**. The chord name is written first, followed by a backward slash (**/**) which is followed by the desired bass note. E.g. the symbol **G/B** **indicates a** G **chord over a** B bass note. This is a first inversion **G** chord, but if the chord symbol just said **G**, you would probably play a root position chord instead. In the following example, the slash chords (**G/B** and **C/E**) are used as a way of creating a smooth bass line, rather than jumping between the root notes of all the chords.

 **47.**

This piece alternates between the relative keys of **C major** and **A minor**. The arpeggio style of playing used here is particularly effective when playing a Rock ballad.

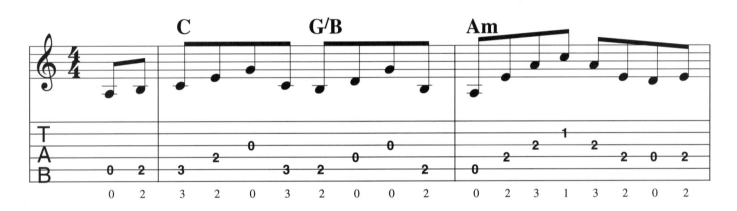

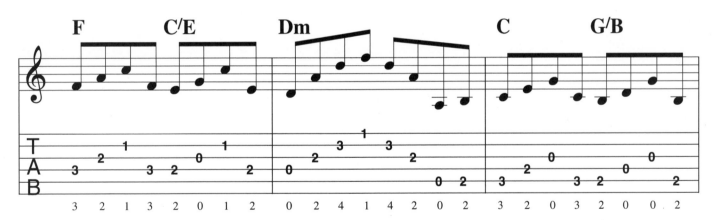

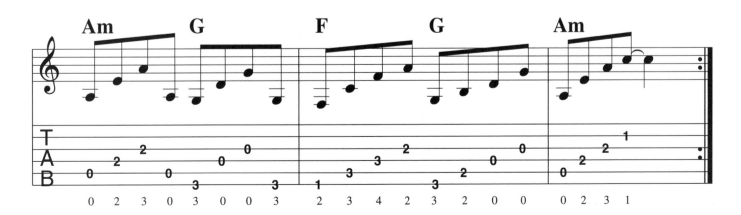

176

Slash chords can be used to create many different harmonic effects. Each combination has a specific name and often creates an entirely new chord. Basically you can play **any** chord over any bass note as long as it sounds good. Experiment with playing all the chords you have learnt over various bass notes from the scale of the key you are playing in.

The following example demonstrates a series of major triads played over an **A** bass note, indicated by the use of slash chord symbols. The triads move through all the notes of the **A natural minor** scale.

 **48.0**

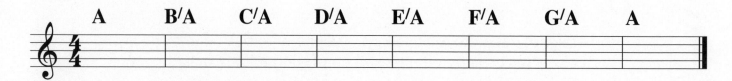

PEDAL TONES

When the same bass note is used under several consecutive chords, it is called a **pedal tone**. This is demonstrated in the following guitar part which uses chords from the previous example. Experiment with pedal tones under other types of chords, and then under a whole chord progression.

 **48.1**

 **49.**

Sometimes the reverse process is used i.e. moving chords under a single melody note as demonstrated in this example.

MOVING BASS LINES UNDER A CHORD

In some musical situations, it sounds good to sustain one chord while the bass plays a line underneath it, as demonstrated in the following example. The chord symbols change every two beats, but the guitar part on the recording is simply a **C triad**. The changing symbols indicate the moving bass part which descends through the C major scale under this triad. Try this process on the guitar and listen to each new bass note changes the effect of the chord.

 50.0 C Triad over Descending C Major Scale

| C | C/B | C/A | C/G | C/F | C/E | C/D | F/G |

This technique can be used with any type of chord in both major and minor keys. In the following example, a **Cm** triad is played over a bass line which descends through the key of **C minor**. Both the natural and flattened 7th degrees are used in the bass line.

 50.1 Cm Triad over descending C min Hybrid Scale

| Cm | Cm/B | Cm/B♭ | Cm/A | Cm/A♭ | Cm/G | Cm/F | Cm/E♭ | Cm/D |

CHORDS WITH MORE THAN ONE NAME

On page 151 you learnt a chord shape using 4th intervals which has more than one name. This is true of many chords. The name of a chord often depends on the context in which it is used. E.g. the notes **E**, **G** and **B** make up an **E minor triad**. If you see an **Em** chord symbol, you can simply play any fingering of an E minor chord. However, if the bass plays a **C note** under this chord, the effect of a **Cmaj7** chord is created. E, G and B are then functioning as the 3rd, 5th and 7th of the chords. This means you could play an E minor triad anywhere you see a **Cmaj7** chord symbol. This is an example of **scale tone substitution**, which is explained on page 192.

E minor Triad ⟶ B
G
E

C Bass Note ⟶ C

=

B
G
E
C
⟵ C Major 7 Chord

178

Most slash chords also add up to another chord type. Sometimes it makes more sense to describe the chord as a slash chord, (e.g. when a pedal tone is being used) and other times it makes more sense to describe the chord as what the notes add up to. Here is an example featuring the slash chord **D/C**. Its notes are **D**, **F#** and **A** over a **C** bass note.

 51.0 Slash Chord Context

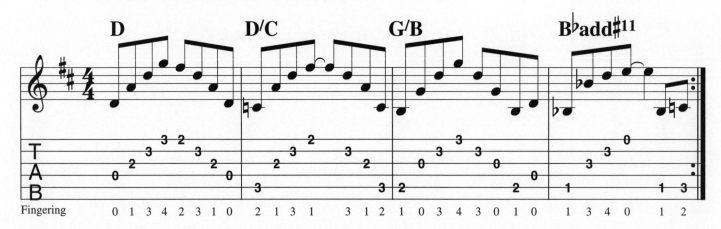

If you analyze the chord **D/C**, you will find that the notes add up to a **D7** chord - **C** is the flattened 7th degree. This means the same chord could also be described as a **3rd inversion D7** chord. Here is an example using the chord in this way.

 51.1 D7 Context

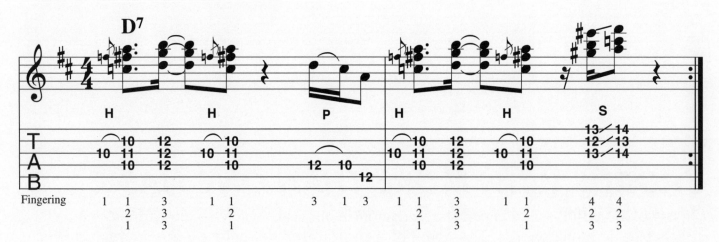

Another possible use for the same group of notes is as a **C13#11** chord. The **C note** is the root of the chord, the **D** note functions as the **9th** degree of the chord, the **F#** is the **#11** and the **A** is the **13th**. Try the following progression using the same chord voicing as the **D7** from the previous example. Notice how the context completely alters the effect of the chord.

 51.2 C13#11 Context

Db13   C7(#11)   Gb13   Eb7(#9)   Eb7(b9)   Db13   C7(#11)   Gb6/9

MODES

The term "**mode**" is another name for a scale. There are **seven** different modes which can be derived from the major scale by starting on each of the seven notes of the major scale. These modes were first used in ancient Greece and have been widely used throughout history in all types of music. Each of these modes can be played in **any key**. Just as there are twelve major keys, there are also twelve possible starting notes for each of the modes. Any note of the chromatic scale can be used as a starting note for any mode. This requires a knowledge of the formula for each mode. The names of the seven modes derived from the major scale are listed below along with their scale degrees.

MODE   FORMULA

Ionian = 1 2 3 4 5 6 7

Dorian = 1 2 ♭3 4 5 6 ♭7

Phrygian = 1 ♭2 ♭3 4 5 ♭6 ♭7

Lydian = 1 2 3 ♯4 5 6 7

Mixolydian = 1 2 3 4 5 6 ♭7

Aeolian = 1 2 ♭3 4 5 ♭6 ♭7

Locrian = 1 ♭2 ♭3 4 ♭5 ♭6 ♭7

Some of these modes are particularly useful for creating chord progressions which don't sound like a typical major or minor key. The Ionian mode is the major scale, so you already know what its possibilities are. The aeolian mode is the natural minor scale, which has also been dealt with earlier in the book. After these, the most commonly used modes are the mixolydian and the dorian, followed by the phrygian, lydian and lastly the locrian. The example below demonstrates a typical Mixolydian Rock riff. The three chords used here - G, D and A also occur in the key of D Major, but as you can hear, the tonality is clearly based around **A** rather than D. To learn more about modes in general, see *Progressive Scales and Modes for Guitar*, or *Progressive Complete Learn to Play Jazz Guitar Manual*.

52.

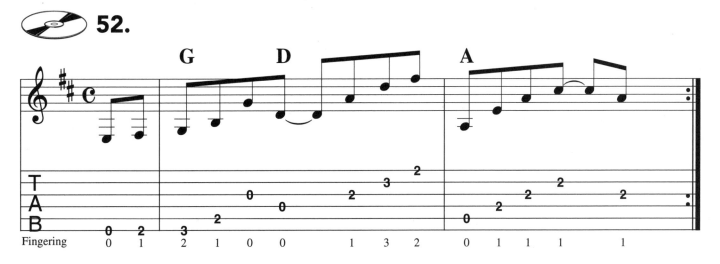

HARMONIZING MODES

All the various modes can be harmonized the same way as major and minor scales. The following example demonstrates the scale tone triads of **D Dorian** played over a **D bass.**

 53.0 D Dorian scale tone triads

| Dm | Em/D | F/D | G/D | Am/D | Bdim/D | C/D | Dm |

 53.1 E Phrygian scale tone triads

By starting with an **E minor** chord and playing over an **E** bass note, an **E Phrygian** tonality is created.

| Em | F/E | G/E | Am/E | Bdim/E | C/E | Dm/E | Em |

MODES IN MINOR KEYS

The same process can be used with minor scales. The following example demonstrates the scale tone chords of **A Harmonic minor** played over an **A bass note.**

 54.0 A harmonic minor

| Am | Bdim/A | C+/A | Dm/A | E/A | F/A | G♯dim/A | Am |

By starting on the other degrees of minor scales, other types of modes can be created. The following example demonstrates the scale tone chords of A harmonic minor starting on **E** which is the 5th degree. The chords are played over an **E** bass note, thus creating an **E Phrygian dominant** tonality. To learn more about this, see *Progressive Complete Learn to Play Jazz Guitar Manual.*

 54.1 5th mode of A harmonic minor

| E | F/E | G♯dim/E | Am/E | Bdim/E | C+/E | Dm/E | E |

Section 5
Chord Progressions

12 BAR BLUES

12 Bar Blues is a pattern of chords which repeats every 12 bars. There are hundreds of songs based on this chord progression, i.e. they contain basically the same chords in the same order. 12 bar blues is commonly used in many styles of music

Some well known songs which use this 12 bar chord pattern are:

Be-bop-a-lula – Gene Vincent/John Lennon
Hound Dog – Elvis Presley
Johnny B. Goode – Chuck Berry
Boppin' the Blues – Blackfeather
The Wanderer – Dion
Going up the Country – Canned Heat
Makin' Your Mind Up – Bucks Fizz
Green Door – Shakin' Stevens
In the Summertime – Mungo Jerry
Rock Around the Clock – Bill Haley & The Commets
Barbara Ann – The Beach Boys
Let's Stick Together – Bryan Ferry
Long Tall Glasses (I Know I Can Dance) – Leo Sayer
Blue Suede Shoes – Elvis Presley
The Thrill is Gone – BB King
School Days (Ring Ring Goes the Bell) – Chuck Berry
Roll Over Beethoven – Chuck Berry
Spirit in the Sky – Norman Greenbaum
Turn Up Your Radio – The Masters Apprentices
Tutti Frutti – Little Richard
Dizzy Miss Lizzy – larry Williams/The Beatles
Peggy Sue – Buddy Holly
Jailhouse Rock – Elvis Presley
Get Down and Get With It – Slade
Good Golly Miss Molly – Little Richard

Lucille – Little Richard
In the Mood – Glen Miller
Surfin' Safari – The Beach Boys
Peppermint Twist – Sweet
Boogie Woogie Bugle Boy – The Andrew Sisters/Bett Midler
I Hear You Knocking – Dave Edmunds
Boy From New York City – Darts/Manhattan Transfer
Mountain of Love – Johnny Rivers
I Love to Boogie – T-Rex
Shake Rattle & Roll – Bill Hayley
Lady Rose – Mungo Jerry
Theme to Batman
Theme to Spiderman
Stuck in the Middle with you – Stealers Wheel
Hot Love – T-Rex
The Huckle Buck – Brendan Bower
Way Down – Elvis Presley
I Can Help – Billy Swan
Rockin' Robin – Michael Jackson
Red House – Jimi Hendrix
Texas Flood – Stevie Ray Vaughan
Killing Floor – Jimi Hendrix
The Jack – ACDC
Ice Cream Man - Van Halen
Oh Pretty Woman – Gary Moore

182

In a basic 12 bar Blues, there are usually three different chords. Each of these relates to one basic **Key.** In Blues, the most common chords are those built on notes **1**, **4** and **5** of the major scale. So in the key of C, these chords would be **C**, **F** and **G**. In the Key of E they would be **E**, **A** and **B**. The example below demonstrates the 12 bar Blues progression in the key of E. In the most basic version, chords I̱ and I̱V̱ are major, while chord V̱ can be major or a dominant 7th.

 55.   12 Bar Blues in E

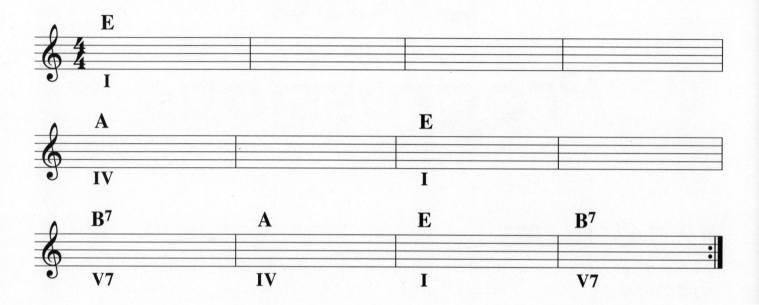

There are many variations on the 12 bar Blues form. Most traditional Blues songs have a **dominant** tonality: i.e. they are played using dominant 7ths, or variations such as 9ths and 13ths. Depending on the style there may be only three different chords, or there may be many other changes throughout the 12 bars. The following progression is a typical example of how a Jazz player might play a Blues in C.

 **56.   Jazz Blues in C**

Blues can also be played in minor keys. Two great examples of this are **"The Thrill is Gone"** by **BB King** and **"Stolen Moments"** by **Oliver Nelson**. The following example demonstrates one version of a Blues in **C minor**.

 57.   Blues in C minor

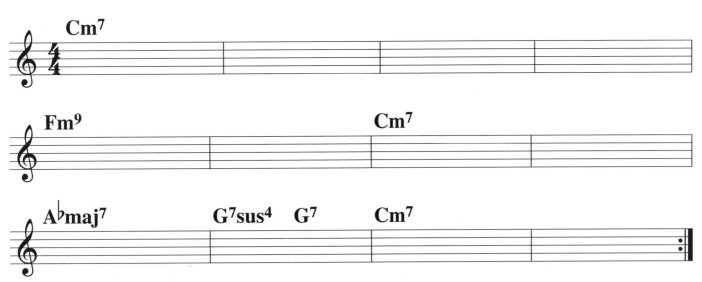

There are also many progressions which have a "bluesy" tonality but do not use the 12 bar form. Here is an example in the key of **A minor**.

 **58.**

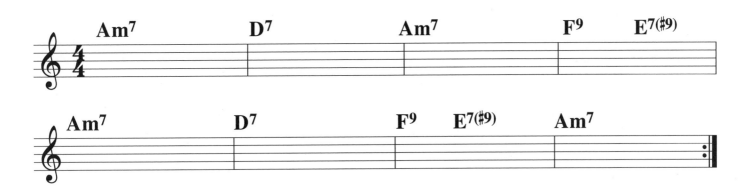

A common variation on the Blues form is an **Eight bar Blues**. Like the 12 bar form, there are many variations. Here is a simple example of an eight bar Blues in the key of **E**.

 59.   Eight Bar Blues

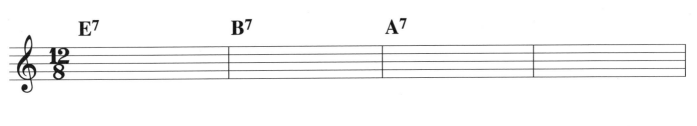

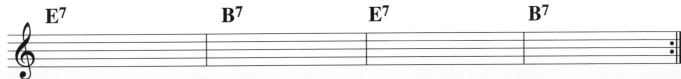

184

Here is more sophisticated version of an eight bar Blues which contains single note runs as well as chords. To learn more about this style of playing, see *Progressive Complete Learn to Play Blues Guitar Manual.*

For More Blues books and recordings by Peter Gelling, visit: **www.bentnotes.com**

60.

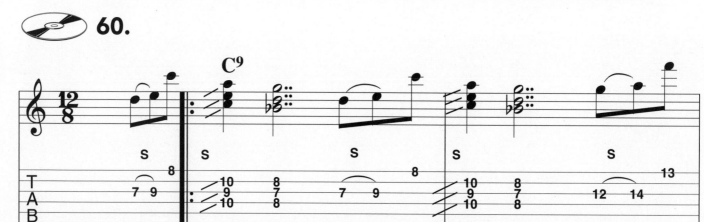

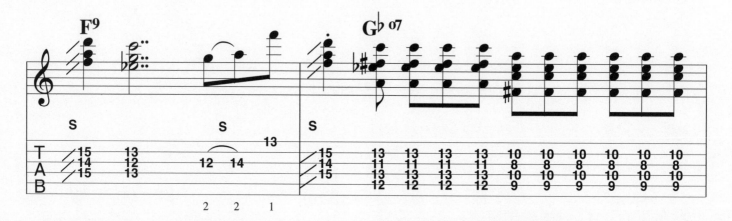

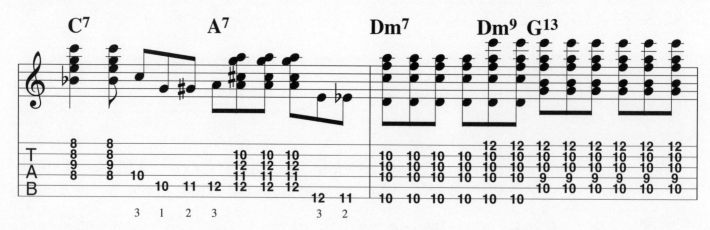

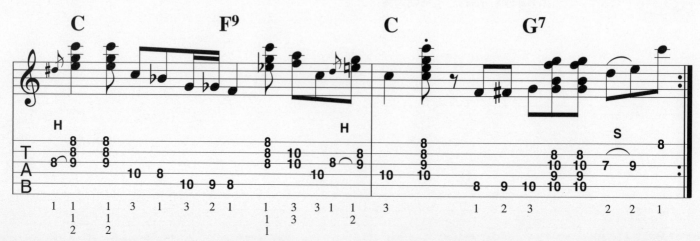

TURNAROUND PROGRESSIONS

The **turnaround** is another very common chord progression, occurring in many Rock, Pop (Top 40) Jazz and Folk songs. There are two variations of the basic turnaround; namely, **Turnaround One**, which is based upon the **I-VIm-IV-V7** chords, and **Turnaround Two**, based upon the **I-IIIm-IV-V7** chords.

There are two basic forms of turnaround, however there are many variations of both.

Turnaround No. 1— I   VIm   IV   V7

E.g. in the **key of C**.

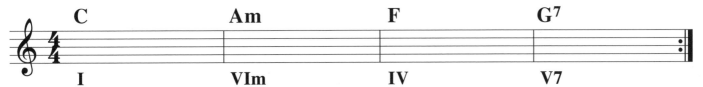

E.g. in the **key of G**.

The VIm chord is the relative minor to the **I** chord. Practice playing Turnaround No. 1 in the above keys and the other keys with which you are familiar.

Turnaround Variations

Unlike the 12 bar Blues, where the progression occurs over a fixed number of bars, the turnaround progression may vary in length.

E.g. 1, two chords in each bar.

E.g. 2, one chord lasting two bars.

It is the **chord sequence**, not the length of bars, that makes a progression a turnaround. Here are some songs which are based, entirely or in part, upon turnaround one.

Turnaround One

I Will Always Love You – Whitney Houston
The Night Has a 1000 Eyes – Bobby Vee
It's Raining Again – Supertramp
More – Various Artists
Ti Amo – Umberto Tozzi
Crocodile Rock (chorus) – Elton John
One Last Kiss – Various Artists
Stand By Me – John Lennon
Dream – Everly Brothers
Return to Sender – Elvis Presley
Telstar – Tornadoes
Always Look on the Bright Side of Life – Monty Python
Why do Fools Fall in Love – Frankie Lyman/Diana Ross
Sarah – Fleetwood Mac
Take Good Care of my Baby – Bobby Vee/Smokey
Where have all the Flowers Gone – Various Artists
Turnaround Sue – Dion & the Belmonts
Tell Me Why – The Beatles
Let's Twist Again – Chubby Checker
Stay (Just a Little Bit Longer) – The Four Seasons/
    Jackson Browne
Cool for Cats – U.K. Squeeze
Y.M.C.A – The Village People
Tired of Toein' the Line – Rock Burnett
You Drive Me Crazy – Shakin' Stevens
Should I do it – Pointer Sisters
Poor Little Fool – Rick Nelson
You Don't Have to Say You Love Me – Dusty Springfield/Elvis Presley
Oh Carol – Neil Sedaka

Two Faces Have I – Lou Christie
Every Day – Buddy Holly
Poetry in Motion – Johnny Tillotson
Sweet Little 16 – Neil Sedaka
Big Girls Don't Cry – Four Seasons
Sherry – Four Seasons
How Do You Do It – Jerry & The Pacemakers
Shour, Shout – Rocky Sharp & The Replays
Aces With You – Moon martin
Houses of the Holy – Led Zeppelin
Uptown Girl – Billy Joel
Buils Me Up Buttercup – The Foundations
'Happy Days' – Theme
Joane – Michael Nesmith
Goodnight Sweetheart – Various Artists
Looking For An Echo – Ol'55
Summer Holiday – Cliff Richard
Be My Baby – The Ronettes/Rachel Sweet
Everlasting Love – Rachel Sweet/Love Affair
I Go To Pieces (verse) – Peter & Gordon
Love Hurts – Everly Brothers/Jim Capaldi/Nazareth
Gee Baby – Peter Shelley
Classic – Adrian Gurvitz
Teenage Dream – T-Rex
Blue Moon – Various Artists
Bizarre Love Triangle – New Order
Dennis – Blondie
It Ain't Easy – Normie Rowe
Breaking up is Hard to do – Neil Sedaka/
    Partridge Family

My World – Bee Gees
Hey Paula – Various Artists
It's Only Make Believe – Glen Campbell
Can't Smile Without You – Barry Manilow
Take Good Care of My Baby – Bobby Vee/Smokie
Crossfire – Bellamy Brothers
Bobby's Girl – Marcie Blane
Do That To Me One More Time – Captain & Tenile
Please Mr Postman – Carpenters/ The Beatles
Sharin' The Night Together – Dr Hook
9 to 5 (Morning Train) – Sheena Easton
Diana – Paul Anka
Telstar – Tornadoes
Enola Gay – Orchestral Manoeuvres in the Dark
Some Guys Have All the Luck – Robert Palmer
So Lonely – Get Wet
Hungry Heart – Bruce Springsteen
Land of Make Believe (chorus) – Buck Fizz
Daddys Home – Cliff Richard
The Wonder of You – Elvis Presley
So You Win Again – Hot Chocolate
Hang Five – Rolling Stones
Paper Tiger – Sue Thompson
Venus – Frankie Avalon
Costafine Town – Splinter
If You Leave – OMD
True Blue – Madonna

Turnaround No. 2 — I IIIm IV V7

E.g. in the **key of C**.

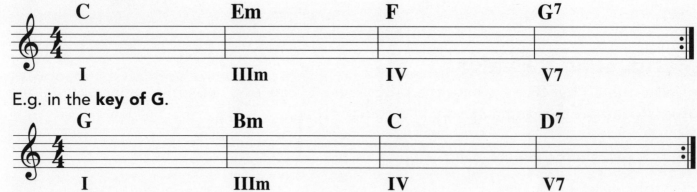

Practice playing Turnaround No. 2 in the above keys and the other keys with which you are familiar.

Examples of some songs which use Turnaround No. 2 are:
Turnaround Two

Crocodile Rock (verse) – Elton John
I started a Joke – The Bee Gees
Different Drum – Linda Ronstadt
Key Largo – Bertie Giggins
Black Berry Way – The Move
Georgy Girl – Seekers
Where Do You Go To My Lovely – Peter Sarsted
Mrs Brown, You've Got a Lovely Daughter –
    Hermans Hermit
Toast and Marmalade for Tea – Tin Tin
Movie Star – Harpo

It's A Heartache – Bonnie Tyler
I Don't Like Mondays – The Boomtown Rats
My Angel Baby – Toby Beau
Land Of Make Believe (verse) – Bucks Fizz
I'm In the Mood for Dancing – The Nolans
What's in a Kiss – Gilbert O'Sullivan
My Baby Loves Love – Joe Jeffries
Dreamin' – Johnny Burnett
Cruel To Be Kind – Nick Lowe
Where Did Our Love Go – Diana Ross &
    The Supremes

Hurdy Gurdy Man – Donovan
I Go To Pieces (chorus) – Peter & Gordon
Get It Over With – Angie Gold
Sad Sweet Dreamer – Sweet Sensation
Down Town – Petula Clark
Easy – Oakridge Boys
Only You Can Do It – Francoiose hardy
Costafine – Splinter (chorus)
Where Did Our Love Go? – Phil Collins

CHORD SUBSTITUTION

Chord substitution involves playing a different set of chords for a given chord progression. This is useful for both beginners and advanced player. Beginners will be able to substitute easier chords for a given chord line (e.g. working from sheet music); and advanced players will be able to embellish a chord progression, often creating a 'jazz' flavour.

The table below summarises common substitutions for beginners. These substitutions can be used because the chords contain similar notes and hence have a similar sound.

Given Chord	Use	Given Chord	Use	Given Chord	Use
6		m6		7$\sharp$5	
6/9		m7		75	
add9		m6/9		7$\sharp$9	
maj7		m9		7$\flat$9	
maj9	**MAJOR**	m11	**MINOR**	9	
maj11		m13		11	
maj13		m(maj7)		13	
maj7$\sharp$11		m7$\flat$5		7$\sharp$5$\sharp$9	**7TH**
sus		m9$\flat$5		7$\sharp$5$\flat$9	
				7$\flat$5$\sharp$9	
				7$\flat$5$\flat$9	
				7$\sharp$11	
				9$\sharp$5	
				9$\flat$5	

Here is an example of simplifying a chord progression, by using the substitutions outlined in the previous table.

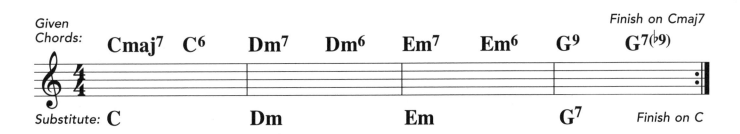

More advanced players can use a **reverse** of the above table. E.g. for **Am**, play **Am7**, **Am6** or perhaps use a combination of the two. This type of substitution is called **direct substitution**, and here are two examples.

Turnaround in A

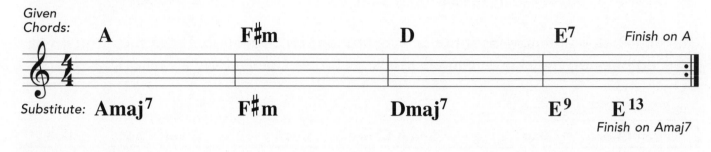

Blues in B♭

LEARNING CHORD SUBSTITUTION

You could go even further with the progressions shown above, and use 11ths, 13ths or altered chords. You could also add in extra chords, e.g. in the final bar you could play **F9** for the first two beats and then play **F13** for the final two beats. Most Jazz and Fusion players get a basic chart and substitute higher extensions to create a Jazz sound. Substitution is usually done on the basis that the chord to be substituted has **at least one** (but usually two or more) **note in common with the original chord**.

To substitute chords successfully, you really need to know your chords well. It is recommended that you purchase a Jazz theory book and study it until you are confident playing any chord, mode or scale in any key without having to think first. It is also a good idea to study chord substitution with a Jazz teacher who will be able to show you some transcriptions of guitar parts by great players which use chord substitution. This aspect of playing can take a long time to become comfortable with, so be patient with it.

TURNAROUND CHORD SUBSTITUTION

Relative Minor

It is common to substitute the relative minor chord for the **IV** chord. This is a **IIm** chord. E.g. in the **key of C** the **IV** chord is **F**. The relative minor of **F** is **Dm**, which is the **IIm** chord (in the **key of C**).

E.g. Turnaround No. 1 becomes –	I	VIm	IIm	V7
E.g. in the **key of C** –	C	Am	Dm	G7

E.g. Turnaround No. 2 becomes –	I	IIIm	IIm	V7
E.g. in the **key of C** –	C	Em	Dm	G7

Practice playing turnarounds No. 1 and No. 2 in various keys, using the above substitution.

Chord Extensions

Turnarounds can also be played using chord extensions of the base chords. E.g. using major seventh and minor seventh chords.

Turnaround 1 Chord Extensions

E.g. Turnaround No. 1 becomes –	Imaj7	VIm7	IVmaj7	V7
E.g. in the **key of C** –	Cmaj7	Am7	Fmaj7	G7

If we substitute the relative minor (**IIm**) for the **IVmaj7** chord,

E.g. Turnaround No. 1 becomes –	Imaj7	Vim7	IIm7	V7
E.g. in the **key of C** –	Cmaj7	Am7	Dm7	G7

Turnaround 2 Chord Extensions

E.g. Turnaround No. 2 becomes –	Imaj7	IIIm7	IIVmaj7	V7
E.g. in the **key of C** –	Cmaj7	Em7	Fmaj7	G7

If we substitute the relative minor (**IIm**) for the **IVmaj** chord,

E.g. Turnaround No. 2 becomes –	Imaj7	IIIm7	IIm7	V7
E.g. in the **key of C** –	Cmaj7	Em7	Dm7	G7

Ninth Chords

It is possible to substitute the **V7** chord with a ninth chord.

E.g. Turnaround No. 1 becomes –	**Imaj7**	**Vim7**	**IVmaj7**	**V9**
E.g. in the **key of C** –	**Cmaj7**	**Am7**	**Fmaj7**	**G9**

If we substitute the relative minor (**IIm7**) for the **IVmaj7** chord,

E.g. Turnaround No. 1 becomes –	**Imaj7**	**VIm7**	**IIm7**	**V9**
E.g. in the **key of C** –	**Cmaj7**	**Am7**	**Dm7**	**G9**

E.g. Turnaround No. 2 becomes –	**Imaj7**	**IIIm7**	**IVmaj7**	**V9**
E.g. in the **key of C** –	**Cmaj7**	**Em7**	**Fmaj7**	**G9**

If we substitute the relative minor (**IIm7**) for the **IVmaj7** chord,

E.g. Turnaround No. 2 becomes –	**Imaj7**	**IIIm7**	**IIm7**	**V9**
E.g. in the **key of C** –	**Cmaj7**	**Em7**	**Dm7**	**G9**

The second exercise on page 148 is a turnaround in the **key of F**, substituting a **C9** for a **C7** chord.

Starting on the IV Chord

Instead of starting all the above turnarounds on the **I** chord, you can start on the **IV** chord.

E.g. Turnaround No. 1 becomes –	**IV**	**V7**	**I**	**VIm**
E.g. in the **key of C** –	**F**	**G7**	**C**	**Am**

E.g. Turnaround No. 2 becomes –	**IV**	**V7**	**I**	**IIIm**
E.g. in the **key of C** –	**F**	**G7**	**C**	**Em**

As shown on page 186 there are hundreds of songs which use turnaround progressions. As well as the ones listed here, there are many Jazz Standards with more complex chord changes which are also based on turnaround progressions. The more familiar you are with these progressions and their various substitution possibilities, the more songs you will be able to learn quickly and the more you will be able to participate in Jam sessions.

SUBSTITUTION AND CONTEXT

When you start to learn how substitution works, it is easy to get carried away and substitute almost every chord in a progression. Sometimes this works well, but at other times it is not desirable at all. If you were playing in a Chicago Blues band and started adding altered chords and Major 9ths, you would be asked to leave the band very quickly. Where and when to substitute depends on the musical context and understanding the idiom you are playing in. The following example demonstrates two ways of playing a turnaround. The first, as in a 1950's or 60's Rock song, and the second as in a Swing tune. Unless you use different chord types, you can't distinguish one from the other.

61.

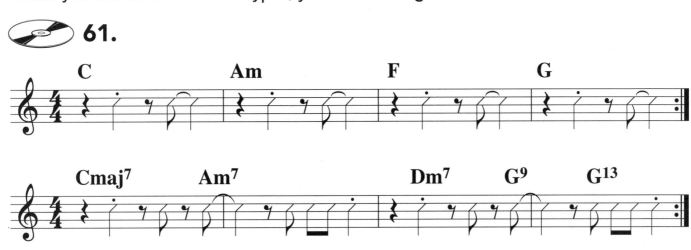

The next example demonstrates a Ⅰ Ⅴ progression in A played in various ways to create different styles. Notice the particular substitutions used fo the various styles and listen to the CD to hear the difference between them.

62.

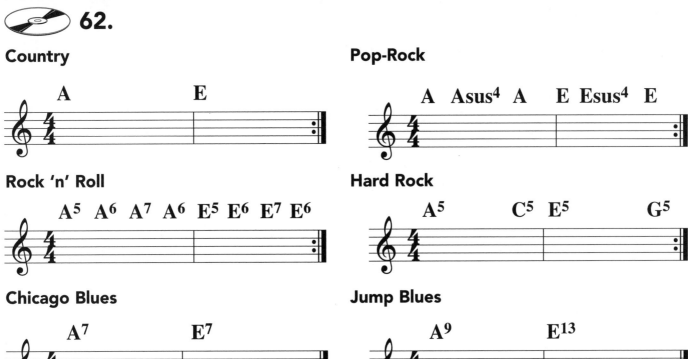

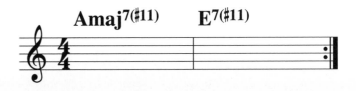

TRIAD OVER ROOT SUBSTITUTIONS

On page 177 the following chords were used to demonstrate that chords can have more than one name. This is valuable to know when it comes to chord substitution. Notice that an E minor triad contains the notes E, G and B. A Cmaj7 chord contains the notes C, E, G and B. Therefore, a Cmaj7 chord can be implied by playing an E minor triad over a C root note. This is called **triad over root substitution**.

E minor Triad ⟶
$$\begin{matrix} B \\ G \\ E \\ \hline C \end{matrix} = \begin{matrix} B \\ G \\ E \\ C \end{matrix}$$
⟵ C Major 7 Chord

C Bass Note ⟶

On of the most common forms of this type of substitution is to use triads from within the same key as the original chord. In any key you can always substitute the chord two degrees ahead in the scale, thus creating a higher extension of the chord. This is shown below in the key of C major.

Ⅰ	Ⅱ	Ⅲ	Ⅳ	Ⅴ	Ⅵ	Ⅶ
B	C	D	E	F	G	A
G	A	B	C	D	E	F
E	F	G	A	B	C	D
C	D	E	F	G	A	B
Cmaj7	**Dm7**	**Em7**	**Fmaj7**	**G7**	**Am7**	**Bm7♭5**

The same principle applies to modes. The example below shows a series of triads from the key of **D major** played over an **A** bass note. Since **A** is the **5th** degree of the key of D, this suggests a **mixolydian** tonality. Mixolydian based triad over root substitution is useful in a Blues context, as each of the triads can suggest upper extensions of dominant chords.

 63. Mixolydian Blues Triads in A

F♯m/A Bm/A C♯dim/A Bm/A Em/A F♯m/A Em/A F♯m/A

Also try down an octave

```
        5       7       9      10      12      14      15      17
T       7       7       8      12      12      14      17      19
A       6       7       9      11      12      14      16      18
B       0       0       0       0       0       0       0       0
```

The following Blues in the key of A uses triad over root substitutions to suggest various higher extensions of dominant chords built on **A**, **D** and **E** which are Ī, ĪV̄ and V̄ in this key. This is a way of creating interesting parts over one chord symbol.

 **64. Blues Using Triad Over Root Substitutions**

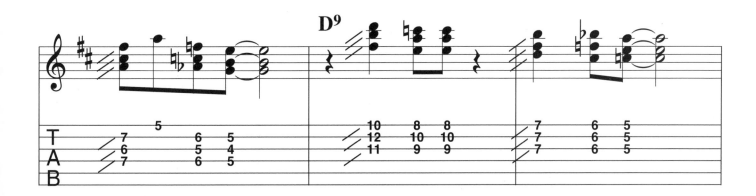

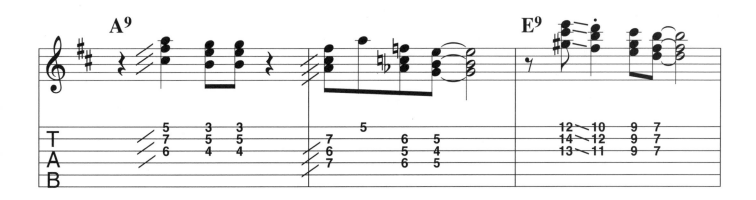

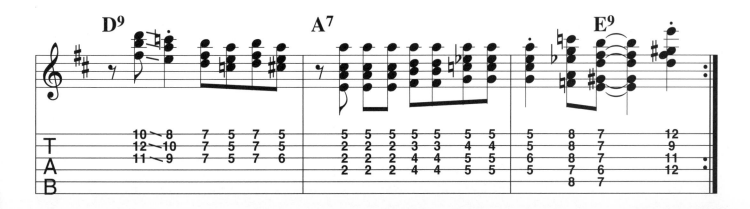

USING 7TH CHORDS TO CREATE 9THS

The triad over root principle can also be used to create 9th chords by placing a different root note under a 7th chord as shown below. By placing an **Em7 chord over a** C **bass note, a CMaj9 chord is created.**

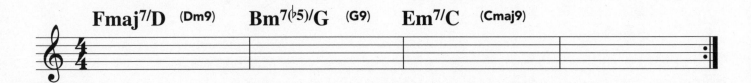

Like triads, this process works for every note of the scale and can therefore be applied to scale tone 7th chords in any key. The following example shows the scale tone 7th triad over root substitutions for chords $\overline{\text{II}}$, $\overline{\text{V}}$ and $\overline{\text{I}}$ in the key of C.

 **65.0**

$\text{Fmaj}^{7}\text{/D}$ (Dm9) $\text{Bm}^{7(\flat 5)}\text{/G}$ (G9) $\text{Em}^{7}\text{/C}$ (Cmaj9)

SUBSTITUTIONS IN MINOR KEYS

All the types of substitution which apply to major keys (relative substitutions, scale tone triads or 7ths two degrees ahead in the key, dominant minor, and tritone substitutions) can be applied to minor keys as well. The main difference you will find is that when you start to go into the upper extensions of chords built on the harmonic and melodic minors, you will get alterations to the chords. Shown below are the chords resulting from substituting scale tone 7th chords two ahead for the standard scale tone 7ths of **A melodic minor.**

 **65.1**

$\text{Cmaj}^{7(+5)}\text{/A}$ $\text{D}^{7}\text{/B}$ $\text{E}^{7}\text{/C}$ $\text{F}\sharp\text{m}^{7(\flat 5)}\text{/D}$

$\text{G}\sharp\text{m}^{7(\flat 5)}\text{/E}$ $\text{Am}^{(\text{maj}7)}\text{/F}\sharp$ $\text{Bm}^{7}\text{/G}\sharp$ $\text{Cmaj}^{7(+5)}\text{/A}$

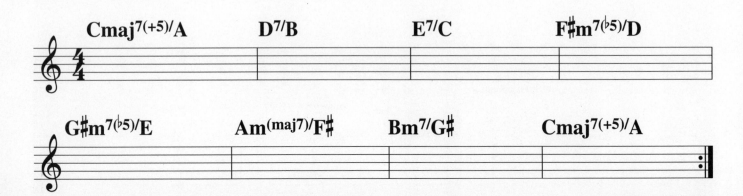

SECONDARY DOMINANTS

In simpler forms of music, dominant 7ths most frequently occur as chord $\bar{V}7$ of a major or minor key. However, it is possible to substitute a dominant 7th chord for any scale tone chord (e.g. $\bar{II}7$, $\bar{III}7$, or $\bar{VI}7$. These are referred to as **secondary dominants**. The use of secondary dominants is useful for implying a series of $\bar{V}$ $\bar{I}$ progressions in different keys, while harmonizing a melody which stays within one key. Secondary dominants can be used in any style of music, and are particularly common in Jazz and Blues. Here is a progression demonstrating the use of secondary dominant chords.

 **66.0**

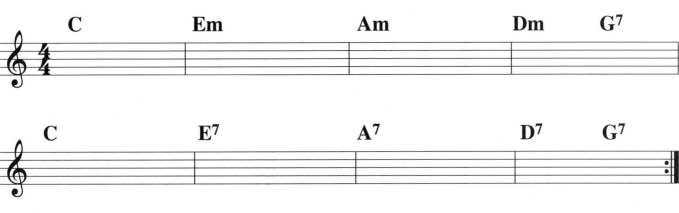

 **66.1**

This example shows secondary dominants applied to a turnaround progression. Altered dominants can sometimes be used instead of a simple 7th chord.

 **66.2**

In this example, secondary dominants are used to suggest a series of $\bar{V}$ $\bar{I}$ movements in various keys leading back to the starting point of C major.

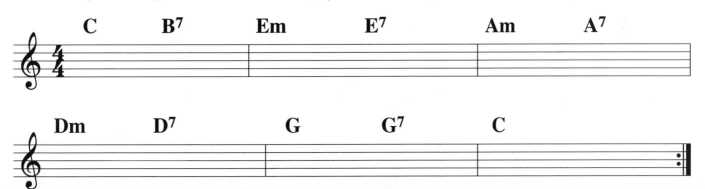

TRITONE SUBSTITUTION

Another common method of substitution is to use a chord whose root is a **tritone** (flattened 5th or augmented 4th) above that of the original chord. This is known as **tritone substitution**. Like other methods of substitution, the reason this works is that there are notes common to both chords. Shown below are the chords **G7** and **D♭7**. As you can see, the note **F** occurs in both chords. The note **B** is enharmonically the same as **C♭** which is the 7th of **D♭7**, so this note is in both chords too.

$$
\begin{array}{ll}
\text{F} & \text{C}\flat \\
\text{D} & \text{A}\flat \\
\text{B} & \text{F} \\
\text{G} & \text{D}\flat \\
\textbf{G7} & \textbf{D}\flat\textbf{7}
\end{array}
$$

In the second half of the following example, **D♭7** is substituted for **G7**, creating a $\overline{\rm II}$ $\flat\overline{\rm II}$ $\overline{\rm I}$ progression in the key of **C** instead of a standard $\overline{\rm II}$ $\overline{\rm V}$ $\overline{\rm I}$. Notice how the notes **D♭** and **A♭** in the **D♭7** chord give the progression a different flavor to the $\overline{\rm II}$ $\overline{\rm V}$ $\overline{\rm I}$ using a **G7** chord.

 **67.**

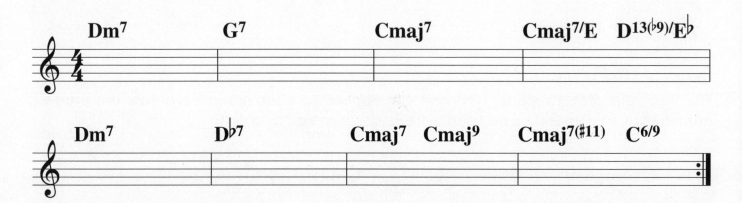

Tritone substitutions are most commonly used with dominant chords, but can be used with any chord type and on any degree of a scale. In some cases, every chord except for $\overline{\rm I}$ can be a tritone substitution. The following example shows a $\overline{\rm I}$ $\overline{\rm VI}$ $\overline{\rm II}$ $\overline{\rm V}$ progression and then a second version where $\flat\overline{\rm III}$ is substituted for $\overline{\rm VI}$, $\flat\overline{\rm VI}$ is substituted for $\overline{\rm II}$, and $\flat\overline{\rm II}$ is substituted for $\overline{\rm V}$. This type of substitution throughout the progression is sometimes called **backcycling**. This is followed by two more variations. These are only a few of the many possibilities. Experiment and come up with some of your own.

68.

A good way to practice substitutions is to learn a basic progression and then try out various substitution possibilities with some or all of the chords once you have the progression memorized. The following example is based on the chord changes to George Gershwin's "I Got Rhythm", and is commonly referred to as "Rhythm Changes". It has been recorded on the CD without a guitar part so you can jam along with the rhythm section. Play it along with the CD until you have the form memorized.

 69. Rhythm Changes Jam-Along

Shown below is another version showing some possible substitutions. Play it along with the recording and listen to the different sound produced by the substituted chords. With any chord progression there are many substitution possibilities. The trick is knowing which ones to use in a particular musical context, and also when **not** to use substitutions. This knowledge comes from knowing the sounds of a particular idiom and is best developed by lots of listening and lots of playing with other musicians.

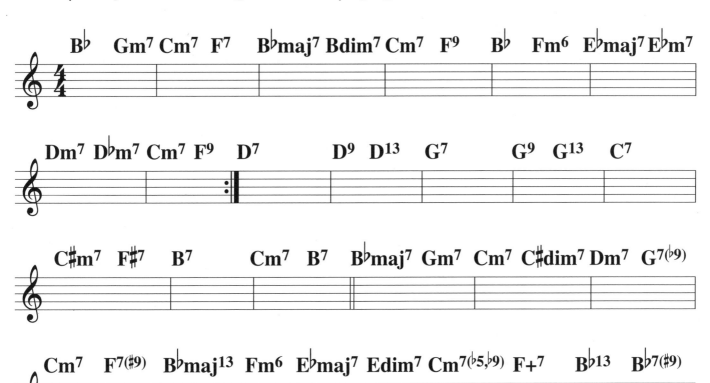

THE $\underline{II}$ $\underline{V}$ $\underline{I}$ PROGRESSION

One of the most common progressions used in Jazz and all popular music is the $\underline{II}$ $\underline{V}$ $\underline{I}$ progression. As the name implies, this progression begins on the second chord in the key ($\underline{II}$m7), progresses to the fifth ($\underline{V}$7) and then progresses to the chord which the key is named from ($\underline{I}$maj7).

A good way to become familiar with this (or any) progression is to repeat it many times using a different set of chord voicings on each repeat. This is demonstrated on the recording with the following example which is a repeating $\underline{II}$ $\underline{V}$ $\underline{I}$ progression in the key of **G.** You could play it using voicings in a particular area of the fretboard on the lower strings and then the higher strings, then move to a different area of the fretboard and repeat the process. There are many possibilities. The more you practice like this, the more freedom of expression you will have when playing with other musicians.

 **70.**

Am⁷	D⁷	Gmaj⁷	Am⁷	D⁷	Gmaj⁷

Am⁷	D⁷	Gmaj⁷	Am⁷	D⁷	Gmaj⁷

$\underline{I}$ BECOMES $\underline{II}$

There are many Jazz standards where a $\underline{II}$ $\underline{V}$ $\underline{I}$ progression is followed by another $\underline{II}$ $\underline{V}$ $\underline{I}$ progression in a key whose $\underline{I}$ chord is a tone (major 2nd) lower. In this situation, chord $\underline{I}$ **Maj7** of the first key becomes chord $\underline{II}$ **min7** of the next key. This means that all you have to do to play the new $\underline{II}$ $\underline{V}$ $\underline{I}$ is change chord $\underline{I}$ from a Major 7th to a minor 7th by lowering the 3rd and 7th degrees a semitone. Here is an example.

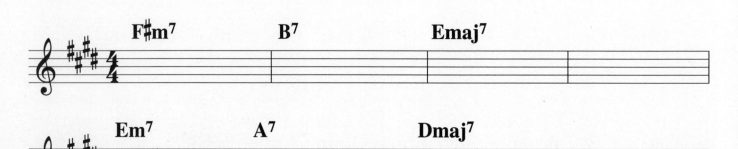

MEMORIZING CHORD PROGRESSIONS

As with chord shapes, a great way to memorize a progression is to play it through all the keys in the key cycle. This is demonstrated below with a Ⅱ Ⅴ Ⅰ progression played clockwise around the cycle. Once you are comfortable with it, try playing the progression anticlockwise around the cycle.

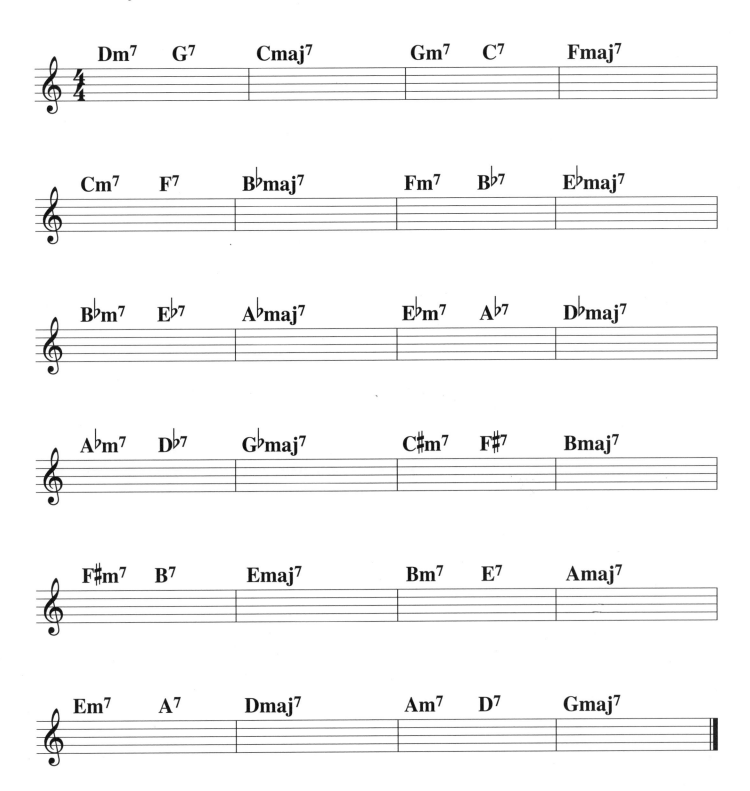

As well as using the key cycle, try playing a chord progression in one key and then move through other keys by starting the progression up or down by a specific interval, e.g. chromatically (minor 2nds), major 2nds, minor 3rds or major 3rds. If you make a habit of this, it won't take long before you can play a progression in any key. This will make you popular with other musicians because it saves a lot of time at rehearsals.

MODULATION

Modulation can be defined as the changing of key within a song (or chord progression). It is very important to be able to recognise a modulation.

In sheet music, a modulation is sometimes indicated by changing the key signature. This will usually be done if the modulation occurs between one section of the song and the next (e.g. between one verse and another). Where there is no change of key signature, a modulation may be detected by examining the melody and/or the chords. When examining the melody, remember that each key is recognisable by the notes of its scale. If different notes appear it may indicate a modulation. For example, if a melody in the **key of C** suddenly features **F♯** notes, it could suggest a modulation to the **key of G**. When examining the chords, a modulation may be determined by following the chord/key relationship, i.e. looking for chords that 'fit into' a certain key. Consider the following progression.

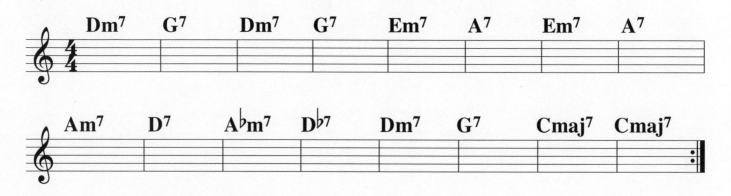

which can be analysed as such:

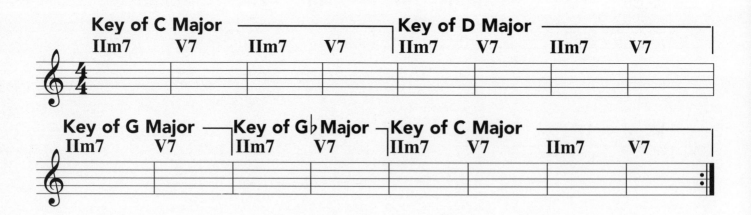

The use of Roman numerals makes the lay-out of this progression very clear, it is based on the IIm7-V7 chords, modulating through four different keys. This type of modulation is most common in Jazz songs. You will find that many Rock songs, although featuring modulation, will not do so to such a great extent.

One of the most common modulations in songs is from the major key to its relative minor:

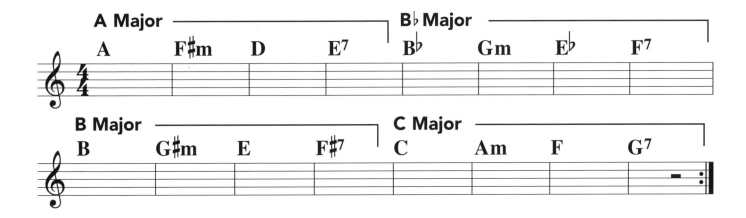

Another common form of modulation is to change up to the key one semitone or one tone higher. This can be done successively, as in the following example:

V̱ BECOMES II̱

Another common modulation technique is where you have a II̱ V̱ progression which does not progress to I̱, but in the next bar, the V̱7 chord becomes II̱ **min7** of the next key. In this case, all you have to do is lower the 3rd of the chord by a semitone to change from a dominant 7th to a minor 7th. Here is an example.

Here is a whole song form making use of short Ⅱ Ⅴ progressions moving through several different keys. It is based on the chord progression from Duke Ellington's "Satin Doll". Learn it as written and then try substituting some of the chords.

 **72.**

Dm⁷   G⁷   Dm⁷   G⁷   Em⁷   A⁷   Em⁷   A⁷

Am⁷   D⁷   A♭m⁷   D♭⁷   Cmaj⁷

Gm⁷   C⁷   Gm⁷   C⁷   Fmaj⁷

Am⁷   D⁷   Am⁷   D⁷   Dm⁷   G⁷   Em⁷   A⁷

Dm⁷   G⁷   Dm⁷   G⁷   Em⁷   A⁷   Em⁷   A⁷

Am⁷   D⁷   A♭m⁷   D♭⁷   Cmaj⁷

LEARNING SONGS

It is important to remember that the reason you learn chord shapes and progressions like II V I's is so you will be able to play freely over the changes to real songs. To learn to play Jazz well, you will need to know lots of popular songs which have become standards. There are many books available which are compilations of standards, often combined with more contemporary tunes. Probably the most famous of these is "The Real Book". Staff in most music stores will know about this book and it is recommended that you purchase either this book or a similar one and learn both the melodies and chord changes to as many standards as possible.

To get you started, here are some progressions to practice which are based on standards. Each one has been recorded on the CD without a guitar part so you can jam along with the rhythm section. Learn each one using the chords indicated and then try out various substitutions using the methods described in the book.

73. 12 Bar Blues in A (Jam-Along)

No chord changes are written here because the Blues progression is one you will need to be able to play by ear. If you need to work out the changes, look at the Blues in E on page 182 and transpose it to the key of **A**. However, it is better if you get away from the page as soon as possible. Your eventual aim should be to play any progression by ear in any key. This is a lifetime study, but all good Jazz players can do this to a large extent.

74. Jam-Along

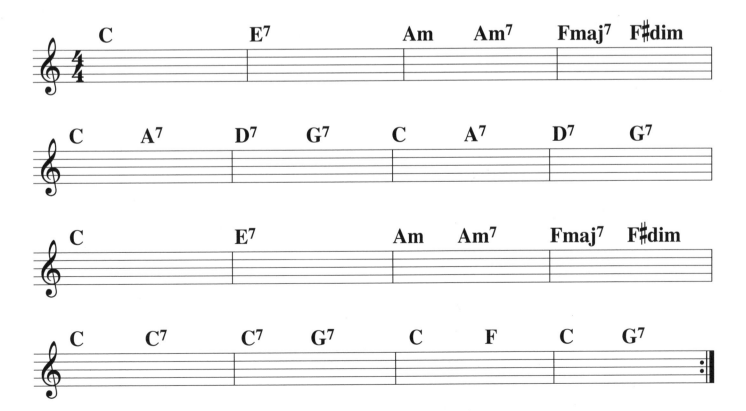

75. Jam-Along

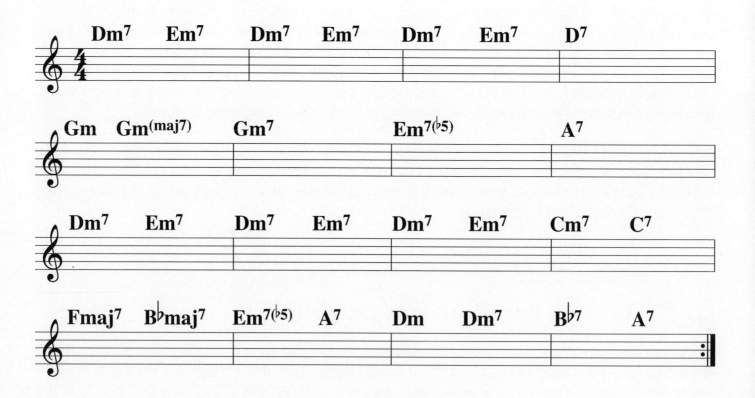

 76. Jam-Along

77. Jam-Along

Line 1: Em | C7(♭5) | Em | C7(♭5) | Em | C♯m7(♭5) | F♯m7(♭5) | B7(♭9)

Line 2: Em | C7(♭5) | Em | A7 | C7 | B+ | Em | F♯m7(♭5) | B+7(♭9)

Line 3: Em | C7(♭5) | Em | C7(♭5) | Em | C♯m7(♭5) | F♯m7(♭5) | B7(♭9)

Line 4: Em | C7(♭5) | Em | A7 | C7 | B7 | Em | E7

Line 5: Dm7 | G7(♭9) | Cmaj7 | A7(♭9) | Dm7 | G7(♭9) | Cmaj7

Line 6: C♯m7 | F♯7 | Bmaj7 | Emaj7 | Fm(6/9) | A♯7 | Em(maj7) | B+7

Line 7: Em | C7(♭5) | Em | C7(♭5) | Em | C♯m7(♭5) | F♯m7(♭5) | B7(♭9)

Line 8: Em | C7(♭5) | Em | A7 | C7 | B7 | Em

LISTENING

Apart from books, your most important source of information as a musician is **recordings**. If you are serious about your chord study, listen to albums which feature piano or keyboard players as well as those featuring guitarists. All music is an extension of what has come before it, so you need to be aware of the development of keyboard playing throughout the history of music. Studying **Classical** music will give you a solid grounding which can be used in any style of music. For more recent styles such as Jazz, Blues and Rock, it is essential to listen to a wide variety of players, some of whom are listed below. There is a lot of crossover between styles which come under the headings of Rock, Jazz, Blues, R&B and Funk. There are many great players in these styles, but the following list is a good start.

Blues Guitar: Robert Johnson, Son House, T-Bone Walker, Robert Junior Lockwood, BB King, Magic Sam, Gatemouth Brown, Hollywood Fats, Stevie Ray Vaughan, Ronnie Earl, Duke Robillard and Robben Ford.

Blues Piano: Otis Spann, Memphis Slim, Champion Jack Dupree, Dr John, James Booker, and Professor Longhair.

Soul/Gospel: Cornell Dupree, Booker T and the MG's (featuring Steve Cropper on Guitar) Mildred Falls (with Mahalia Jackson - "Live at Newport 1958"), Ray Charles, Aretha Franklin, and Richard Tee.

Funk: The Meters (featuring Leo Nocentelli on guitar), James Brown (lots of Funk guitar here), Parliament/Funkadelic, Nile Rogers, Herbie Hancock, Stevie Wonder, and Prince.

Rock/Pop/Metal: Lynyrd Skynyrd, ACDC, The Rolling Stones, The Police, Steely Dan, Black Sabbath, Metallica. All these bands feature great rhythm guitar playing.

Jazz: Guitar: Django Rinehardt, Joe Pass, Barney Kessell, Herb Ellis, Kenny Burrell, Jim Hall, Wes Montgomery, Jimmy Raney, Tal Farlow, Emily Remler, Bruce Forman, Pat Metheney, John Abercrombie, John Scofield and Bill Frisell.

Jazz: Piano: Jelly Roll Morton, Lil Hardin (with Louis Armstrong) Fats Waller, Teddy Wilson, Count Basie, Duke Ellington, Mary Lou Williams, Art Tatum, Thelonious Monk, Bud Powell, Horace Silver, Wynton Kelly, Red Garland, Oscar Peterson, Bill Evans, McCoy Tyner, Herbie Hancock (Jazz as well as Funk), Jimmy Smith (Hammond Organ), Keith Jarrett, Joe Zawinul (with Weather Report), Mike Nock, John Medeski, Jacky Terrason, and Brad Mehldau.

As well as this, it is valuable to listen to albums featuring great singers such as Billie Holiday, Ella Fitzgerald or Mel Torme and pay careful attention to what the accompanying musicians are playing. The art of accompaniment is a lifelong study.

TRANSCRIBING

When you are listening to albums, try to sing along with the solos and rhythm parts, and visualize the fingerings and techniques you would use to achieve the sounds you are hearing. **Write down** anything you really like, or anything you can't immediately transfer from your ear to the fretboard. This is called **transcribing**. All the great players have done **lots** of it. Transcribing helps you to understand and absorb the music and before long, it starts to come out in your own playing. It is also valuable to play along with albums, sometimes imitating what you are hearing and other times improvising. This is great ear training and is lots of fun.

ALTERED CHORDS CHART

The chord chart below features chords which have one or more alterations to one of the given formulas, and are therefore called **altered chords**.

CHORD NAME	CHORD FORMULA	EXAMPLE	
Major Flat Fifth	1 3 ♭5	C♭5:	C E G♭
Minor Seventh Flat Fifth	1 ♭3 ♭5 ♭7	Cm7♭5:	C E♭ G♭ B♭
Seventh Sharp Fifth	1 3 ♯5 ♭7	C7♯5:	C E G♯ B♭
Seventh Flat Fifth	1 3 ♭5 ♭7	C7♭5:	C E G♭ B♭
Seventh Sharp Ninth	1 3 5 ♭7 ♯9	C7♯9:	C E G B♭ D♯
Seventh Flat Ninth	1 3 5 ♭7 ♭9	C7♭9:	C E G B♭ D♭
Seventh Sharp Fifth Flat Ninth	1 3 ♯5 ♭7 ♭9	C7♯5♭9:	C E G♯ B♭ D♭
Ninth Sharp Fifth	1 3 ♯5 ♭7 9	C9♯5:	C E G♯ B♭ D
Ninth Flat Fifth	1 3 ♭5 ♭7 9	C9♭5:	C E G♭ B♭ D
Ninth Sharp Eleventh	1 3 5 ♭7 9 ♯11	C9♯11:	C E G B♭ D F♯
Minor Ninth Major Seventh	1 ♭3 5 7 9	Cm9(maj7):	C E♭ G B D
Thirteenth Flat Ninth	1 3 5 ♭7 ♭9 11* 13	C13:	C E G B♭ D♭ F* A
Thirteenth Flat Five Flat Ninth	1 3 ♭5 ♭7 ♭9 11* 13	C13♭5♭9:	C E G♭ B♭ D♭ F* A

In altered chords, the notes to be altered are always written as part of the chord name, enabling you to construct the chord. For example, a **Cm7♯5♭9** (not listed above) is a **Cm7** chord with the fifth sharpened (**♯5**) and the ninth flattened (**♭9**). When you are working out a suitable shape for this chord, remember that the root note and/or the fifth note may be omitted.

Another type of alteration occurs when chord symbols are written thus:

Example 1: **G/F♯** bass
This indicates that a **G** chord is played, but using an F♯ note in the bass.

Example 2: **C/G** bass
This indicates a **C** chord with a **G** bass note.

Sometimes the word 'bass' will not be written (i.e. the symbol will be just G/F♯), but the same meaning is implied. These chords are often referred to as **slash chords**.

TUNING YOUR GUITAR

TUNING TO ANOTHER INSTRUMENT

If you are playing along with another instrument, it is essential that your guitar be in tune with that instrument. Tune the open strings of your guitar to the corresponding notes of the accompanying instrument. E.g., To tune to a piano, tune the open 6th string to the **E** note on the piano, as shown on the keyboard diagram. Then tune your guitar to itself from this note, using the method outlined below, or tune each string of your guitar to those notes of the piano shown on the keyboard diagram.

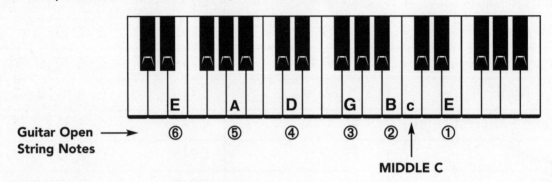

Guitar Open → ⑥   ⑤   ④   ③   ② ↑ ①
String Notes

MIDDLE C

TUNING THE GUITAR TO ITSELF

If you do not have another instrument to tune to, you can tune the guitar to itself by using the following method. However, this usually requires many months of practice. You will probably need your music teacher or musician friend to help you tune when you are learning.

1. Place a left finger on the **6th** string (thickest string) at the **fifth** fret, and play the string.
2. Play the **open 5th string** (an **A** note). If this note sounds the same as the note you played on the **6th** string at the **fifth** fret, the **A** string is in tune.
3. If the open A string sounds **higher**, it means that it is **sharp**. Turn the tuning key slowly in a clockwise direction. This will lower the pitch of the string. Play the two strings again and compare the notes. Keep doing this until the open A string sounds the same as the E string at the fifth fret.
4. If the open A string sounds **lower**, it means that it is flat. Turn the tuning key slowly in a counter-clockwise direction. This will raise the pitch of the string. Play the two strings again and compare the notes. Keep doing this until the open A string sounds the same as the E string at the fifth fret.
5. Tune the **open 4th string** (a **D** note), to the note on the **fifth** fret of the **5th** string, using the method outlined above.
6. Tune all the other strings in the same way, except for the **open 2nd string** (a **B** note), which is tuned to the note produced on the **fourth** fret of the **3rd** string (see diagram).